STRANGER ON T

STRANGER ON THE LINE

The Secret History of Phone Tapping

Patrick Fitzgerald
and
Mark Leopold

THE BODLEY HEAD
LONDON

British Library Cataloguing
in Publication Data

Fitzgerald, Patrick
Stranger on the line: the secret history
of phone tapping.
1. Criminal investigation   2. Wire-tapping
I. Title   II. Leopold, Mark
363.2'52   HV8073.5

ISBN 0–370–31086–1

Phototypeset by Falcon Graphic Art Ltd
Wallington, Surrey
Printed in Great Britain for
The Bodley Head Ltd
32 Bedford Square, London WC1B 3EL
by Biddles Ltd, Guildford and King's Lynn

Contents

Introduction

Consider an industry with a multi-million pound budget, employing hundreds of skilled technicians and clerical staff, equipped with the most advanced computer and electronics technology and potentially in contact with every person who ever uses a telephone, yet operating in (almost) total secrecy. Tapping is that industry. In this book, we offer a comprehensive study of this controversial subject.

The current and future importance of tapping, and of the telecommunications on which tapping preys, is neatly explained by this extract from a Conservative Party draft policy document, prepared in 1979:

> *The battle lines are already being drawn for the struggle to control information in Britain. Government administration, worker collectives, corporations, police and security forces, and foreign corporations and Governments all seek to preserve their own privacy while finding out as much as possible about everyone else. Information is the commanding height of tomorrow's economy.*[1]

The political and economic significance of telecommunications itself (often abbreviated these days to telecomms) is indisputable. The march of the British empire in the nineteenth century and, later on, the spread of multinational companies were only possible because efficient international telegraph and telephone links were available. For every nation, as Sir Donald Maitland, a former civil servant with a wide knowledge of the subject, comments:

> *effective communication has a catalytic effect on economic development, and countries which don't have good communica-*

7

tions are therefore at an immediate economic disadvantage.[2]

From a different perspective, the telephone has become indispensable to the organisation of anything from a picket to a picnic which involves a number of people. The computer has brought telecomms into a new era in which it is more than a valuable ancillary service, but a vital economic resource in its own right.

Since its election in 1979, the Thatcher Government has invested much political capital in the ability of information technology to replace and revitalise Britain's declining, traditional, manufacturing industries. The expectation is that a new kind of economy will emerge in which the principal activity is the production, processing and distribution of electronic information through the combined technologies of computing and telecomms. Automation reduces human involvement in manufacturing, design and administration to the common denominator of operating a terminal – a telephone or a computer keyboard, for example – in some information network. Social activities like shopping and entertainment are and will be similarly affected.

The catalyst for this new economic order was the way in which the technology of computing and that of telecomms were increasingly using the same techniques and equipment. The major obstacle to this convergence was that the structures of the two component industries were completely different. When the Conservatives took power in 1979, all Britain's public communications networks were operated by the General Post Office (GPO). The single exception was the city of Hull, whose council was allowed to run local telephone services under licence from the Post Office.

From 1912 until the end of the 1960s, the GPO was a government department with its own minister, the Postmaster-General. The 1969 Post Office Act turned it into a public corporation (a 'nationalised industry', so to speak) but left its monopoly powers intact. The British computer industry, by contrast, was evolving at a rapid, if uneven, pace, and boasted a population of great diversity and fierce competitiveness. The choice facing the Thatcher Government, succinctly expressed by Robert Gressens, president of the American telecomms company GTE, was 'to expand the monopoly and

8

regulation to include computers or else go in the other direction, and liberalise'.[3]

As might be expected, the administration opted for the latter course of action. In 1980, the Post Office telecommunications division was established as a separate corporation, British Telecom. The 1981 British Telecommunications Act granted licences to a rival national public telecomms operator, Mercury Communications, as well as to Hull city council, and to other applicant companies offering certain types of data transmission service. Three years later, after another Act of Parliament, British Telecom was restructured as a private company, and half of it was sold to private investors.

One of the main reasons that public communications services were subject to state control in the first place was to guarantee official access to the information which could be derived from tapping. This consideration was very much in the mind of the Government when the Post Office was initially set up in the seventeenth century, and applied with equal force when telegraph and telephone services were introduced in the nineteenth century. The Post Office, and subsequently British Telecom, has enjoyed long and intimate relations with the government agencies involved in tapping.

Tapping is uniformly carried out under conditions of great secrecy, not only for the obvious practical purpose of not alerting the target of the tap, but also to protect the Government from public indignation. The strong cultural antipathy towards the eavesdropper generally is reinforced where the state is concerned, not least through popular appreciation of Orwell's hideously omniscient creation, 'Big Brother'. The organs of Government most involved in tapping are consequently those most concerned with matters of secrecy, namely the security and intelligence services. Enforcement agencies, principally the police and the Customs and Excise service, also use taps, but on a much smaller scale. It is these customers who decide, in accordance with their own priorities, what is tapped from the vast quantity of communications flowing through the nation's telecomms networks.

The organisation and operations of the customers are the subject of Chapter 2. It will become apparent that there are two traditions in tapping, motivated by different intelligence

9

demands and using different methods. The administration and technology of these two systems are covered by the next two chapters which describe how tapping is done. Chapter 3 traces the history of taps fitted against an individual telephone line, from primitive origins in the manual telephone exchange to the modern national tapping centre. Chapter 4 describes a more intangible form of tapping, which we call 'trawling', in which a large number of lines – especially international circuits – are intercepted simultaneously and then filtered to extract any potentially interesting material.

The political and legal controls on tapping are discussed in Chapters 5 and 6. Chapter 5 charts the parliamentary and legal face of tapping through the twentieth century. A picture emerges of a seemingly impervious administrative wall around tapping, fiercely defended from all but the tamest scrutiny. Chapter 6 describes how tapping legislation was finally forced on the Government, and offers a critique of the statute which resulted. Chapter 7 surveys the legal frameworks governing tapping in other Western countries, comparing these with the British system.

Tapping is mostly, but not exclusively, the preserve of the Government, where it is generally carried out under official sanction. Chapter 8, 'The Wilder Shores', examines the unofficial aspects of tapping, taking in other forms of electronic surveillance, especially hidden microphones or 'bugs'. Returning to the official domain, Chapter 9 reviews forms of telecomms surveillance concerned with the source and destination of phone calls, rather than their actual contents, and looks at more overt ways of using the telephone system against perceived enemies of the State. Chapter 10 looks at the future of tapping: technological advances in telecomms networks will benefit the State's tappers by easing the process of interception, but they may be confounded by the sheer volume of information with which they have to cope. New methods of collating and analysing intercepted communications will be necessary.

The nature of contemporary tapping is not easily recognised through the haze of myth and mystique which envelops the topic. Popular folklore abounds with tales of sinister occurrences during telephone calls. As evidence of phone taps, most of these are as spurious as the Government's continual referral to 'national security'. Nevertheless, enough anecdotes have accumulated to produce a sort of culture which serves, in the absence of an alternative, as a popular conception of tapping. This culture, the 'fear of tapping' is the subject of Chapter 1. In the remainder of the book, it will become clear that the technology of interception and processing, and the priorities of Government intelligence-gathering, lie at the true heart of tapping.

Chapter 1

Fear of Tapping

Many people fear their phones may be tapped. Tapping is a subject about which there is widespread suspicion, confusion, and downright paranoia. This is scarcely surprising when official sources tell us so little about who is tapped. The Government argues that the very purpose of the exercise would be negated if those whose phone calls are intercepted knew that someone was listening. However, as we shall show in Chapter 7, many other governments are much more open about the targets of official phone tapping. Throughout the Western world, the law tightly defines the circumstances in which tapping is allowed, or provides for targets to know of the interception after a fixed period of time has elapsed. These countries do not yet seem to have collapsed from proliferating crime and subversion. In Britain, the 1985 Interception of Communications Act enshrined deliberately vague criteria for tapping, and the Government almost invariably refuses to confirm whether or not a particular individual or organisation has been tapped.

In these circumstances, there has grown up a kind of 'culture' of tapping, a series of popular myths and stories, many of which have little basis in fact. Some people, for example, believe that behind all the clicks and buzzes on their line there is a little man in a dirty raincoat with a pair of headphones attached to a telegraph pole or junction box. This is absurd. The first thing a professional tapper tries to do is clear the line of 'squeaks and farts' (as they are known in the trade). This interference is a characteristic feature of our antiquated telephone network and is, if anything, even more of a nuisance to the tapper than to the rest of us.

Even among those who are aware that the reality of telephone interception is different, there is much mythology about tapping. Apart from the purely paranoid, there are many who perhaps wish they were more of a threat to the State than they are. As the Labour MP Austin Mitchell has said, 'In some political circles it is a demonstration of virility to have one's phone tapped'[1] (though there is little evidence to suggest that such delusions are confined to the male sex). Among those who most certainly *are* sometimes tapped, for example peace movement or trades union activists, many tales are circulated, ranging from the bizarrely unlikely to the convincingly sinister. Before looking at this folklore of tapping, however, it is worth examining the official answers to the question 'who is tapped?'

Perhaps the best starting place is to consider *how many* people are tapped. In 1980 and 1985, the Government produced White Papers[2] giving the numbers of warrants to tap signed in each year since 1937 by the Home Secretary or the Scottish Secretary, together with the Foreign Secretary's warrants since 1980. In 1984, the latest year on record, only 538 warrants were signed by these three gentlemen, while in no year does the published figure rise above 600. Surely (the innocent might ask) there can be little cause for concern, if so few telephones are being tapped? Unfortunately, the number of warrants quoted in the White Paper bears little relation to the number of phone calls tapped by the authorities.

Far more tapping goes on than has ever been admitted. We can be sure of this for several reasons. In the first place, the numbers of warrants signed by the Northern Ireland Secretary, which may include taps in mainland Britain, have never been released. According to the 1985 White Paper, this is because 'It would not be in the public interest to reveal these because of the terrorist threat in the province.'

Secondly, the figures relate to those warrants *signed* in a particular year, not to those *in force* during that year. Warrants only stay in force for a matter of months, but they may be renewed indefinitely. Many of those signed in previous years may, therefore, still be operative. A former Home Secretary, Merlyn Rees, told the Commons in 1985 that:

Some taps continue for a long time. I do not intend to spell it out, even in this House. However, I imagine that every Hon.

14

Member knows what I am talking about. They are blanket tappings.[3]

Moreover, warrants can cover any telephones which may be used by a named target, so one warrant can cover a number of people's phones. It has also been suspected that warrants have been signed for *organisations*, rather than individuals, enabling one warrant to cover any number of members of, for example, a political party.

In addition, there is considerable evidence to suggest that the State sometimes taps without any warrant at all. During the debate quoted above, John McWilliam MP (a former telecomms engineer, who probably knows more about tapping than anyone else in Parliament) reported that:

It is wrong to say that interception has not happened without warrants. In addition to officially authorised taps certain official tappings do not require warrants. That derives from an institutional relationship between the police, the CID or the Special Branch, and the Post Office – subsequently British Telecom.[4]

In the same debate, Ian Mikardo MP said that:

The problem is not phone taps authorised by the Secretary of State, it is the very much larger number of phone taps that are made without any application for an authorisation.[5]

From time to time, stories have emerged in the media about such unauthorised tapping. Two cases in particular, both involving the police, are worth mentioning. In a book on the 'Operation Julie' drugs investigation of the mid-seventies, Inspector Dick Lee (who ran the operation) told how he persuaded an unnamed organisation to tap a suspect's telephone, in order to avoid the official police channels for applying for warrants. More recently, when armed police from C11 (the Criminal Intelligence unit of Scotland Yard) shot, and seriously wounded, an innocent man named Steven Waldorf in his car, it emerged that the trigger-happy constables had become convinced that the vehicle contained an armed fugitive, David Martin, after tapping the phones of

15

some of Martin's friends. The subject of tapping did not come up at the policemen's trial, apparently because the taps were unauthorised. It was only afterwards that the full story emerged in the press, after the police had finally obtained official authority to tap, and Martin had been apprehended.[6] It is not clear why they did not apply for warrants in the first place. Perhaps it was simply inconvenient.

Although both these stories involve the police, there is no reason to think that unauthorised tapping is not done by the security services as well. Indeed, there is evidence to suggest that it is easier for them to get a tap placed without a warrant. The magazine *Police Review* in 1985 quoted a British Telecom source as saying:

> *When it is a police matter, we always see the warrant. When the tap is being made for the security services, we never see the warrant. We never know if there is one.*[7]

An intelligence officer told *The Observer* in 1984:

> *Most of the phone taps are done in a terrible hurry, and the thing is to know the boys in British Telecom and say 'Look, we need this done. Can you help?'*[8]

Apart from unauthorised taps on particular phones, the authorities also intercept phone calls, not because of a tap on one of the telephones itself, but in the course of a 'trawling' operation. The process is described in full in Chapter 4. The Foreign Secretary's warrants, which authorise this sort of operation, do not specify addresses or phone numbers in Britain (except for warrants covering suspected terrorist activity), but categories of material to be intercepted, for example calls in which a particular Middle East construction project is mentioned. There is no limit to the number of calls that could be tapped under such a warrant.

Also not included in the official statistics are calls from tapped phoneboxes, calls recorded with the permission of one of the parties to the conversation, and those picked up by bugs, infinity transmitters and similar devices (see Chapter 8). Similarly uncounted are calls intercepted by foreign intelligence agencies, private detectives, industrial spies, and the like.

The published numbers of warrants, therefore, give us no real idea of how many phone calls are tapped. Informed estimates in the early eighties put the number of phones in Britain tapped by the authorities at over a thousand.[9] We can add to this the trawling methods which enable calls to be intercepted without tapping particular phones, and unauthorised taps, as well as tapping by anyone other than the British authorities. If our homes are supposed to be our castles, the telephone is a convenient and secret entrance for those who might wish to lay siege to them.

If the published figures for warrants were broken down into those granted to the police, to the intelligence services, to customs, etc., this would at least provide some information about who is being tapped; unfortunately, they are not. We are unable therefore, to know for sure how much tapping is directed at suspected criminals, and how much is carried out by the Security Service against less obvious 'enemies of society'. Nor are the figures broken down according to the grounds on which the warrants are signed. According to the Interception of Communications Act, warrants may be issued for three reasons:–

(1) For the purpose of preventing or detecting serious crime
(2) In the interests of national security

and (3) For the purpose of safeguarding the economic well-being of the United Kingdom.

The first of these sounds unobjectionable enough. Who would quibble at the prevention or detection of serious crime? However, the definition of 'serious crime' has steadily broadened over the past couple of decades. The current meaning of the term is:

An offence for which a man with no previous record could reasonably be expected to be sentenced to three years imprisonment, or *an offence of lesser gravity in which* either *a large number of people are involved,* or *there is reason to apprehend the use of violence,* or *in which the financial rewards of success are very large.*[10]

17

This definition begins objectively enough, but quickly becomes far too vague to give us any idea of who the police might be tapping. For example, how many is a large number of people? Certainly, plenty of minor public order offences such as 'obstruction' could come under this heading. There seems to be nothing here to stop the police tapping the organisers of pickets or demonstrations, almost all of which might well cause an obstruction.

The second kind of warrant is issued to the intelligence services 'in the interest of national security'; these probably make up the majority of warrants. The term 'national security', although it appears in over fifty Acts of Parliament, is nowhere defined. The then Home Secretary, Leon Brittan, said in 1984 that it:

> . . . *encompasses the protection of the country and its institutions from internal and external threats of the safety of the realm, for example from terrorists, espionage, or major subversive activity.*[11]

Although they are presented as mere examples of what 'national security' might include, in themselves these criteria are very broad. Few would object to the use of tapping against terrorists or spies, but the inclusion of 'major subversive activity' caused some dissent when the Interception of Communications Bill was being debated in the House of Commons. This was despite the fact that subversion had always been grounds for tapping, under both Labour and Conservative administrations.

Who qualifies as a 'subversive'? Again, the official definition has broadened in recent decades. Since 1975, governments have relied on the explanation used by the then Labour Minister, Lord Harris of Greenwich. He held that subversive activities were:

> *Those which threaten the safety or wellbeing of the State, and which are intended to undermine or overthrow Parliamentary democracy by political, industrial or violent means.*[12]

This vague and contentious definition is not applied solely to those who contemplate illegal activities. The Home Secretary said in 1984 that:

18

Tactics which are not themselves unlawful could be used with the aim of subverting our democratic system of government.[13]

In the following year, he elaborated on this:

It has been a long standing view that, unfortunately, there are threats to our society and security represented by people who have not committed criminal offences.[14]

The third type of warrant, for the purpose of safeguarding the economic well-being of the country, is issued only by the Foreign Secretary. The Government have been even less forthcoming about the targets of these warrants. 'Economic' warrants may only be issued 'when it is considered necessary to acquire . . . information relating to the acts or intentions of persons outside the British Isles'[15], but, clearly, the people who are to be tapped will be inside Britain. Who are they? When the clause was debated in Parliament, the Home Secretary referred to the need to:

protect the country against adverse developments overseas, which do not affect our national security . . . but may have grave and damaging consequences for our economic well-being such as a threat to the supply of a commodity on which our economy is particularly dependent.[16]

It is probable that prime targets for this sort of tapping would include people working in the financial and commodity markets of the City of London, but one cannot be sure that it is restricted to them. After all, any threat to the stability of the apartheid regime in South Africa could be interpreted as a threat to the supply of several commodities vital to the UK, especially certain metals. We are not suggesting that anti-apartheid campaigners in Britain *are* being tapped under Foreign Secretary warrants, but there would appear to be nothing in the legislation to prevent this.

The official criteria, then, seem to make a very wide range of people vulnerable to tapping, yet they tell us nothing specific about who is actually tapped. For a fuller picture, we are forced to rely on information provided by former participants in the tapping industry and the evidence of the victims

19

of interception. Leaks by ex-intelligence officers are rare, partly because of the fierce loyalty that is inculcated into those who inhabit the secret world, but one rare glimpse of how targets are chosen was provided by a former MI5 officer, named Cathy Massiter, in 1985.

Massiter had entered the intelligence world with no qualms about its aims and activities but she became convinced that her employers were undermining democracy in the guise of defending national security. She resigned and decided to tell her story on a Channel 4 television programme called *MI5's Official Secrets*. In it she revealed that, during the mid-1970s, the National Council for Civil Liberties was targetted by MI5 as a 'subversive' organisation:

> *Anyone who was on the National Executive of NCCL, who worked for NCCL, or who was an active member . . . would be placed on permanent record . . . The police were asked to identify Branch Secretaries in their area and report on the activities of the NCCL in their area . . . The reports that we received about NCCL were such as to indicate quite clearly that there were* [Special Branch] *agents in* [the organisation].[17]

Other pressure groups monitored in this way, according to the programme, included Friends of the Earth, SHELTER, the housing charity, and the Campaign for Nuclear Disarmament. Radical lawyers and trades unionists were also said to be under surveillance.[18]

In the case of CND, as it was not itself officially regarded as 'subversive', a tap was authorised on the telephone of its vice Chair, John Cox. He was a member of the Communist Party, and this provided a convenient pretext to find out what CND were up to, especially as Cox lived in Wales, and had to keep constantly in touch with CND headquarters in London by phone. Other CND members were put under surveillance by similar ruses. In the case of CND Chair, Joan Ruddock, her lack of any vestige of a 'subversive affiliation' proved a severe handicap to MI5, until she gave an interview to a Soviet journalist who, unbeknownst to Ruddock, was also a KGB agent. This gave the Security Service the chance they wanted, and she was instantly entered in MI5's files as a 'contact of a hostile intelligence service'. At last, surveillance could begin.

MI5's Official Secrets included a sworn statement by an ex-MI5 clerk who preferred to remain anonymous. Her job had been to transcribe the tapes of telephone calls that had been tapped. Amongst other targets, she listed trades union officials such as Margaret Witham and Mick Duggan of the Civil Service union, the CPSA; Ken Gill, General Secretary of TASS; Mick McGahey and Arthur Scargill of the NUM, and Syd Harraway and Derek Robinson, both shop stewards in the motor industry. Naturally, as with CND, the taps were often justified in the name of subversion, rather than as straightforward snooping on active trades unionism. Cathy Massiter explained the process:

> *Whenever a major dispute came up, something at Fords or the mines, or the Post Office . . . immediately it would become a major area for investigation: what were the communists doing in respect of this particular industrial action, and usually an application for a telephone check would be taken out on the leading comrade in the particular union concerned.*[19]

By picking out particular 'subversives' active in striking unions, MI5 are able to get a clear picture of the organisation of industrial action. According to the ex-transcription clerk, when she was listening to the conversations of Syd Harraway, a Fords shop steward:

> *I was instructed by my superiors to listen out particularly for any reference to the Ford unions' bottom line in the pay negotiations. It was considered of vital importance to obtain the unions' private position.*[20]

Sometimes, bugs were placed in rooms where crucial union meetings were to take place. When the draughtsmen's union, TASS, were discussing a merger with the Engineering Union, a room in Ken Gill's house where officials from the two unions were to meet was broken into and bugged.

The information produced by these taps and bugs was not restricted to MI5. Asked about the Harraway tap, Cathy Massiter said:

> *I can only assume that [the unions' bottom line] . . . was*

21

requested because the Department of Employment wanted . . . this information. It surprises me in a way that it was done so blatantly.[21]

The revelations of the Massiter programme left many people similarly surprised. After the Opposition had made a fuss in Parliament, the Government responded by asking Lord Bridge, the Judicial Monitor of tapping (see Chapter 6), to investigate whether the Home Secretary had ever improperly authorised any taps over the period covered by the programme. These ludicrously inappropriate terms of reference failed to include the possibility of wholly *un*authorised tapping by the Security Service, and even ensured that any properly authorised taps mentioned by Massiter or the unnamed clerk would not be mentioned in Bridge's report. This document duly exonerated all Home Secretaries from 1970 to 1984 from ever having improperly authorised a tap. When it came out in 1985, the report was attacked from all quarters. In a savage letter to *The Times*, the former Home Secretary, and SDP MP for Hillhead, Roy Jenkins wrote:

> *A judge of status and quality ought not, in my view, to have agreed to conduct such an enquiry within the limitations of time and scope imposed by the Prime Minister. He has made himself appear a poodle of the executive.*[22]

Massiter's uniquely specific evidence confirms the long-held suspicions of those who believe themselves to be victims of tapping. However, in the atmosphere of rumour which surrounds the subject, it would be unwise to conclude that *all* such suspicions are well-founded. In order to round out Massiter's picture, then, we have to examine in detail some of the many allegations of tapping. In the rest of this chapter, we take a sceptical look at such victims' tales. Sceptical, not because we do not believe that they were tapped, but because of the startling lack of hard evidence. It is extremely difficult to 'prove' that one is tapped, but even the most sceptical analysis of the evidence, erring always on the side of caution in classifying stories as paranoid or self-serving, could not dismiss them all.

However, even where the targets of tapping correctly

22

identify the interception, we cannot treat the published cases as a representative sample of all those who are tapped. Some kinds of tap are more likely to be discovered than others. Some people are more likely than others to get a tip-off that tapping has occurred, either from people inside the police and security services, or from British Telecom staff. Finally, some people have better access to the media, or make a 'better story' in terms of Fleet Street's news values than the rest of us. For example, a large proportion of tapping reports in the press cover the tapping of VIPs: nationally known people such as Members of Parliament, or even Royalty. Similarly, we have far more stories about the tapping of national trades union officials than of shop stewards; far more about the surveillance of CND national office holders than the interception of the humble peacenik. Yet it is clear from *MI5's Official Secrets* that even local activists in 'subversive' or other radical groups, or those engaged in strike action, may be targetted for tapping and other forms of surveillance. Despite this imbalance in the published stories, and despite the startling lack of hard evidence to back up many tapping allegations, the tales of the tapped form an important part of the 'culture of tapping'.

To veterans of the Aldermaston marches and Trafalgar Square sit-ins of the early 1960s, Cathy Massiter's revelations about the tapping of peace activists came as no surprise. The nuclear disarmament movement had worried the British intelligence services since the 1950s, but tapping seems to have really got under way during the heyday of the direct action organisations, such as the Committee of 100, in the early sixties. The philosopher, Bertrand Russell, who helped organise sit-down demonstrations, together with others from the Committee, is said to have developed the tactic of organising fake meetings over the phone, and then recording the arrival of the police at the supposed scene of assignation. In the mid-sixties the Hampstead Group of the Committee of 100, a peace group which advocated non-violent direct action against the State's nuclear infrastructure, produced a pamphlet entitled *Mail Opening and Telephone Tapping in Britain*, which included comments and contributions from sympathetic postal and telecommunications workers. According to the leaflet:

Most Committee of 100 groups have alleged, and could reason-

23

ably suppose, that their calls and calls to them had been intercepted. . . . Occasionally, mischievous Committee members or those who have got tired of police tampering have arranged a fake, supposedly hush-hush demonstration, and have made absolutely sure that the phone call was the only way the information was passed: then one person has gone along to see a group of policemen standing aimlessly around waiting for a belated and non-existent demonstration.[23]

On one occasion, according to the Hampstead Group:

A supporter rang the Committee office to suggest a picket at the Egyptian Embassy, and the writer was the only person he spoke to on the phone. A meeting was arranged for 3pm the following day at Bond Street underground station. In order to avoid being tapped, the Committee member did all his phoning from public call boxes, yet the police were waiting for them.[24]

This is frustratingly circumstantial evidence, but another story in the leaflet would strain anyone's sense of coincidence:

A young sailor, Paul Valentine, absent without leave from his ship, told Douglas Kepper, then Secretary of London Committee of 100, on the telephone that he was meeting his girlfriend at Charing Cross Station at 3pm that day. When he got to the station, an Assistant Provost Marshal [naval policeman] was waiting to arrest him.[25]

The slow collapse of CND in the mid to late sixties presumably led to a diminution in surveillance, for it is not until the resurgence of the peace movement in the early eighties that we again hear CND tapping stories, this time accompanied by a variety of 'active measures', such as cutting off activists' telephones at crucial moments. Joan Ruddock, among others, recalls some strange experiences.

I replaced my receiver to regain the dial tone, and suddenly heard my own voice repeating a part of the conversation I'd just had. Therefore I now always assume that a third party is listening to my private phone conversations.[26]

On another occasion, an organiser at CND headquarters picked up a switchboard extension to hear, not the dialling tone, but the background noise of what he described as 'some form of control room'[27]. Others heard the same effect.

It is difficult to assess this type of tapping story. It is hard to believe that a legally authorised official tap at the local exchange, installed and run by professional tappers, would lead to such a clumsy playback. Professional tappers tend to use one-way links, which carry no signal back to betray their presence to the target. There is considerable evidence, though, to suggest that the police and intelligence services sometimes use clumsier, less orthodox methods of electronic surveillance (described in Chapter 8), and such unofficial taps might be repeated or work both ways in this manner. There could be legitimate reasons for the 'control room' effect, for example engineers working on the line, or even not uncommon faults in the network. As for the played-back conversations, they might be a form of harassment, an 'active measure' akin to those described in Chapter 9. It is difficult to see an *innocent* explanation for this effect, however, unless one casts doubt on the word, or the sanity, of the person who hears their conversation played back.

Playbacks may appear to be incontrovertible evidence of State tapping but, even here, one has to be cautious. There has been such a case, not involving CND, with a (comparatively) innocent, if rather bizarre, explanation. The then editor of *The Economist* magazine, Andrew Knight, became convinced that he was being tapped after his wife heard a playback of a call she had made to a cook, concerning a recipe for stuffed veal. Eventually, a Mr James Hazan, who claimed to tape his own calls because of having a bad memory, admitted to recording the recipe after overhearing Mrs Knight's conversation on a crossed line. Mr Hazan was quoted as saying:

I am very interested in cookery, so instead of hanging up, or asking them to get off the line, I listened . . . it is my hobby, and the recipe sounded good.[28]

It is, however, unlikely that the recorders of Joan Ruddock's telephone calls were after any sort of culinary information. What the tapped chef story does illustrate is the danger of assuming that State surveillance is behind even the strangest telephonic events.

The inconclusive nature of the evidence does not mean that CND activists are not being tapped. The government's attitude is that groups such as CND should be placed under surveillance, even if they are not, in themselves, regarded as subversive, on the grounds that there may well be Soviet infiltration into such organisations. This argument could apply to almost any organisation, from the Freemasons to the Brigade of Guards. In fact, recent history seems to show that British Intelligence, the Royal household, or Cambridge University are more likely places to find *bona fide* Russian agents than a public pressure group like CND. In reality, to argue that the possibility of infiltration justifies tapping the peace movement, is to justify any amount of surveillance of anyone involved in any campaigning group whatsoever.

This cavalier attitude is exemplified by the reaction of the government to the strange case of Tim and Bridie Wallis, a couple of CND supporters living near the Molesworth missile base. When friends rang them at their Cambridgeshire home, an answering machine replied, politely informing the callers that the Wallises were not at home, and asked them to leave their name, address, and phone number. The odd things were that this happened while Mr and Mrs Wallis *were* at home, and that they do not possess an answerphone machine. When the matter was raised in Parliament, the Chairman of the Commons Foreign Affairs Committee, Sir Anthony Kershaw, asked Home Secretary Leon Brittan:

Is my Right Honourable and Learned Friend aware that if he is not tapping these people, I want my money back?

The Secretary of State replied

Without going, as is customary, any further into these details, I can only say that my Honourable Friend should not expect a refund.[29]

The over-serious or the paranoid might interpret this as a clear confirmation that the Wallises, and presumably other local peace activists, were under surveillance. Without going this far, the exchange is nevertheless symptomatic of the attitudes of those in authority to the civil rights of peace activists.

The tapping of trades unionists has an even longer history than snooping on CND. It dates back at least as far as 1926, the year of the General Strike. Papers now removed from the Public Records Office show that Ernest Bevin, then head of the transport workers (and a future Foreign Secretary), had his phone tapped throughout the strike.[30] It was not until the 1970s, however, that complaints about tapping from trades unionists of all kinds began to proliferate, since when virtually no major strike has been without its tapping allegations, a rich contribution to the culture of tapping.

There are many such stories about the railworkers' dispute of 1972. An ASLEF official named Neil Milligan has told how he received a tip-off from a 'mole' on the same evening that his line was wired up.[31] Such information quite frequently reaches striking workers, often because a sympathetic telecom engineer in the exchange has noticed the tap. Although it is usually rigged up out of sight and sound of ordinary British Telecom staff, evidence of unusual wiring occasionally comes to light in the course of routine maintenance work. There is even a tale of a tapper being discovered by a group of exchange engineers, while in the process of wiring up a union telephone line. The technicians proceeded to regale him with a sarcastic chorus of 'Land of Hope and Glory'![32]

Multiple confirmation of tapping was obtained by the National Executive of the Fire Brigades Union, during their dispute with the Labour government in 1977. The Leeds strike HQ, run from the local Trades Council office, was equipped with a single payphone. An FBU official told the *MI5's Official Secrets* team:

> We had one man in that telephone box all the time, and he became aware that there were voices in the background saying 'They have just made a call; have you logged it?', and 'Have you got it?'. Now, we thought 'He's got to be crazy', – until we all heard it in turn over the nine week period.[33]

Another official received independent confirmation of surveillance:

We had long periods of discussion, negotiations in the HQ with our national employers, and a fairly senior civil servant happened to make a comment about something that we had decided as an Executive Council very shortly before, a day or two before, which was a tactic we would intend to use. One of my colleagues said to him 'Have you buggers been tapping our phone?', and he said 'We've got to know what you're gonna do', and I think that from that moment on, certainly all our Executive Council have been absolutely clear . . . that our phones have been and are being monitored.[34]

The next strike to get major attention from the tappers was the Grunwicks dispute, a local fight over union recognition that developed into a major *cause célèbre* for the Left. On one occasion, local exchange technicians actually removed a tap from the Grunwicks strike committee's line. It was speedily replaced.[35] Like the Leeds fire fighters, the strike committee used a local Trades Council offices, and they amused themselves one day by using a variation on the old Committee of 100 trick of the fake demonstration. Over the re-tapped phone, they arranged to vandalise a Grunwicks director's car. The director in question was, in fact, sympathetic to the strikers, who had no intention of touching his property; instead, the strike convenor, Jack Dromey, together with a couple of his colleagues went to see who turned up at the director's home. Sure enough, both ends of the street were covered by plain clothes detectives.[36]

A rather more humorous rendezvous with the forces of law and order was set up over the phone by a strike committee during the 1980 steel workers' strike. It involved a pretend mass picket of Granelli's Ice Cream Factory, in Rotherham. This time, the strike committee was waiting in a car, outside the cornet works, to watch the police turn up in force; expecting, no doubt, to find brawny steelmen wrestling in the street with the ice cream van drivers.[37]

By making these fake arrangements, groups of people are able to test their suspicions of tapping for themselves. Convincing the public at large, however, is a rather more difficult task. For a start, it is always possible that the police information comes from a spy infiltrated into the group, or from a bug in the offices, rather than from tapping. Both these tactics have often been used by the Special Branch and MI5 in the past. However, bugging is usually more expensive and time consuming than a tap, while information from agents within suspected organisations is notoriously less reliable than more objective surveillance techniques. There may, therefore, be a *prima facie* suspicion of tapping, but this is very different from proof.

For the 'fake picket' test to be at its most reliable one would have to attempt to screen out the possibility of other forms of surveillance, by limiting the number of people who know of the fake plans, checking for bugs (if possible), and avoiding the use of public call boxes. For maximum credibility, the whole process, and particularly the arrival of the police at the scene of the false picket, should be witnessed by a neutral figure, perhaps a solicitor or a trustworthy journalist. Unfortunately, there is no recorded case that measures up to these standards.

Despite this, there is no doubt that many trade disputes are monitored closely by the security services. When the Post Office Engineering Union, whose members are in a better position than most of us to know about tapping, issued a report on the subject in 1980, their General Treasurer, David Norman, told the TUC:

> *Whether you're on the General Council or a Branch Secretary, if your union's engaged in industrial action, then there's plenty of evidence to suggest that your calls are being monitored by the Security Service.*[38]

The POEU itself suffered from tapping in 1983, during a dispute over the privatisation of BT. David Norman wrote afterwards:

> *I suspect that their long hours monitoring my calls proved to be of little interest, because all of us were well aware of the dangers of electronic eavesdropping, and devised a series of cryptic codes to prevent advance warning of our action being given . . . I suppose it was not long before our security services became aware that we were using some form of code, but, given its crude nature, they probably found difficulty in cracking it.*[39]

Despite the fact that British Telecom is now a private company, all its employees have to sign the Official Secrets Act. The National Communications Union (as the POEU is now known) is therefore wary of its members making public all they know about tapping. On one occasion, when some BT engineers were due to talk about tapping on a television programme, their employer issued a public warning to all its staff about the dangers of transgressing the Act. The would-be whistleblowers did not turn up at the studio.[40]

This incident occurred during the 1984–5 miners' strike, when allegations of tapping reached a new pitch. The POEU described official assurances that the miners' phones were not being tapped as 'laughable', and demanded to be allowed to investigate and report on the allegations without risk of prosecution under the Official Secrets Act. The government did not agree to the request.[41]

In fact as *MI5's Official Secrets* later disclosed, the leaders of the NUM had been tapped for a long time before the strike began. Arthur Scargill had complained of tapping as head of the Yorkshire miners as early as 1980. No dispute was going on at the time, so presumably Scargill himself was classified as a subversive. According to Cathy Massiter, his phone had been tapped since the late seventies 'in view of his particular history and his known political views'. According to the unnamed transcription clerk, the NUM President 'would occasionally shout abuse into the phone at the people who were tapping him'.[42]

Also under surveillance before the start of the strike was the Scottish miners' leader, Mick McGahey. The tap on his home telephone became the subject of in-jokes among the staff at MI5's Curzon Street HQ, owing to the supposed garrulousness of his wife, whose calls were laboriously transcribed by the patriotic minions on the fifth floor. Even these calls, however, were grist to the intelligence mill, which was 'able to get information from her chattering [about her husband's movements] which he himself was careful to conceal'.[43]

If its leaders had always been tapped, it was not until the strike was under way that ordinary NUM members found themselves under such surveillance. Sometimes the tapping seems to have been fairly amateurish. On one occasion, the industrial correspondent of the *Sheffield Morning Telegraph* was interviewing a Yorkshire NUM official by telephone when the two men heard police radio messages coming over the phone. When the NUM representative shouted 'Hello copper, can you hear me?', the interference ceased.[44] Another time, the owner of a bus company in Pontypridd, South Wales, was rung up by strikers wanting a bus to Derbyshire. Minutes later, the Derbyshire police phoned to ask how many pickets he was bringing.[45]

Allegations of tapping during the miners' dispute were sometimes denied by the police and the Home Office, but more usual was the refusal to comment. Home Secretary Leon Brittan said:

> *What we are seeing is the smear a week technique . . . I am not going to deal with allegations that fly around like confetti.*[46]

It could, of course, be that the stories of tapping during the miners' strike and other disputes are all paranoia, or even pure lies, but it is difficult to discount the word of people not involved in the dispute, such as journalists and the owners of bus companies. In the end we cannot know for sure, but for those who heard the Prime Minister describe striking miners as 'the enemy within', it is difficult to believe that all the allegations of tapping during the dispute were untrue.

No one can be absolutely sure that they are not tapped. Even people who may themselves be above suspicion of being subversive or engaged in serious crime may be tapped, because of what they know, or because of what they may be told. The fact that the Left are the most vocal on the subject of tapping should not convince others that they themselves are not tapped. In many ways, the VIP denizens of Westminster and the City of London are far *more* likely to be of interest to the intelligence world than is the average would-be agitator. Unfortunately, they seem less anxious to tell the rest of us about their experiences. The schoolboy code of silence which helps to bind the British Establishment together also discourages any mention of matters which could be interpreted as coming under the holy rubric of 'national security'.

The Left do not, however, have a monopoly of paranoia. Although tax evasion is widely regarded as one of the least

31

reprehensible (if most lucrative) of crimes, avid supporters of free enterprise have still accused the Government of tapping tax evaders.[47] In 1980 the Conservative MP for Huddersfield West, Geoffrey Dickens, wrote to the Prime Minister about an anonymous company director, who believed that tax and excise officials were tapping his phone. Dickens asked:

> Are there any circumstances whereby officers of the Inland Revenue or VAT officials can be given authority to either bug . . . tap telephones [or] intercept the Royal Mail, and use any such information as evidence?[49]

Mrs Thatcher replied that the only circumstances in which this sort of white collar crime would justify tapping would be:

> A case involving a substantial and continuing fraud which would seriously damage the revenue or the economy of the country if it went on unchecked.[49]

One fraud case in which there were allegations of tapping occurred in 1985, when a company named Ultraleisure was accused of using the Government's Export Credit Guarantee Scheme to trade in Europe, contrary to EEC law. The Chairman of Ultraleisure claimed, through his solicitor, that calls made by his wife from a public call box were played back to her when she was questioned by Lincolnshire police. The police and the Home Office were unable either to confirm or deny these allegations.[50]

Complaints from businessmen, however, are rare. There have never, for example, been any reported cases in which one of the Foreign Secretary's taps, for the purpose of defending the economic wellbeing of the nation, has been used. This is hardly surprising: apart from the code of silence, it would be virtually impossible to discern such a tap, as it would be unlikely to be used in such a way that the source of the material would be compromised.

More frequent than complaints from the business world are allegations of tapping from MPs, despite the fact that successive governments since 1966 have maintained that MPs are immune from such surveillance.[51] In 1976 Bob Cryer MP read in his local newspaper that his phone was being tapped by the security services to check his suitability for a Cabinet post.[52]

At about the same time, many other Labour Members, including Michael Meacher, were alleging that they had been tapped because of the leak of a secret Department of Health and Social Security document on child benefit.[53] Neil Kinnock, too, believed that he was tapped in the seventies.[54] Yet at the time the idea was pooh-poohed by Labour officials. When a former counter-intelligence officer discovered by accident that telephones at Transport House, the Labour Party's HQ, were tapped, the General Secretary of the party was quoted as saying that he was not losing any sleep over the matter. 'This is London', he said, 'this is Britain'.[55]

Some MPs are lucky enough to be granted a privilege not available to other targets of tapping: the intervention of the eavesdropper to say precisely what he and his colleagues find offensive in the conversation. This happened to the Tory MP, Sir Tufton Beamish, in 1950. He was having a conversation with someone at the War Office, when a voice broke in and warned, 'Please remember that I have been listening to your conversation. Please remember to be more careful in future'.[56] Two and a half decades later, Labour MP Tom Litterick was talking with the social services correspondent of *The Times*, Pat Healy, when a voice interrupted to tell the journalist, 'You had better not print that'. When asked his identity, the voice replied, 'That doesn't matter, but don't you dare print that'.[57]

Even serving ministers have been tapped. In 1974, it has been alleged, the Minister for Overseas Development, Judith Hart, had her conversations with a Communist Party official recorded by MI5.[58] In an earlier Labour government, in 1964, the Lord Chancellor, Lord Gardiner, was accustomed to holding his more sensitive conversations with the Attorney General in a car, for fear of being tapped or bugged by the Security Service. Fifteen years later Lord Gardiner said:

I have had some experience in this field, and I am still not certain whether or not my telephone was bugged by MI5, but I still think it probable.[59]

It is possible to go higher still than the Lord Chancellor. It has even been claimed that King Edward VIII was tapped, before and after his abdication in 1936, on the orders of the

Prime Minister, Stanley Baldwin.[60] On a slightly lower level of State drama, in 1965 two telephonists claimed that they had learned the names the Royal children called the Queen. *The Wiltshire Echo*, a local paper owned by Woodrow Wyatt, Labour MP for Bosworth, alleged that it was common practice among Post Office operators to listen in to Royal calls.[61] The Post Office responded with the devastatingly logical argument that the allegations:

> *Were said to be based on statements by two telephone operators . . . Both the operators were girls, one has since been suspended from duty, and the other was a telephonist who recently resigned while under disciplinary notice in connection with another matter.*[62]

It seems that, in the world of the tappers, nothing is sacred. Even the police themselves have complained of tapping. At one London police station in the 1970s, the officers became suspicious that their phones were being tapped. This went on for some weeks, until a constable was arrested for selling the addresses of wealthy householders who were going on holiday to a gang of burglars.[63] In 1984 the Police Federation lodged an official protest with the Chief Constable of Greater Manchester, James Anderton, after a tape recorder was built into the switchboard at Chester House, the headquarters of the Manchester police. It was alleged that the recorder was used, not only for taping 999 calls, but for eavesdropping on the private conversations of the officers themselves. As a result there were a number of transfers out of the district, and two resignations, one a policewoman forced to leave after the discovery of her affair with a senior officer.[64]

This is by no means an exhaustive account of tapping allegations. Apart from the three areas on which we have concentrated – CND, the trades unions and VIPs – we may be pretty certain that others are under such surveillance: for instance, officials of the Communist Party, the various Trotskyist sects, Left groups in the Labour Party, and nationalist parties such as Plaid Cymru and the Scottish National Party, as well as far-Right groups. Particularly targetted, too, are investigative journalists and pressure groups that engage in direct action such as Friends of the Earth and Greenpeace.

One does not have to protest about anything as sensitive as defence matters to come under the beady eye of the Security Service. The published stories of tapping are, moreover, the merest tip of the iceberg of State surveillance, which looms under a wide sea of people. In one way or another, almost all of us are potential protesters, potential dissidents, potential subversives. In one way or another, virtually any of us might be tapped.

However, very few people are regularly tapped, and many of the more paranoid critics of tapping might be surprised at how few calls are actually recorded. Britain in the eighties is not a police state in the classic, Orwellian sense. What has prevented this, however, are not the laws and administrative regulations governing tapping which pass as 'accountability' in the case of the intelligence services. Rather, our current defences against total surveillance lie in the institutional and financial constraints put on the spies, and, above all, on the restraining influence of precedent.

This means that, in order to get closer to answering the question 'Who is tapped?' we must take a look at the agencies involved in tapping, both the 'customers' for taps, such as the police and intelligence services, and the people who often run the physical operation of tapping, GCHQ and British Telecom. Who are the tappers? This is the subject of the next chapter.

Chapter 2

The Tappers and Their Targets

It is almost axiomatic that with each new method of communication comes the shadow of a new method of surveillance. The two original techniques of transmitting speech over long distances – wire telephony and radio – were both developed in the late nineteenth century. The complementary surveillance operations were under way early in the twentieth century. The technological differences between the two methods of communication naturally encouraged the evolution of two separate systems of official eavesdropping, but the fact that this was what actually happened was equally the result of two very different sets of demands for surveillance facilities from two distinct quarters within government. Later in this chapter, we see how the almost casual interception of foreign radio transmissions led to the rise of signals intelligence and the growth of the electronic eavesdropping empire run by the Government Communications Headquarters (GCHQ). First we look at the tapping of calls carried on the domestic telephone network from the perspective of the customers – the agencies which initiate the taps and make use of the intercepted conversations.

The principal sponsor of domestic tapping is the Security Service, better known as MI5. The agency began life as the home section of the Secret Service Bureau, an organisation set up in 1909 to compensate for a dearth of information about Germany, then Britain's main imperial rival. (The foreign section became the Secret Intelligence Service, SIS.) Combatting German espionage in Britain was, in the early days, MI5's main task. The agency was not granted powers of enforcement (arrest, right of search and so on) and was required to work in total secrecy, which it did using agents recruited by MI5 officers and a vast 'Registry' of personal records acquired from police forces around the country. From the very beginning, MI5 also established valuable contacts with two other official bodies.

The first was the Post Office with which MI5 made arrangements for letter and telephone interception. The Post Office already had many years' experience of meeting State intelligence requirements – indeed, one reason Cromwell set it up in the seventeenth century was to facilitate letter-opening – and as it was also a government ministry, an agreement to cooperate with MI5 was a formality. In the context of phone-tapping, the Post Office was asked to make the necessary physical connections and ensure that the taps worked properly, while MI5 selected the target lines and took receipt of the intercepts. This division of responsibility, which continues to this day with British Telecom, also governs domestic tapping by other agencies.

The second link forged by MI5 was with the Special Branch of the Metropolitan Police. The Branch had been formed in 1883 specifically to uncover Irish nationalists then engaged in a major bombing campaign in the capital. (Its original, more descriptive name – the Political Branch – had been dropped as too controversial.) By the time of MI5's appearance in 1909 the Branch's remit had grown to include detection of bombing and assassination plots, VIP protection, and occasional scrutiny of travellers passing through British ports. The Branch had both the personnel (about fifty officers) and the experience of intelligence-oriented work to support MI5. Branch officers, under Security Service direction, carried out the labour-intensive physical surveillance of suspects, although MI5 did eventually form its own team of 'watchers'.

The work of MI5 and Special Branch was radically and permanently altered by the Russian revolution of October 1917. The British Government anticipated some form of alliance between disaffected British workers and the new Russian regime, mediated through Bolshevik agents and sympathisers within Britain. A wave of strikes had begun the previous year which had threatened, among other things, armaments production. Monitoring this new foe precipitated a demarcation dispute between MI5 and Special Branch over who should be snooping on whom. The dispute was resolved in 1921, after protracted Whitehall politicking, in favour of

37

MI5, which during the ensuing decade established complete hegemony over the Special Branch. It made no difference, however, to intelligence priorities: as the 1920s progressed, in the words of the writer Anthony Verrier, 'Russophobia increased to the point . . . where anyone in Britain who professed sympathy with Russia – not necessarily with communism – was likely to come under surveillance'.[1]

The Security Service's primary, continuous targets – aliens (official or otherwise), trades unions and political dissenters – were fully established in its corporate mind by the early 1920s. They have remained essentially the same ever since, although there have been significant changes in the relative importance attached to each. The tacit blessing of Whitehall and of governments of all political parties has supported them throughout.

The agency's main contribution to the Second World War was a largely successful scheme of converting captured German spies into double agents to act as conduits for disinformation to their erstwhile controllers. Even during the war against fascism, however, left-wing subversion was not forgotten: an official Committee on Communism, fed with reports from MI5, deliberated between 1941 and 1945.[2]

After the war, Communist agitation came to be seen as the power behind the growing nationalist movements in the colonies, where a large number of MI5 officers were posted at the time to prop up the local security and intelligence organs. Military signals units handled most of the tapping in the colonies, a tradition which continued into the 1970s in Northern Ireland where the British Army was responsible for most of the phone tapping in the province.

Meanwhile, MI5's major domestic target, the Communist Party of Great Britain, had lost its attraction to the Soviets as a local political instrument, while the Party's own domestic influence shrivelled before the chill of the Cold War. Despite its ever-declining fortunes and membership, the Party has been of constant interest to MI5. The telephone lines into Communist Party headquarters have been monitored since at least the 1920s, making the Party the front-runner for the honour of being subject to Britain's longest-running telephone tap.[3]

Surveillance of the Communist Party was motivated by two

factors. Firstly, MI5 needed a complete membership list to fulfil the requirements of Positive Vetting, a screening system for Government employees introduced in 1951 at American behest, which was designed to prevent Soviet penetration by excluding individuals with subversive inclinations or unseemly personal circumstances from access to classified material. The defection that year of Donald Maclean, a senior British diplomat specialising in Anglo-American relations, prompted the American demand. Maclean had been under investigation by MI5 who had followed a standard pattern of physical surveillance, telephone tapping and mail interception.[4] (By contrast, a phone tap was *not* allowed in the Mitchell case, a decade later, when MI5's own deputy chief came under suspicion as a Soviet agent. Mitchell was eventually cleared by the investigation.)[5]

The second reason was the Party's perceived support within a number of trades unions. Industrial reports to Labour Cabinet ministers during the late 1960s were couched in terms of the influence and attitude of the Communist Party in a particular dispute. This was partly because of the political climate but also because MI5 had, since 1952, been governed by a ministerial directive, stipulating that its sole function was

> the Defence of the Realm as a whole, from external and internal dangers arising from attempts at espionage and sabotage, or from actions of persons and organisations whether directed from within or without the country, which may be judged to be subversive of the State.[6]

This clause entrusted MI5 with considerable discretion in its investigation of 'subversion', with the result that pressure groups seeking only to change Government policy by legitimate means came under surveillance as well as those actively seeking the overthrow of the State. Delegating the policy decision of what constitutes 'subversion' to MI5 allowed the agency to choose its own surveillance priorities on the basis of its own political perceptions. These perceptions became hopelessly distorted – particularly investigations of organised labour, which were increasingly conducted on the premise that trades unionism was inherently subversive.

MI5 was not wholly responsible for such developments:

during the 1960s, Labour ministers (who could hardly condemn trades unions as 'subversive') gratefully received regular reports from its industrial section, albeit couched in terms of the influence of such-and-such a political grouping.[7]

At the beginning of the 1970s, the realignment accelerated: MI5 began to shift 'from being essentially a counter-espionage organisation, aimed at hostile foreign powers, to a domestic surveillance organisation'.[8] Around this time there were increasing demands on the agency in the form of growing industrial militancy, the return of urban terrorism and the rise of the 'New Left' – an amorphous, fluid combine of Trotskyist and anarchist groups, and organisations campaigning on single issues. The emergence of a new breed of union shop steward, more militant than its predecessors and less hidebound by the diktats of union bureaucracy, caused a problem. Conversely, the scale of Soviet intelligence operations in Britain was drastically and irreversibly reduced after September 1971 when the Government ordered the expulsion of 105 Russian diplomats. The miners' strike of the following year was a watershed in consolidating the new priorities. However, the change in MI5's policy was also supported, and perhaps stimulated, by a major reappraisal of threats to internal security conducted in the late 1960s, as a result of which,

> long-term contingency plans were made to deal with a . . . state of emergency, a general strike, an insurrection in one region of the country, and ultimately, a general insurrection leading to revolution.[9]

These plans, drafted by the military and incorporated in a subsequent Army operations manual, drew extensively on the experience of counter-insurgency campaigns in former colonies and referred specifically to the need for an effective intelligence system. Although they have no doubt undergone subsequent revision, the very existence of the plans attests to the State's concern with defending itself from its own citizens. Such preoccupation continues, not only in the Cabinet, but also inside MI5. One commentator invited to speak to a group of MI5 staff early in 1985 was 'shaken to hear the agency's head, Sir John Jones, talking about the dangerousness of trade unions and of the "threat within" '[10]. Even when the overall political atmosphere did not favour such trenchant attitudes, the security services were still able to dictate domestic intelligence policy because of governmental unwillingness to impose effective control.

Curzon Street House, a bleak, imposing building in London's Mayfair district, distinguished only by an encircling concrete apron at first floor level, is MI5's current headquarters – the nerve centre of an intelligence organisation employing 2,000 staff and dispensing an annual budget (for 1985/6) of £160 million. Its priorities are reflected in the fact that F Branch, which monitors domestic subversion, is larger than the other main operational division, K Branch, which is responsible for counter-espionage. Within K Branch, numbered sections each deal with a set of legations and with investigations of suspected agents recruited by a foreign power, liaising closely with SIS and allied security services. F Branch work is divided between two categories of target: terrorism in Britain and the movement of sensitive items, such as arms and explosives, make up the 'hard' targets; the other category – the 'soft' targets – comprise trades unions, political factions and certain professions (teachers, lawyers, journalists and MPs have been cited). Both Branches attempt to recruit and control agents in their areas of interest, a delicate business which is carried out by special sections within each. F Branch desk officers who study domestic politics also spend a certain amount of time reading party literature and union journals to keep themselves aquainted with the policies and personalities of target organisations. The information acquired is stored in the Registry which has been computerised since the late 1960s and now runs on British-built ICL machines accessible through a network of some 200 terminals. The system has a reported capacity of 20 billion characters (20 Gigabytes), enough for a 1,000 word dossier on each of 3 million people.[11]

Beyond these sources, K and F may call upon the sinister technicians of A Branch, formally entitled 'Intelligence Resources and Operations'. A Branch units handle MI5's dirty work – breaking into private houses, planting and operating bugs (but not taps), extracting information from other Government departments without authorisation, following people in cars and on foot – with a recipe book of bizarre and jokey codenames to label each source (Cinnamon, Ratcatcher, Still

Life). Other A Branch sections transcribe the recordings from bugs and telephone taps and liaise with GCHQ.

K and F between them generate most of MI5's phone tap business. A smaller amount is carried out on behalf of C Branch, whose main function is the supervision of personnel vetting for Government departments, quasi-official bodies like the BBC and private companies whose employees have access to State secrets; it also vets the members of juries selected for Official Secrets and terrorist trials. Some of the domestic surveillance information finds its way to the Civil Contingencies Unit, a semi-clandestine Cabinet Office creature which plans government strategies to counter major strikes, and hijacking or hostage incidents. Phone taps are also common during inquiries into leaks of official information, documentary or otherwise. These are handled in various ways, sometimes internally; alternatively an outside agency, usually either MI5 or the Metropolitan Police Serious Crimes Squad, is brought in to conduct the investigation.

Much low-level and routine surveillance work, particularly outside London, is farmed out to the local police Special Branch. Before 1961, only the Metropolitan force had a Special Branch: in the provinces, comparable duties were carried out by officers seconded from the regular CID. Today, there are approximately 1,250 officers engaged in Special Branch duties in Britain's fifty-one constabularies. The Chief Constable of each force is nominally in charge of the individual Branch but in practice operations are directed nationally from London under MI5 direction or by MI5 regional liaison staff.

The Metropolitan squad, with some 400 officers, is by far the largest of the British Special Branches and is similar in size to that of the Royal Ulster Constabulary. It has a particular responsibility, dating from its Victorian origins, for Irish activism on the mainland – which MI5 has not managed to take over – and for guarding diplomatic premises, most of which are located in the London area. The Metropolitan Branch's greater experience and expertise has allowed them to be less subservient to MI5 than provincial Branches. Official publications indicate that only the Metropolitan Branch applies for tapping warrants directly and on the same terms as MI5, while others are channelled through MI5.

Members of the Metropolitan Special Branch, in common

with their counterparts outside the capital, have little contact with their colleagues in the remainder of the police force. The regular police have long used phone taps during major criminal investigations although the level of demand has never matched that of MI5 and Special Branch. Recent trends in policing, particularly those emphasising the role of surveillance and information-gathering, portend an increase in the volume of police tapping. There have been repeated allegations, for example, of police monitoring of phone calls on the Broadwater Farm estate in North London since the disturbances of September 1985.[12] The archetype of this style of policing is the Metropolitan Police C11 Criminal Intelligence squad. C11 is concrned with organised crime, particularly armed robbery and drug trafficking, but only for the purpose of collecting intelligence on suspects rather than making arrests. Part of their work, as described by one C11 officer, involves the construction of detailed personality profiles based on a period of continuous surveillance, very likely including a phone tap:

At the end of it we knew everything about him. We knew what credit cards he was using, what he was buying, how many times he would go to the bank, and what he went there for. We knew what his wife was buying in the shops and how much she was spending. We even knew where his daughter went at night, who she was mixing with and what she was spending.[13]

Drugs are also a particular interest of the third main customer for domestic phone taps: the Customs and Excise, particularly its secretive Investigation Division. Drug importation did not become a major Customs interest until the 1970s, when an accelerating influx of heroin and cocaine forced a change of focus away from the smuggling of diamonds and watches, against which most taps had been directed since Customs first began to use them in 1946.[14] Then, in the early 1980s, another new priority emerged affecting both the intelligence and Customs services. This was the export of high technology products, mainly computers, which have potential military applications. Sales of such equipment to the Soviet bloc have been regulated since the late 1940s under the auspices of the trans-national Co-ordinating Committee for

Multilateral Export Controls, commonly known as COCOM, staffed by government trade officials from most NATO countries plus Japan. The Reagan administration in the United States has made strenuous and successful efforts to augment both the scope of the COCOM embargo and the vigilance of individual members, as a result of which the Soviet bloc has increased its efforts to procure Western hardware.[15] In Britain, where there have been a number of convictions for illegal export of computer systems in the last few years, telephone taps are a key part of the enforcement programme, 'Project Arrow'.

The demand for intelligence on the international trade in illicit or sensitive items like drugs, weapons and computers can hardly be met by tapping only the domestic telephone network. Here we enter the arcane realm of signals intelligence, known to its practitioners as SIGINT.

SIGINT is officially defined today as the 'reception and analysis of foreign communications and other electronic transmissions for intelligence purposes'.[16] The key phrase here is 'foreign communications' which covers everything from private international phone calls to radio messages between army units to despatches between governments and their embassies. Its origins can be traced to the interception of radio messages by British wireless stations in the first few days of World War One. The transmissions seemed to emanate from Germany; moreover, many of the intercepts turned out to have been encoded, an obstacle which the new British intelligence machine was not immediately equipped to tackle. Both the Admiralty and the War Office set up rival sections to break the German cyphers and unravel the encrypted messages. The Admiralty unit, commonly known as 'Room 40' after its habitat, fared considerably better than its War Office counterpart, called MI1b.

Initially, Room 40's intercepts were all naval messages, easily acquired through a network of receiving stations, variously run by the Admiralty itself, the Post Office and the Marconi company, collectively dubbed the 'Y Service'. In the summer of 1915, however, Room 40 formed a diplomatic section which eavesdropped on German Government messages carried on submarine telegraph cables. The successes of this particular section over the next three years strengthened the hand of the Whitehall faction which favoured retaining a SIGINT agency during peacetime. In 1919 the squabbling wartime SIGINT units were fused into the Government Code and Cypher School, which was located in the same premises as Secret Intelligence Service (SIS) and put under the nominal control of the Chief of SIS, although it operated with almost complete autonomy. Its success with Soviet diplomatic codes during the 1920s proved of immense value to Britain's diplomatic duel with the Soviet government and guaranteed the School's future.

Two important developments in the late 1930s had a lasting impact on British SIGINT. The first was the establishment of an overseas eavesdropping station in Hong Kong, in order to monitor Japanese expansionism in the region, which set the pattern for the creation of similar installations in other British colonies. The second was the emergence of the German military-industrial complex which led the School to devote special attention to commercial communications for items relevant to the Reich's burgeoning military economy. It was the Second World War, however, which established the preeminence of SIGINT as the most productive source of foreign intelligence. It also produced collaborative agreements between the British and American SIGINT agencies which had profound consequences for the subsequent development of the British tapping industry.

In August 1939 the Government Code and Cypher School was evacuated to the green fields and loud architecture of Bletchley Park, a Victorian mansion in Buckinghamshire. At Bletchley, academics and engineers, many of them recruited from the Post Office, wrestled with 'Engima', the new machine-generated German cypher system. Some versions of 'Engima' were solved in 1940 and read for the rest of the war; others remained largely impregnable.

Across the Atlantic, at the end of September 1940, the American SIGINT agency, the Signal Intelligence Service, had decoded the most secure Japanese diplomatic messages, also encrypted by machine and known as 'Purple'. The British discovered the American breakthrough and by the end of the year, American neutrality notwithstanding, the two nations had negotiated a secret agreement allowing for *a full exchange of cryptographic systems, cryptanalytical techniques, direction finding, radio interception, and other technical communication matters pertaining to the diplomatic, military, naval and air services of Germany, Japan and Italy.*[17]

In 1942 British SIGINT was reorganised under the new title – still in use – of Government Communications Headquarters (GCHQ) and given a new home at Eastcote in north-west London. By the spring of 1943 GCHQ and its American partners felt sufficient mutual confidence to take their cooperation a stage further. The BRUSA (Britain-USA) SIGINT agreement, signed on 17 May, authorised the exchange of personnel as well as technology; it also established common procedures for the processing and distribution of SIGINT products, and set down joint regulations on security.

BRUSA was the principal link in the wartime intelligence co-operation between Britain and the United States, and both parties intended that SIGINT collaboration should continue after the war. Intelligence-gathering from within the Soviet Union, the main enemy after Hitler's defeat, was especially hazardous because of formidable internal security. Defectors, as opposed to agents who stay inside, were the main human source of information; SIS and CIA ran a joint defection programme – one of the products of a 1946 accord between Prime Minister Attlee and President Truman.[18] However, until the era of satellite photography, SIGINT produced the best intelligence on the Soviet Union and continues to be a vital source of information today.

The inequality of the SIGINT partnership was self-evident in most fields: essentially, the Americans had more money and more resources. The secret UKUSA pact of 1947, which superseded BRUSA and is still in force today, did two things to realise that objective: first, it confirmed that the BRUSA arrangements for exchanges and common procedures would continue in peacetime; secondly, Canada and Australia, both of whom were involved in Japanese SIGINT operations up to 1945, were formally included as signatories. The UKUSA pact also established a hierarchy of members. At the top is the US National Security Agency (NSA), formed in 1952 under Presidential directive to assume control of all American SIGINT operations. NSA is described as the 'First Party' to the agreement; the other English-speaking signatories – Britain, Australia, Canada and New Zealand – are 'Second Parties' although Britain was, by one account, given the slightly elevated status of a 'senior partner'.[19] Other NATO allies qualify for 'Third Party' status. NSA and GCHQ have SIGINT agreements outside UKUSA with a dozen countries including Japan, South Africa, Brazil and, more recently, China. GCHQ has an especially close relationship with the South Africans.

The main signatories aimed to monitor the world's entire electronic and telecommunications output through a global network of eavesdropping facilities. Arrangements were made to try to avoid duplication, while 'a general agreement not to restrict data'[20] was supposed to guarantee equal access to all intercepts. The Americans tended to ignore these aspects of the agreement, despite the inefficiency of overlapping. This was partly because their UKUSA allies had only enough resources to intercept a limited number of channels, partly because their newly-adopted global foreign policy stimulated a considerable appetite for intelligence.

Transatlantic SIGINT diplomacy prospered in the early 1950s as the implementation of UKUSA's numerous provisions continued. Special communications facilities were established to link monitoring outposts and headquarters buildings. Liaison offices sprang up at the major SIGINT complexes, some of which were jointly operated by several agencies. GCHQ now has an office of more than fifty staff at Fort Meade, the Maryland headquarters of the National Security Agency. GCHQ itself moved its headquarters once again in 1953 to its current residence on two large sites in Cheltenham in Gloucestershire. NSA alone exercised the general right under the pact to operate its own SIGINT stations on the territory of other signatories.

In the autumn of 1956, the entire infrastructure of Anglo-American relations was put in jeopardy by the Suez crisis. NSA became temporarily involved in recriminations after the event because of allegations published in Britain that the US had been decoding British military communications. The British had no cause for complaint, having eavesdropped on American submarine cable traffic since the early part of the century. For a while it seemed possible that UKUSA would become a casualty of this transatlantic dispute. However, GCHQ's whole operation was organised around the pact. Financial strictures meant that its only future outside was the unappetising prospect of retrenchment to a SIGINT establishment appropriate to a moderate European power and largely bereft of American-derived intelligence material. NSA was equally keen to restore the transatlantic link-up. Britain's most attractive asset was the imperial residue, an incongruous assortment of territories peppered around the globe. Some of these are well suited to SIGINT activities: Cyprus, Hong Kong, Tristan da Cunha, Ascension Island, Gibraltar, St Helena and the Indian Ocean fortress of Diego Garcia all play host to UKUSA SIGINT stations.

GCHQ's financial dependency on NSA is apparent from a letter, written in 1969, from GCHQ boss Leonard Hooper to his NSA counterpart, Marshall P. Carter:

I know that I have leaned shamefully on you, and sometimes taken your name in vain, when I needed approval for something at this end.[21]

Carter's response to this missive, unearthed from his private papers by the American writer James Bamford, is not recorded but the genuine friendship between the two intelligence bosses fortuitously coincided, it seems, with one of the smoothest periods of the partnership. The imbalance continued to grow, however, in correspondence to the relative economic fortunes of the two nations. During the 1970s and into the 1980s, GCHQ steadily relinquished more and more of the transatlantic bed, while the intricate liaison structures and an increasing technological dependence ensured that the agency was firmly bound into the UKUSA system. Since GCHQ is Britain's major supplier of foreign and economic intelligence, the independence and viability of the foreign and trade policies for which GCHQ's information is used is called into question. Britain was co-opted, for example, into providing SIGINT support for the American war effort in Vietnam, in defiance of declared Government policy, by virtue of the strategic position occupied by GCHQ monitoring stations in Hong Kong.

GCHQ is now 'the majority shareholder in British

intelligence'[22]. The agency provides at least three-quarters of Britain's foreign intelligence itself from intercepted radio and other communications traffic, and provides vital technical support for the other intelligence services. It now controls 11,500 full-time staff, composed of 7,000 civilians and 4,500 service personnel. Of the civilians, between 4,000 and 5,000 work at Cheltenham in a disciplinary pot-pourri of crypt-analysts, linguists, administrators, radio technicians, computer specialists and every flavour of engineer. The Cheltenham estate is divided between two main complexes at Oakley and Benhall, located four miles apart on the eastern and western outskirts of the city. The Oakley site houses the administrative headquarters and, up the hill away from the town, GCHQ's computer facilities. Laboratories and workshops populate Benhall.

GCHQ's functions are split up between alphabetically-labelled divisions grouped under four directorates: Operations and Requirements, Organisation and Establishment, Plans, and Communications Security. The most important of these, Operations and Requirements, contain those divisions reponsible for processing and analysing the raw material picked up by GCHQ's monitoring sites. The outposts are variously staffed by civilian and military personnel: the civilians belong to the Composite Signals Organisation (CSO), a GCHQ annexe which evolved from the old 'Y Service', while military SIGINT staff are generally attached to specialist army and air force units (the navy has only a minor SIGINT capability). In addition, RAF pilots have long conducted electronic reconnaissance missions against the Soviet bloc and other nations, latterly Argentina. Ground SIGINT facilities are located on British or British-controlled soil, in friendly or pliable countries (including West Germany, Oman and Belize), and inside a handful of British embassies. Within the boundaries defined by UKUSA, GCHQ targets are chosen according to the intelligence priorities set by its major British clients, including SIS, which has ultimate responsibility for all overseas intelligence gathering. Under another old wartime arrangement, overall direction of SIGINT operations is exercised by the London Signals Intelligence Board, with representatives from GCHQ and military intelligence, and presided over by SIS.

Some two-thirds of GCHQ's work comes from intercepted

49

military communications, largely radio messages, which the UKUSA partners use to monitor the ground units, vessels and aircraft of foreign armed forces, with particular emphasis on the Soviet bloc. Part of the remaining third is composed of diplomatic messages, transmitted in text form rather than spoken, between embassies and their respective foreign ministries at home. London embassy radio traffic is monitored by a GCHQ Composite Signals unit located in the Earl's Court district of west London. The transmissions of neutral and hostile countries (non-allied diplomatic communications or NDC in SIGINT-speak) are an obvious target but UKUSA partners suffer the same treatment. In fact, the UKUSA treaty allows for mutual interception to ensure that the correct security procedures are being followed in partners' own communications. The advantage here rests with NSA, who seek to read all Washington embassy traffic, including the British, and, from the NSA installation at Chicksands in Bedfordshire, a large amount of London diplomatic communications as well.

Some embassy communications rely on radio contact with the home government, others are entrusted to commercial operators, like British Telecom and the state-run telecommunications authorities in Europe, who run the world's public networks. These organisations are known collectively as International Licensed Carriers (ILCs). However, GCHQ monitors not only foreign embassy traffic on public networks but *every* international telex and data transmission and a significant proportion of telephone conversations passing in and out of Britain. (This programme is described in detail in Chapter 4.) From some of its out-stations, GCHQ is also able to eavesdrop on several other key international routes and some foreign internal channels.

The main reason for GCHQ's interest in commercial telecommunications is the acquisition of economic intelligence, since most international communications relate to business activity. Economic intelligence-gathering is not a recent phenomenon: it has had a long-standing application in assessing the military potential of possible adversaries. Since the Second World War, however, it has assumed greater (if fluctuating) prominence as a determinant of the British Government's whole trade policy. A similar development of economic intelli-

50

gence occurred across the Atlantic, with NSA at the forefront. Between 1952 and 1966, the NSA station at Kirknewton in Scotland eavesdropped on commercial telecommunications. One ex-employee has described part of his work as looking out for 'details of commodities, what big companies were selling, like iron, steel and petrol. . . . Some weeks the list of words to watch for contained dozens of names of big companies'.[23]

ILC intercepts are pooled between the UKUSA agencies and commercial intelligence reports drawn up by liaison groups at Cheltenham and elsewhere. Diplomatic intercepts, too, are scrutinised for information of possible commercial interest. A target list compiled in the mid-1970s and obtained by the *New Statesman* specified:

> – *diplomatic messages related to international oil negotiations and investment of oil revenue by producer countries;*
> – *diplomatic messages covering world currency problems and national responses;*
> – *Japanese diplomatic messages in general, and in particular those with economic content.*[24]

Some parts of Whitehall have periodically adopted a dismissive attitude towards this kind of intelligence collection. During the late 1970s, for example, the Treasury and Department of Trade were reportedly

> *sceptical of the need for economic intelligence on western European nations and Third World countries not posing a threat to British security.*[25]

Since the quality of intelligence reporting was sometimes no better than that of the financial press, such a view is not surprising. This spell of neglect ended early in 1984 after a review initiated by the Permanent Secretary to the Treasury, Sir Peter Middleton. Economic intelligence is now a high priority.

Producing polished intelligence reports from the raw intercepts is often a complex business. Almost all military and diplomatic intercepts are encoded or scrambled in an attempt to make them indigestible to SIGINT. Some of the simpler guises are unravelled at the point of interception and the

51

results despatched to Cheltenham along with the less accessible items.

Those coded messages which have not been broken in the field are sent to H Division (Cryptanalysis). Where much early codebreaking could be done by hand, the complexity of modern cyphers demands an ever-increasing level of computer support. Despite regular success with some Third World and a few low-level Soviet cyphers, GCHQ's cryptanalysts have, for the most part, been defeated by high-level Soviet bloc cyphers. According to one account, GCHQ and NSA 'couldn't do anything except read externals . . . They couldn't read the messages themselves because they couldn't break the stuff'.[26]

'Externals' is a blanket term covering all characteristics of an intercept other than the contents. The origin, destination, length, format and level of encryption of a message or series of messages can reveal discernable patterns of organisation and activity. Against the leading SIGINT nations, however, even this kind of study, known as 'traffic analysis', can be redundant because the messages can not actually be found: 'they send telecypher in constant streams twenty-four hours a day. . . . You get pages and pages and pages of letters, random letters, with no beginnings and no endings'.[27] (In Chapter 4, externals will emerge as key parameters in the techniques developed by NSA and GCHQ for sorting through large volumes of communications intercepted from commercial carriers.)

Even when codes are broken and conversations unscrambled, there remains the barrier of language. GCHQ employs a small army of skilled translators under the cover title of the Joint Technical Language Service (JTLS). The cream of the Government's linguists, JTLS staff are also used on occasion by the rest of the intelligence establishment. Their range of interest is apparent from a 1985 recruitment advertisement which sought applicants skilled in 'Arabic, Bulgarian, Czech, Finnish, German, Hungarian, Italian, Japanese, Persian, Polish, Russian and Serbo-Croat . . . Dutch, Norwegian, Portuguese and Swedish'.[28]

The decoded, translated products and traffic studies arrive on the desks and video terminals of Cheltenham's two analytical divisions – J (Special SIGINT) which handles the Soviet bloc, and K (General SIGINT) which covers everything else.

The analysts of J and K Divisions produce reports for distribution to GCHQ's customers, covering political and economic affairs as well as military topics.

The finished reports, sanitised as far as possible to erase traces of the original source, are sent to a range of customers. David Kahn recounts the distribution of a 1941 diplomatic intercept as: the War Office, Foreign Office and Director of the Government Code and Cypher School (three copies each); the India Office (two copies); the Admiralty, Air Ministry, Colonial Office, Dominion Office, MI5 and Secretary to the Cabinet (one copy each)[29]. Today's mailing list, assisted by post-war Whitehall streamlining, is rather slimmer. Items immediately relevant to other intelligence agencies or to GCHQ's sponsor ministries are sent directly to them. The biggest single customer, however, is the Joint Intelligence Organisation (JIO).

JIO evolved from the support staff attached to the wartime Joint Intelligence Committee which was established in 1939 to co-ordinate the plethora of existing and ad hoc intelligence combines. In 1957, when the Committee was switched from military to civilian control, these analysts and administrators were put under the wing of the Cabinet Office, where JIO now resides. Its work, as described by the Franks Committee report on the Falklands war, involves

> *making assessments for Ministers and officials of a wide range of external situations and developments. It draws for its assessments on all relevant information: diplomatic reports and telegrams, the views of Government departments and publicly available information, as well as secret intelligence reports. It also has a co-ordinating role in respect of the work of the security and intelligence agencies.*[30]

The only significant omission here concerns information obtained through liaison arrangements. JIO exchanges analyses with allied intelligence organisations, notably the CIA station at the American embassy in London (another practice inherited from the Second World War).

JIO's political and military reports are put before the Joint Intelligence Committee, which today comprises the chiefs of the intelligence services, military representatives and senior

53

civil servants. After approval by this Committee, the reports are sent to selected ministers in a weekly 'Red Book'. JIO's economic section reports to a separate group entitled the Overseas Economic Intelligence Committee, chaired by a senior Treasury official, which also feeds a small coterie of Ministers. The contents of its reports are further made available to other concerned ministries (Trade and Industry, Energy and Agriculture, for example), official bodies such as the Bank of England and favoured private companies including ICI, British Petroleum, Rio Tinto Zinc and major British defence contractors.[31]

Both official Intelligence Committees (Joint and Overseas Economic) answer to the supreme entity in the intelligence mandarinate. This is the Permanent Secretaries Committee on the Intelligence Services, which brings together the Whitehall bosses of the Treasury, Foreign and Commonwealth Office, Home Office and Ministry of Defence. The Committee's power derives quite simply from its control of the intelligence budget of slightly under £1 billion for the financial year 1985–86. The bulk of intelligence financing has, since at least 1935, been salted away in the budgets of other ministries. GCHQ's running costs were fixed at £600 million for the twelve months ending in March 1986.[32] Two-thirds of this bill is met by the Ministry of Defence, who also cover capital expenditure (although some equipment is loaned); the Foreign and Commonwealth Office pays the rest. The fiscal carve-up between the two ministries broadly reflects the distribution of GCHQ's work. The Permanent Secretaries Committee is also in charge of a third intelligence coordination group, the Official Committee on Security, which supervises Government security procedures and the work of MI5.

Inside this bureaucratic phalanx, populated by the myriad Whitehall-based entities described above, are the labyrinthine channels of direction and dissemination which separate the operational arms of the intelligence complex from the Cabinet Ministers who make use of the information derived from them and who are nominally entrusted with their supervision. A comprehensive analysis of the role and control of Britain's intelligence services is beyond the scope of this book. Our concern here is to indicate the function of communications interception – both at home and abroad – in intelligence gathering and, to a lesser extent, law enforcement. On the face of it, there are two very different tapping systems in operation, splitting neatly between domestic and foreign targets, and between an active and passive use of the intercepted material: in the former case, MI5, for example, actually use the material to support, say, an espionage inquiry; GCHQ, on the other hand, merely collate and analyse their intercepts before passing their conclusions on to Whitehall and other government agencies.

In subsequent chapters, it becomes apparent that technological changes and the loosening of GCHQ's guidelines (allowing it a domestic role) have effected a partial convergence of the two systems at an operational, if not administrative, level. There is, however, a similarity between them in the broader context of intelligence collection, namely that tapping is frequently the bottom line in clandestine surveillance. Cathy Massiter's testimony to the *MI5's Official Secrets* documentary (see Chapter 1) indicates that, once the request for monitoring of CND came through, two things were done: MI5 agent Harry Newton was sent out to spy on the organisation; and CND executive member John Cox had his phone tapped. In general, MI5 prefer agents to phone taps in terms of the amount of information garnered, but even if Newton or some similar character had not been available to the agency, the tap would have gone ahead anyway. In the foreign arena, it is most unlikely that any Western intelligence agency has become privy to the deliberations of the Soviet Politburo by recruiting an agent from within its ranks; however, the US National Security Agency was able to monitor the conversations of various Soviet leaders, including General Secretary Brezhnev, conducted from the radiotelephones installed in their official limousines. (The intelligence yield was not spectacular in this instance – the most significant information appears to have been that Brezhnev suffered from regular hangovers.)[33] Intelligence, like politics, is the art of the possible, and tapping is often the most feasible and reliable method of collecting intelligence.

Chapter 3

Local Exchange Tapping

Britain's intelligence complex conducts two forms of communications interception: one is specific, aimed at individuals and organisations in order to acquire pre-determined information; the other is indiscriminate, picking up everything within reach in the expectation of finding something useful in the catch. Historically, these categories have roughly corresponded to the tapping of domestic and foreign communications respectively. The distinction, which was the product of technical factors (see below) as well as the influence of different intelligence demands, resulted in two separate tapping systems. In Chapter 4, we examine GCHQ's blanket monitoring techniques, which have been mainly directed against international communications. Here, we look at the mechanics of telephone tapping within Britain, which is predominantly used for domestic security and criminal investigations, and at the evolution of the supporting administrative and technical facilities.

Since 1937 Government agencies who want to use a phone tap have been required to seek ministerial approval in the form of a signed warrant (see Chapter 5). At MI5 the normal procedure for doing this begins with the desk officer in charge of the investigation. The officer prepares details of the target, including name and telephone number, and a supporting explanation justifying the use of a tap. The application is submitted for approval to the officer's section chief and then to MI5's deputy director. Usually the volume of applications exceeds the available tapping resources, so that those with the highest priority – as assessed from desk officers' submission – are selected for Home Office approval.

Metropolitan Police officers apply for warrants, through a Chief Superintendent or Commander, to the Assistant Commissioner in charge of criminal investigation. He vets all applications before they are sent to the Home Office. Provincial police officers apply through their own Chief Constable. Customs and Excise warrants sought by the Investigation Division are submitted through the chief of division or the deputy in charge of operations.

All applications for telephone and mail interception warrants are received and processed by a section of F4 Division at the Home Office; this division is responsible for departmental policy on 'counter terrorism, security liaison, subversive activities, use of firearms by the police, security of explosives, protection'.[1]

In England and Wales the final, crucial link in the chain of authorisation leading to the Home Secretary is the Permanent Under-Secretary at the Home Office, the department's most senior civil servant. It is at this stage that the decision on authorisation is effectively made. Asked in February 1985 how many applications he had rejected while in office, Home Secretary Leon Brittan replied that:

> the process is not a straightforward one by which the agency says 'Here is an application. Yes or no?'. Unless there is urgency, there is much interchange between the agency and those who advise the relevant Secretary of State. An application might not be made formally if it is made clear that it is unlikely to be granted.[2]

This answer came close to an admission – the essence of which is supported by other sources – that ministerial approval of warrant applications is a rubber stamp on decisions taken by the Permanent Under-Secretary and F4 Division at the Home Office in consultation with the applicants.

In Scotland authorisation procedures are identical to those in England and Wales, except that the Secretary of State for Scotland and appropriate civil servants at the Scottish Home and Health Department carry out the functions of the Home Secretary and Home Office.

The lack of ministerial control, in the absence of legislation, gave considerable scope for abuse. In the past, MI5 have arranged taps without a warrant in cases where there was insufficient evidence to support an application; if the tap proved productive, an application followed. Once the Home Secretary had signed, the date was altered to cover the period *before* the application. The connivance of Home Office officials was essential since records of each warrant, including the date of issue, are kept by F4.

Not only MI5 benefited from a Home Office helping hand. Towards the end of 1976, Inspector Dick Lee, the Thames Valley Police officer leading the 'Operation Julie' drugs inquiry put in applications for three taps. According to Lee's own account, 'a kind official at the Home Office brushed aside the usual red tape and these went on in a few days'.[3]

Special Branch officers, in contrast to their MI5 overlords, have been more inclined simply to ignore the warrant system and make a direct approach to the GPO, via the area head of the Post Office Investigation Division. (Before 1937 all tapping requests were made in this way.) There are a variety of circumstances, not necessarily involving any kind of interception, under which the police would seek the co-operation of the Post Office. The administrative relationship between the two was governed by a set of Home Office guidelines to the police, issued in 1969 and again in 1977, which described in detail the restrictions on the disclosure of information to the police by area Telephone Managers. It then added, in a brief paragraph, that

> *if the police are in urgent need of information which the Post Office may be able to furnish in connection with a serious criminal offence, the police officer in charge of the investigation should communicate with the Duty Officer, Post Office Investigation Division who will be ready to make any necessary inquiries.*[4]

Although interception is not specifically mentioned, it is not excluded. An internal Post Office memorandum of the same period also refers to this procedure which, according to several sources, was regularly used by Special Branch officers, particularly outside London, to secure phone taps and metering information (see Chapter 9).

Before the splitting of the GPO in 1981, the 300-strong Post Office Investigation Division (POID) functioned as an internal police force for the corporation and as the main point of contact in the Post Office for the law enforcement and intelligence agencies. POID officers were mostly recruited from the ample ranks of former police officers; and until the mid-1970s they were supplemented by serving police sergeants seconded from the Metropolitan force. A coterie of experienced GPO telephone engineers were also engaged to carry out tapping work. (No applicant taller than five feet nine inches in height could serve with the POID because, according to GPO folklore, the Division's investigators needed to spend long hours crouched in telephone exchange cubbyholes, known as 'towers', awaiting suspected miscreants.)

Most POID officers, including the headquarters staff, were based in London. Outside the capital, a single POID liaison officer was attached to each Telephone Area Office (the headquarters for an area typically covered by a provincial telephone directory). The majority of their work was concerned with the investigation of alleged crimes against the Post Office, covering everything from Girocheque fraud to the theft of GPO van parts, but the Division was also involved in the interception of communications. The POID 'Special Section'[5], with offices near St Paul's cathedral, opened, copied and (sometimes) resealed letters and packages destined for target addresses – and continues to do so. Until the turn of the 1970s, the Division's telecomms specialists were responsible for installing a large proportion of taps on behalf of the major customers. POID participation then declined considerably following the inauguration of the national tapping centre, although the Division continued to arrange taps for Special Branch and carried out some of its own during investigations into obscene and fraudulent phone calls. (Since GPO reorganisation, the POID telecommunications section has been reconstituted as the British Telecom Investigation Department, BTID.)

The close contact between POID and Special Branch police officers (who are expected to cultivate such relationships) easily subverted the feeble efforts of central government to regulate tapping. The overall lack of executive scrutiny meant that the procedures for arranging taps evolved according to administrative convenience, with scant regard to the scope for abuse. The recent law on interception, as we illustrate in Chapter 6, has done little to rectify the situation. Over the years, the sole political demand on the tappers has been that their business should be conducted in the utmost secrecy: the discovery of a tap by the target may render it useless or even counter-productive.

The pursuit of invisibility has been a dominant trend in the history of Britain's tapping system, even though it has sometimes hindered that system's development. Apart from the need for security, the main constraints on tapping have always been technical. The mechanics of telephone tapping necessarily depend on the technology and configuration of the telephone system. The way in which telephone calls are transmitted determines how a conversation is intercepted, while the structure of the network determines where the interception can take place. Furthermore, the amount of tapping in progress at any time is limited by the capacity of the tapping system to extract useful information from the intercepted conversations. This processing stage – involving listening or recording, transcription and delivery to the customer – has undergone enormous change since the dawn of tapping, largely because of technological advances which have increased both the efficiency of the system and the volume of interception which it could support.

Within the boundaries set by mandatory secrecy and the availability of suitable technology, the tapping system was organised and developed in line with the needs of its principal customers. For the regular police, the Special Branch and MI5, taps are most frequently aimed at an individual or a single set of premises. The example of a residential subscriber with a single telephone thus provides a suitable starting point for a description of tapping techniques.

The telephone system links each subscriber to a local telephone exchange via an individual circuit which carries all incoming and outgoing calls. The circuit consists of a pair of conducting wires, made of copper (or occasionally aluminium), which transmit conversation as a continuous, varying electric current; the telephone instrument makes the conversion between sound and electricity. This technology has been used for local networks since the invention of the telephone and is likely to remain in use for a long time to come. The simplest and most effective way to tap this kind of line is by the physical connection – 'hardwiring' – of a second circuit

60

leading to a monitoring site; two wires in the tapping circuit are attached to the two speech-carrying wires in the target telephone line. The principle is essentially the same as that of a domestic extension telephone.

The function of the exchange is to direct each call to the appropriate destination by establishing a connection between the two phones, a process known as 'switching'. Calls to different destinations are switched along different routes, so a tapper who seeks to monitor all the conversations of one particular subscriber should arrange for the tap to be fitted somewhere on, or at either end of, the circuit between that subscriber's telephone and the local exchange.

Local telephone networks are installed according to a standard format, although some variations are inevitable. In a typical arrangement for houses in a residential neighbour-hood, the telephone is connected to a junction box on the exterior of the house, and from there by an overhead line to a wooden pole – a familiar sight in many streets. Each pole serves an average of twenty houses. Here, the circuits are wrapped together into a single multi-strand cable and run into underground ducts. In densely occupied premises – housing estates and office blocks – subscriber circuits often travel straight into the ducts.

The individual telephone lines arrive at the local exchange packed together inside the incoming cables, and have to be sorted out before they can be connected to the switching units. The simplest arrangement of the lines, for both engineering and accounting purposes, is in telephone number order; however, the circuits are assembled into cables on a street-by-street basis, and there is no direct correspondence between number and location – only by coincidence will two neigh-bouring houses have adjacent telephone numbers. The func-tion of the main distribution frame is to organise the lines into numerical order.

The frame consists of two large racks, typically ten feet high by thirteen feet wide, standing face-to-face and covered with arrays of electrical contacts. The incoming circuits are fitted to one of the racks, called the 'line side' in geographical (street-by-street) blocks; on the opposite 'exchange side' of the frame, lines into the switching units are ordered in strict telephone number sequence. Between the two sides of the frame is a maze of multi-coloured wires, called 'jumpers', which cross-connect each incoming line to the appropriate number on the exchange side. The progress of the circuits beyond the main distribution frame varies according to the design of the exchange, but the frame itself is a standard piece of equipment.

The main distribution frame is normally the last point at which a particular subscriber's line can be uniquely separated out from the other lines. The reason is that the path taken by the call through most types of switching equipment varies according to the destination of the call and the availability of appropriate connections. The path does *not* depend on where the call is coming from. Therefore a hardwired tap directed at a particular line should be connected between the main distribution frame and the telephone instrument, or at one of the two end-points. (The situation is different for the new generation of computerised exchanges which British Telecom is currently installing throughout its network. See Chapter 10.)

There are recorded instances of taps installed at cabinets and junction boxes, which are the two most accessible points in the local network, but, as the Post Office Engineering Union point out, such taps 'present formidable technical and practical problems' and are also 'too open to public view and too liable to discovery by Post Office engineers on normal duties.'[6] Given the importance of security, the professional tappers have long preferred to fix taps on the main distribution frame at the local exchange, from which the public is barred. *Any* call from a telephone in the United Kingdom can be intercepted from the local exchange serving one or other of the two callers. The remainder of this chapter is concerned with this kind of tap.

Although the modern telephone user takes it for granted, national direct dialling has only been generally available in Britain since the 1960s. Previously, as many readers and vintage film buffs may remember, calls outside the local area (and, before that, each and every call) had to be connected manually by a telephone operator at the exchange. The historical image of the telephone exchange was a reality: rows of beheadsetted employees removed and inserted plugs from rows of sockets, called 'jackfields', in vertically mounted switchboards, accompanied by the operator's mantra of 'Number please'.

The tapper, perched silently next to the appropriate operator position, could monitor an individual line through the switchboard. The arrangement sometimes caused a faint click when the line was connected, just as a headphone jackplug inserted into a hi-fi amplifier socket does. Apart from contributing to the classic myth in the 'fear of tapping' catalogue, there was a genuine danger that the click could alert the target to the presence of the tap. Moreover, the fact that a particular line was being monitored was instantly obvious to all the operators, further increasing the risk of exposure; for, as one engineer recently commented, '[the] exchanges I worked at are "gossip shops" . . . no security or intelligence officer would operate within a hundred miles of them'.[7] Nonetheless the technique was regularly used before the 1960s by Post Office investigation staff.

The low security and inconvenience of the switchboard tap were unacceptable for sensitive or long-term investigations. Moreover, this rudimentary method was only viable as long as the Post Office continued to rely on manual switching for trunk calls. Conversion to full automatic trunk switching was not begun until 1958 and consumed well over a decade before completion. A better technique – one more akin to the contemporary tap – made the interception on the exchange side of the main distribution frame.

At each connection on the exchange side is a 'test jack' installed as an access point for connecting test equipment. Under the new arrangement, one end of the tapping circuit was inserted in the test jack. This gave greater security than the switchboard method, although the presence of the circuit was clearly visible to exchange engineers. It also presented the new problem of finding a location for the eavesdroppers at the other end of the circuit. In some cases, the monitoring site was located in the exchange building and staffed by members of the Post Office Investigation Division. The favoured alternative, which put the tappers off the premises, used the camouflage of the GPO's Service Observation system.

Introduced in the mid-1930s, and still used today in a modernised form, Service Observation is a primitive form of quality control, based on random listening-in to calls on a small number of selected local exchange lines, listed in a weekly memorandum compiled by area headquarters staff. Under a typical arrangement of the 1940s the chosen lines at each exchange were each fitted with an observation circuit at the test jack; these circuits were connected to an outgoing circuit group which relayed the calls to the observation centre, staff on Service Observation duty, normally experienced telephone operators, monitored calls using an especially designed Observation Panel – essentially a sophisticated switchboard which could, among other things, display numbers dialled by any line under observation. Each observer was provided with a chart on which to record equipment faults, congested lines and errors made by either a customer or an operator.

Service Observation has sometimes been misinterpreted as nothing more than a flimsy disguise for tapping. The official description of the test circuit as a 'tapping relay' added to the confusion.[8] In fact, this kind of monitoring was the only way for the GPO to assess the qualitative performance of the telephone service. Nevertheless, the system *was* exploited as an administrative Trojan horse: lines scheduled for tapping were simply added to the weekly observation list for each exchange. The connections at the exchange were made in an identical fashion, so that engineers were unable to distinguish lines under genuine Service Observation from the taps. The latter, however, were not listened to at the Service Observation unit but by the tappers located at a remote office. Taps at smaller exchanges, which did not have permanent links to an observation centre, continued under Investigation Division control.

The major technical advance of the 1940s, as far as the tappers were concerned, was the development of magnetic tape recorders, the first of which became commercially available in 1948. Primitive, unwieldy recording devices, based on Thomas Edison's invention some sixty years earlier, had been in use for some time. Before the Second World War, the Post Office maintained a separate Telephone Interception Unit, which liaised directly with MI5's counter-espionage division and transcribed conversations on its behalf from recordings made on wax-coated cylinders. The principles of recording and reproduction were similar to those of today's vinyl records.

The GPO Investigation Division was entrusted with arranging MI5's taps: the agency found existing interception arrangements too exposed to involve itself directly, but was equally unwilling to eschew access to such a valuable source of intelligence. When war broke out, MI5 took control of domestic phone tapping from the Post Office. After 1945, the Investigation Division regained its responsibility but the transcription staff, who had spent the war ensconced in the servants quarters at Blenheim Palace, were permanently absorbed into MI5's administrative and technical division as Section A3[9] (since re-labelled A2A).

Magnetic tape recorders spread quickly. By 1952 they were already in service for local police taps. In such cases, a designated exchange engineer installed and maintained the tapping circuits and changed the tapes, which were periodically collected by the Investigation Division and passed on to the customer. Five years later, a team of Privy Councillors under Lord Birkett found that tapping was 'a purely mechanical operation' in the course of which tapped conversations were listened to 'only occasionally and briefly to check whether the machines [were] in order'.[10]

Although improved recording technology eased the interception process, it had little impact on the labour-intensive business of transcribing the tapes. Nor could it address the problem that many investigations demanded an immediate response to certain intercepts from a human listener. A former GPO investigations officer explained that:

It's no good putting a recorder on the line and coming back tomorrow at tea-time to see what you've got. When you play it, you always find a hoarse voice rang at three, said "It's me. See you at the usual in ten minutes." and you weren't there. If you're tapping people who know what it's all about, you have to have relays of good men listening twenty-four hours a day.[11]

*

Babies were not the only boom phenomenon of the 1950s and '60s. A less acknowledged but even more rapid growth occurred in the number of telephone subscribers, which naturally produced an increase in the amount of tapping. Also during this period – and more significantly – the domestic tapping system began to adopt a centralised structure.

The main stimulus came from MI5, which was looking towards a new regime in which it could control the execution of its own taps; as ever, it was also concerned that local involvement in and awareness of interception be kept to a minimum to enhance security. MI5's demands were pressing: positive vetting had recently been introduced under its direction, and assessments of character and habits, which formed a central part of the new scheme, could readily be made from the mundane intelligence typically produced by telephone surveillance. The agency's domestic tapping needs, along with those of its colleagues in SIS, were formulated by officers from MI5's A Branch and discussed with the Ministry of Defence, specifically the Defence Research Policy Committee. This body, one of Whitehall's more spectral residents, held a brief to investigate and monitor various aspects of defence and intelligence technology.[12]

The centralisation programme of this period was concentrated in London, where the level of tapping was highest. The geographical concentration of the capital's telephone network eased the job of laying on the requisite circuitry connecting the new tapping centres to the Service Observation units which supplied their raw material. However, the establishment of a number of tapping centres with different line capacities, equipment and customers suggests a haphazard, ill-coordinated process. A police tapping unit, in operation during the 1950s, was located in the Passport Office building in Petty France, near St James's Park. A tapping school was set up in the same block to train budding eavesdroppers from Britain and elsewhere. The Petty France centre was by far the smallest of the species, with no more than thirty lines, and came to an inauspicious demise later in the decade when its existence 'became known to the underworld [and] one gangster boasted he threw gelignite down a manhole to disrupt the operation'.[13] The building was subsequently demolished by more orthodox means.

The refugees from the Passport Office – Scotland Yard officers attached to criminal intelligence and Special Branch – moved to less vulnerable premises a few miles to the west. The Duke of York's barracks in Chelsea is well-known as the headquarters of several Guards regiments and of the 21st Special Air Service (SAS) Regiment, but during the 1960s it also housed one of the capital's two main phone tapping centres. Several hundred lines, wired into jackfields and fitted with devices to prevent interference and transmission loss, fed a battery of tape recorders assembled on shelves in a suite of first floor offices, with MI5 as the main client. The other big London centre was just half a mile away. This 300-line unit, which occupied part of a block just off Vauxhall Bridge Road, was confined to use by the intelligence services. Smaller centres set up shop elsewhere in the capital.

By the end of the 1960s, the capital's eavesdropping web had reached a capacity of 600 lines, but the expansion brought problems. Service Observation was starting to wear thin as a cover for tapping, particularly in London, where it was becoming overloaded by the ever-growing demand for new tapping circuits. Also the random element at the heart of Service Observation monitoring was incompatible with the orderly, systematic process sought by the tappers.

Service Observation was eventually relieved of its tapping load, leaving it with only its genuine quality monitoring work. Another operator facility called Trunk Offering (abbreviated to TKO) has occasionally been used in the past as a cover for tapping. The term Trunk Offering is a leftover from the era of manual trunk switching. Before connecting an incoming trunk call, the operator had first to check that the line to the intended recipient was clear. If it was found to be engaged on a local call, the operator could use TKO circuits to break into the conversation and ask if the subscriber wished to curtail the call in progress and take the trunk call instead. Trunk Offering in this original form no longer exists, but TKO access to subscriber lines is still used at Control Centres, as one former telephonist explained:

> most people have had the experience of ringing up the operator and saying 'Look, this number I've been dialling has been engaged for the last three hours. Could you try it for me and see if they are actually talking or not?' Now if that number is a local number, the operator will press a switch marked TKO on their switchboard and break into whatever is happening on that line.[14]

The operator breaks into the line by dialling on the switchboard telephone. Trunk Offering could, in theory, be used as a limited 'dial-a-tap' system. Tappers prefer not to use it because TKO access is noisy, tending to produce those much-feared clicks, and the monitoring has to be conducted in the insecure environment of an operator centre.

Throughout the 1960s and '70s, the Special Branch–GPO Investigation Division link was still available. As well as circumventing the warrant procedure, it proved its logistical value in several cases where a concentration of taps was required in a restricted area. A former exchange engineer described how, during the Angry Brigade bombings at the beginning of the 1970s, a team of Special Branch officers and Post Office investigators took complete control of the Colchester telephone exchange for two weeks. The regular staff, with the exception of the exchange manager, were barred from access to the switching equipment during that period. Selected residential lines were tapped, along with every public call box serving the Essex University campus, where some students were thought to be connected with the Angry Brigade. The wholesale monitoring of call boxes in a particular district appears to be standard practice during terrorist investigations: tapping operations of this type have been mounted in Kilburn, London's main Irish quarter, during IRA campaigns.[15]

By the late 1960s the authorities felt that the proliferation of incongruous tapping centres had to be checked. The demand for taps continued to rise, which caused increasing disarray among staff struggling with manually-controlled equipment. MI5's policy shift (see Chapter 2) brought into its purview a new range of 'soft' targets more susceptible to intelligence gathering via interception, while at the same time SIS was assuming greater responsibilities at home, particularly in the fields of counter-espionage and counter-terrorism, and its tapping appetite grew accordingly. On a smaller scale the Metropolitan Police was increasing its use of tapping.

At this point, the tapping administrators from the main departments of State and the intelligence establishment, with the tacit approval of the Post Office, decided on the establishment of a custom-built, integrated tapping centre. (The minister formally in charge of the GPO at the time,

Postmaster-General Christopher Chataway, has declared that he was neither party to nor even aware of this decision.)[16] GCHQ, the doyen of Britain's eavesdropping industry, was brought in to work with the Post Office on the design and equipping of the new complex.[17]

GCHQ's involvement in the tapping project was significant both politically, as its intelligence brief had traditionally been confined to foreign parts, and practically, because of its experience of processing and analysing vast quantities of intercepted communications. In particular, the computer techniques which GCHQ introduced to the jackfield-reared tappers of the day revolutionised the domestic monitoring system: two of these methods – traffic analysis and automatic speech recognition – are examined later in the book.

The tapping centre has since become popularly known as 'Tinkerbell', after London police argot – not so much a reference to the fairy in the play *Peter Pan*, more of an oblique acknowledgement to the inventor of the telephone, Alexander Graham Bell. Tinkerbell was conceived as being more than just a modernised agglomeration of the existing London tapping facilities; for while these may have dealt with a limited amount of provincial traffic, it was intended that Tinkerbell should have coverage as close as possible to national. The objectives were centralised control – in the interests of efficiency and security – and speedy access for the main customers, who were firmly rooted in London, to intercepts from anywhere in the country. To show how the new system worked, it is convenient to divide it into four stages: interception at the local exchange; transmission of the intercepts to the tapping centre; recording and processing at the centre; and dissemination to the client agencies.

The demise of the Service Observation cover meant that the standard method of fitting the tap at the local exchange had to be reconsidered. A new procedure, still used in most exchanges, was devised which no longer made use of the test jack. Instead, the tapping circuit is connected to the line side of the main distribution frame and secreted within the maze of jumpers connecting the two sides of the frame. For reasons explained below, the other end of this false jumper is attached to a connection on the exchange side of the frame reserved for a spare outgoing line (called a 'junction') into the trunk network. The normal fuse fitted to each line side connection as a safety precaution is replaced with a red coloured fuse, to warn exchange engineers not to disconnect that circuit. (Lines used by essential services, such as doctors, are similarly distinguished.)

The revised procedures also caused a problem regarding staff security. Previously, taps had usually been fitted unwittingly by a local exchange engineer assigned to making Service Observations connections, but the new wiring arrangement was so peculiar that suspicions about its purpose were inevitable. The tapping administrators therefore decided to form their own squad of engineers to carry out the work without local assistance.

Protocol under this new model tapping regime consists of a phone call to the local exchange manager announcing the imminent arrival of engineers from outside the area. In pursuit of yet further security, even this simple courtesy is sometimes omitted. Neither the purpose nor any other details of their visit are disclosed. Usually, they arrive in a pair, during the small hours of the morning when telephone traffic, and consequently the number of engineers on duty, are at a minimum. They let themselves into the building. Once inside, explained a former GPO employee, 'they start playing around on the main distribution frame. You're told to keep out of the way and make them a cup of coffee. Then they go away again.'[18]

The exchange visitors book acquires no record of these fleeting guests, whose job it is to fit the tapping circuits at Britain's 6,000 local exchanges. They are recruited, along with 120-odd colleagues, from the ranks of experienced GPO engineers. After positive vetting, they work under the direction of the Tinkerbell centre. The Home Office is formally responsible for their activities, although British Telecom (and the GPO before them) continues to pay their salaries. On taking up Tinkerbell duty, the travelling tappers are, according to one account, allocated a BT staff grade above that of a normal local exchange manager, allowing the tappers to pull rank should they have run into difficulties with uncooperative or obstructive local exchange staff.[19]

A centralised national tapping system only became viable when a secure means was found by which to transmit telephone intercepts from any local exchange to the Tinkerbell complex. The GPO trunk communications network offered a simple and convenient solution. The trunk network links local exchanges through a hierarchy of specially designed 'trunk exchanges' connected by high-capacity circuits capable of carrying hundreds and thousands of calls simultaneously, using both underground cables and microwave radio channels. Microwaves – radio signals with frequencies above 1 GHz (1 billion cycles per second) – have been used in commercial telecomms networks for over thirty years. They follow a 'line-of-sight' path, so that the distance between a transmitter and receiver is limited by the curvature of the earth to around 40 km. The GPO microwave system uses a network of towers adorned with horn-and dish-shaped aerials to receive, amplify and re-transmit incoming signals. Both the microwave and coaxial cable trunk systems were intended to handle military and sensitive government traffic as well as normal long-distance telephone traffic.

Since Tinkerbell began work, the gateway into the trunk network for a call coming through a local exchange has been one of some 350 'Group Switching Centres', each of which handles long-distance traffic for between fifteen and twenty local exchanges. The procedure for installing a tap at the local exchange under this set-up is, as described above, to wire up a false jumper at the local exchange connecting the target line to a spare outgoing junction circuit. After passing through a locked amplifier room, the junction links the local exchange to its parent Group Switching Centre. A small transistor device is wired into the tapping circuit to prevent noise, power loss or other interference which might alert the target to the presence of a tap. The tapping lines are entered in local engineering records as 'defence circuits'.[20]

At the Group Switching Centre, one or more groups of twelve circuits are re-allocated from the defence quota to send the intercepts through the trunk network to Tinkerbell. (The figure of twelve is dictated by technical factors governing trunk transmission.) The intercepts arrive in London at one of the capital's trunk exchanges, from where they are transmitted, along with other military traffic, to the London hub of the secure defence communications network located in a tunnel running beneath Whitehall. Built shortly before the Second

71

World War, this tunnel was subsequently incorporated into a twelve mile underground labyrinth bored by the Post Office, a hundred feet below street level, to protect the telecommunications arteries of central Government.[21]

The choice of location for the Tinkerbell tapping centre was dictated, in part, by the feasibility of laying sufficient circuits to bring the intercepts in from the Whitehall warren: the nearer, the better. Given that, the advantage of proximity to most of the major customers reinforced that preference, as the headquarters of MI5, SIS and the Metropolitan Police all stand within a mile and a half of Whitehall; only Customs and Excise, in the City of London, is further afield. (The main London tapping centres of the 1960s, at the Duke of York barracks and in Vauxhall Bridge Road, were similarly close to the seat of government.) A search through the Department of Environment's (DoE) substantial portfolio of metropolitan property – some owned, some leased – produced a well-situated office block of suitable blandness on Ebury Bridge Road, a street running slightly east of north from near the Thames at Chelsea Bridge towards Victoria Station, half a mile away. The building, numbered 91 to 95, occupies a roughly rectangular site at the southern end of the road, wedged between two blocks of Peabody Trust flats. The site, now jointly owned by the DoE's Property Services Agency and the Pearl Assurance group, had been periodically redeveloped during the 1950s and 1960s for various office uses.

The Ebury Bridge Road complex, seen from above, assumed the shape of a letter 'T': the façade – the cross-stroke of the 'T' – looked westwards onto Ebury Bridge Road; the stem, slightly off-centre, was aligned away from the road to the east, so that it was invisible except from the overlooking flats on either side. The front part of the building was, and still is, host to a group of industrial tribunal offices. The rear portion, designated no. 93, consumed the eastern half of the 'stem': it was sealed off from the industrial tribunals with separate locked entrances. In January 1972, Westminster City Council approved a request by the purported occupants of 93 Ebury Bridge Road, the GPO's London Telecom Region, for the installation of 'a circular plastic cooling tower on the roof of the building, in connection with an air-conditioning system'. The purpose of the intended system was to suppress the temperature of computer equipment operating inside. The application announced the impending arrival of the phone tappers and the initiation of Tinkerbell.[22]

The incoming tapping circuits to Tinkerbell discharged their intercepts under computer control into a bank of magnetic tape recorders. The centre was initially equipped with slow-running 64-channel machines produced by the American-based Ampex corporation, whose then President, Arthur Hausman, had spent twelve years in the US National Security Agency – GCHQ's SIGINT partner – finishing as head of research and development.[23]

Tinkerbell was originally designed to record 1,000 tapped conversations simultaneously, although subsequently its capacity was said to have been greatly increased, perhaps fivefold.[24] Assuming one recording circuit is available at Tinkerbell for each local exchange tap, this latter estimate is consistent with a theoretical value of over 4,000 concurrent taps which can be deduced from the provision of a single 12-circuit group at each of the country's 350 Group Switching Centres.

It is possible, however, to squeeze the traffic from several thousand tapping circuits into just 1,000 recording lines, using the principle of 'trunking'. This is a basic element in the planning of telecommunications networks which, in the case of a local exchange, exploits the fact that only a small proportion of the subscribers connected to that exchange will be engaged on a telephone call at any one time. An exchange with 2,000 subscribers might, for example, be engineered to switch only 200 calls simultaneously; once the number of conversations in progress reaches that threshold, further calls are blocked by the exchange and an engaged tone is returned to the dialling customer. It is likely that a similar kind of trunking system was used at Tinkerbell, with the possible result that some intercepts were delayed or lost.

While trunking arrangements would have improved Tinkerbell's recording efficiency, different techniques were required to streamline other aspects of the tapping operation. The value of tapping has always been depressed by the need to sort through the intercepts to distill useful intelligence from a mass of trivia. This is a tedious, painstaking process better suited to computers than to human analysts. Tinkerbell sought to improve the efficiency of tapping by filtering out spurious traffic on the basis of call destination, as the *New Statesman* explained:

> *computerised retrieval systems enable particular connections to be automatically logged, so that a 'target' subscriber's calls need only be transcribed when he or she makes a call to some destination likely to be interesting.*[25]

There were limits to the processing abilities. Irrelevant traffic still had to be recorded, in case some momentous nugget of information were inadvertently missed; and if the recipient of the call was unknown, the number dialled had to be checked against manual records. Reverse directories, ordered by telephone number rather than alphabetically by name, are kept in each telephone exchange for engineering purposes.

Clerical jobs at Ebury Bridge Road, as elsewhere in the GPO, were probably done by women, a number of whom were seen among the ninety-odd morning arrivals at the Tinkerbell centre. The male employees included managerial staff and the engineers responsible for equipment supervision and maintenance. The engineers working inside the tapping centre held the grade of Technical Officer, a lower level than the roving engineers who travel to local exchanges to connect the tapping circuits. Technical Officers normally belong to the National Communications Union (formerly the Post Office Engineering Union) while the mobile engineers and senior administrative staff are represented by the white-collar union, the Society of Telecom Executives. In all, perhaps 200 personnel were attached to the Ebury Bridge Road centre.

The remainder of the morning arrivals were envoys from the customer agencies, for whom there was a well-defined pecking order. At the bottom, as ever, were the regular police (as distinct from Special Branch) who had the smallest number of lines allocated to them – less than 100 – and the least access to Tinkerbell's advanced processing facilities. The recordings from almost all police-sponsored taps, Metropolitan or otherwise, were passed to C11 Criminal Intelligence at New Scotland Yard. During the mid-1970s, if not since, officers from provincial forces were obliged to go there to study notes

74

and transcripts of calls prepared by C11 officers who were vetted and cleared to handle the tapes and visit Tinkerbell. Some officers were unhappy with the Yard's hegemony, including Dick Lee, head of the 'Operation Julie' drugs inquiry. In October 1976, Lee wanted a tap on Henry Todd, the suspected organiser of a drug distribution network. Instead of going through the normal procedure, Lee persuaded

> *an organisation which for security reasons cannot be named, to put a tap on Todd's phone. The reason for this was the information from Swan* [a pseudonymous informant] *that the major distributors had been paying protection money to unnamed London policemen. As all* [police] *phone taps are channelled through Scotland Yard, Operation Julie could not afford to disclose their interest in Todd.*[26]

Drug-related inquiries also spawned many of the taps set up by the Customs and Excise Investigation Division who, like the police, had a fixed quota on the number of simultaneous taps in operation.

The 'top customers' at Tinkerbell came from MI5 and, to a lesser degree, from SIS and GCHQ, arriving periodically at Ebury Bridge Road to collect tapes and deliver target lists. Photographs of the centre suggest that intelligence representatives even used a separate entrance to the police visitors. However, a large and growing proportion of intelligence taps were relayed over secure lines directly to Curzon House in Mayfair, home of MI5, to SIS headquarters next door to Lambeth North underground station, and to one of GCHQ's London offices – formerly Palmer Street near St James's Park – where foreign language intercepts were tackled by the Joint Technical Language Service (see Chapter 2). A transcription clerk who joined MI5 early in 1978 explained:

> *after about two months training, I went to work in MI5's industrial room* [in Curzon House] *with seven other women, transcribing the tapes of telephone calls which had been tapped. Each morning, I'd collect the actual tapes from a room on the 5th floor which contained banks of recorders operating 24 hours a day.*[27]

Analysis and transcription are normally completed within a week, although some recordings are kept for as long as a month. The tapes are then wiped clean and re-used. According to a 1980 Government White Paper, notes and transcripts taken from the intercepts 'are retained for twelve months or for as long as required for the purposes of investigations, after which they are destroyed'.[28] Since this requirement is judged solely by the investigating officer, transcripts can be stored indefinitely with impunity. The intelligence establishment, in particular, is not inclined to discard any information, however worthless it might appear. 'It is an axiom of internal security,' declared BBC presenter Tom Mangold in 1981, 'that there can never be too much intelligence.'[29]

The publication of the 1980 White Paper was forced from the young Conservative administration by an unexpected breach of security. On the first day of February that year, a spell of nearly ten years of invisible tapping came to an end. Journalists Nick Anning and Duncan Campbell, writing in the *New Statesman* magazine, delivered a lengthy account of the GPO's work on behalf of the intelligence establishment and police: the article tackled the opening of mail and the manufacture of bugging devices, but its main target was Tinkerbell.

Exposure was a major embarrassment to the tappers, but there was also a lesson, which they took with evident seriousness. The two writers made it clear that, despite intense security and swaddlings of official secrecy, there were a number of peculiarites which drew attention to the operation at 93 Ebury Bridge Road. The most visible of these was incessant activity: lights were kept on throughout the night; staff came in and out of the building at all hours, many of them obviously working shifts. The GPO's local planning applications described the site as a 'computer centre'. Although night-time data processing is not uncommon, the comings and goings at this facility seemed excessive for this purpose. The Tinkerbell engineers, whose nocturnal visits to unsuspecting local exchanges added to the hubbub, also contributed to a second anomaly. According to the article:

> these men frequently travel in standard PO vans, which are said by other engineers to be something of a 'giveaway' since they are just labelled 'Post Office Telephones' and do not have the usual

words saying which Telephone Manager is responsible for them.[30]

More bizarre than either of these two suspicious indicators was the official status of the tapping unit within the GPO bureaucracy. Affixed to the wall outside Tinkerbell's main entrance was a plaque inscribed with the cryptic legend 'PO/THQ/OPD/EDD' – the Equipment Development Division of the Operational Programming Department of Post Office Telecommunications Headquarters. An internal directory of the period for PO/THQ – then based in Gresham Street in the City of London – contains a corresponding entry, 'OP5 Equipment Development Division', under the Operational Programming Department. Most of the thirteen divisions in this department were involved in straightforward policy work on matters such as power supply, safety, transport and technical standards; the staff and their office telephone numbers were listed in full, along with explicit descriptions of their jobs – 'Bedford and Commer Vehicles. Electrical, Fuel Injection and Breaking [sic] Equipment', read one entry. OP5's entry, by contrast, listed only four senior staff, including the head of the division in charge of it, and negligible occupational detail. Most of the telephone numbers given for OP5 connected to Headquarters at Gresham Street. But two others had a prefix which corresponded to an ordinary telephone exchange close to Sloane Square in Chelsea, several miles away. These were telephones inside Tinkerbell.

Asked whether the Ebury Bridge Road centre was responsible for telephone tapping, the Post Office quite properly directed inquires to the Home Office, who were unusually blunt: 'We wouldn't answer questions like that . . . you know that very well.'[31] Five years later, questions about another tapping centre from the *New Scientist* magazine drew the drier response: 'If we can deny it, we'll come back to you.'[32] (They did not.)

After the initial exposure of Tinkerbell, the Post Office plugged the lesser security loopholes. The main entrance to the centre was abandoned in favour of a more secluded, if circuitous, route passing through neighbouring offices occupied by the Department of Employment. The 'giveaway' unmarked vans of the Tinkerbell engineers were replaced marked with the code of BT's normal reserve fleet, the letter

'R'. Finally, in the search for a new label to replace OP5, Tinkerbell's administrators took advantage of a reorganisation of GPO Telecommunictions, begun in July 1979 preparatory to its reincarnation as British Telecom, which created an Exchange Services Department. One of its sub-divisions, ES4, was distinguished by both the paucity of its entry in the new staff directory and familiarity of its name, 'Equipment Development Policy Division'. This was Tinkerbell's new official title: it was a flimsy cover and was soon exposed. In response, British Telecom removed ES4 from the directory altogether and issued warnings to employees reminding them that the contents of the directory were not to be shown to anyone outside BT.[33]

These measures were clearly inadequate by themselves to reassert security. At the very least, new premises had to be found for the Tinkerbell centre; but the tapping administrators had also to consider that a simple change of location, even with a liberal application of bureaucratic camouflage, was no guarantee that the new centre would not fall victim to the same fate as Ebury Bridge Road. Several sources declare positively that tapping operations were decentralised after 1980. In any event, by the end of 1981, the tappers had vacated Ebury Bridge Road. The move cost the Property Services Agency, the body responsible for administering government and other official buildings, approximately £500,000.[34] The old Tinkerbell site is now occupied by British Telecom's Mobile Phone Division.

One new tapping centre – predictably dubbed Tinkerbell Two – was established less than a mile to the north, at Chantrey House in Ecclestone Street, opposite Victoria Station, again with easy access to the military communications system. Architecturally, Chantrey House was an improvement. Its red brick façade, set with large bay windows, compared favourably with the rectangular anonymity of its predecessor. Chantrey was built early in the twentieth century as a block of mansion flats with five main storeys crowned by an attic service floor. The exterior design was of sufficient quality to earn it the status of a minor listed building, which in the autumn of 1973 helped to prevent its demolition by the owners, Grosvenor Estates. The interior, declared contemporary planning reports, 'is not of interest'.[35]

Eighteen months later, in May 1975, a less drastic redevelopment plan was approved and the building leased to the Post Office. Once the small businesses already using the premises had been bought out, the new occupants set about converting the existing layout into open plan office space. The top two floors, plus a newly-constructed mezzanine level, were separated off from the rest of the building: only the lower part of the building could now be reached from the main entrance on Ecclestone Street.

From these alterations, it seems that the upper floors of Chantrey House were earmarked for a secure facility as soon as the Post Office obtained the leasehold, years before the original Tinkerbell was closed. The Post Office, and subsequently British Telecom, carried out much sensitive work (apart from tapping) on behalf of various State agencies and the corporation abounded with shadowy groups whose staff isolated themselves from their colleagues in other departments. Before the tappers moved in, upper Chantrey House was occupied by a mysterious Special Studies group, labelled SS–9, attached to Telecommunications Headquarters. Sharing the building with Tinkerbell Two, but occupying the lower three floors, was the Clerical Training Centre for British Telecom's London Region, which also moved in during 1980 and, at the time of writing, is still there. The structural separation of the two parts of the building ensured that, until public disclosure of the tappers' relocation, trainees had no idea what was going on above their heads: unless, that is, they inferred anything suspicious from the constant cloaking of the upper floors by blinds during the day and blackout curtains to mask night-time lights.

During the 1970s, Tinkerbell had been labelled with a Headquarters code to serve as a formal identity – necessary for Post Office administrative purposes. Cover for Tinkerbell Two, however, was supplied, not by THQ, but by the Network Services Division of London Telecom Region. Under the section in charge of Circuit Provision – which records which circuits go where and arranges for new ones to be laid – was the tappers' new pseudonym, a unit entitled 'NS3.4 – Field Projects' with a contact phone number at London Regional Headquarters at Camelford House on the Albert Embankment, south of the River Thames.[36]

Tinkerbell Two seems to have been afforded more spacious premises and a better layout than its Ebury Bridge Road forerunner: 20,000 square feet distributed between two-and-a-bit floors against 12,000 square feet on five floors. Upper Chantrey House could accommodate, at most, 100 people at any one time. The 1984 staff roster included a total of 60 British Telecom employees, working in shifts, including 40 engineers of Technical Officer grade. The roving EEs now seem to work out of alternative depots.

800 lines were installed to carry intercepts into Chantrey House, marshalled on a frame in the basement of the building and run through cable ducts to the monitoring equipment on the upper floors. The recording capacity was less than the lowest estimate made for Ebury Bridge Road, which tends to support the thesis that tapping was decentralised after the latter's exposure. The steady process of automation continued with the installation in October 1984 of two data circuits linking Chantrey House directly to British Telecom's new directory enquiry computers in Leeds, and at Charles House in Kensington, London. Directory enquiry staff are able, on request from a customer, to interrogate these computers to supply the telephone number for a given subscriber and address. It is a simple matter to write suitable software to allow an inverse procedure with which to identify the subscriber for a particular telephone number.

Customer access to Chantrey House intercepts was organised, in a similar manner to the Ebury Bridge Road system, as a combination of regular pick-ups and an increasing proportion of direct lines. These were laid on for the intelligence services as before, but also for the police – at least twenty lines linked Chantrey House to New Scotland Yard – and, it is thought, for the Cabinet Office, which houses the Joint Intelligence Organisation and the Civil Contingencies Unit.

The direct lines to New Scotland Yard may have been used during one of the biggest tapping programmes of recent years, directed against striking miners in the 1984/85 dispute. GCHQ once again assumed an advisory role and despatched a representative to Sheffield, home of the National Union of Mineworkers, early in the dispute. Some of the intercepts, it has been suggested, were relayed straight to the National

Reporting Centre at the Yard, which supervised the deployment of thousands of police officers drafted into the coalfields from all over the country.

The enforced closure of the Ebury Bridge operation was not the only problem which confronted the 1980s generation of tappers. Further administrative upheaval was threatened by the implementation of one of the Thatcher Government's key industrial policies which, as explained in the Introduction, involved the creation of a competitive market in telecomms services and the privatisation.

The problem which this presented for the tappers and their customers was one of control and logistics. A fast decision on the future control of the domestic tapping machinery was needed, as the Government prepared for the sale of half of its shareholding in BT to private investors. Privatisation was scheduled for 1983 but, due to overcrowding in the Parliamentary debating programme, it did not take place until November the following year.

In the summer of 1981, the Home Office – the principal source of funds for domestic tapping – convened a 'Feasibility Study Group', with representatives from GCHQ, MI5, the Metropolitan Special Branch and British Telecom itself, to deliberate on the situation. The Group, described by one source as 'very ad hoc, [with] no formal terms of reference'[37], met three times in the ensuing eighteen months, apparently without reaching agreement. There was no particular reason why the then existing arrangement, under which BT provided tapping services on an 'agency' basis, could not continue: the only stumbling block was that the corporation considered the 1981/82 budget of around £1.5 million per annum[38] to be inadequate. Of the alternatives, none of the intelligence organisations seemed able to stomach a takeover of Tinkerbell by one of their rivals, while a compromise proposal, creating a new Home Office department to run tapping operations, would not have satisifed anyone, least of all Mrs Thatcher's efficiency sleuths. In Whitehall, such an impasse tends to favour the status quo: and indeed, it appears that BT retained the responsibility for operating a tapping centre. The financial terms of the settlement are unknown, although it is likely that all operating costs are now met in full by the Home Office: for a Tinkerbell-sized unit, these may now have reached £5 million per annum.

Uniquely for a private company, British Telecom now has a vital, integral role within the British intelligence complex. Should BT ever do the unthinkable, and suddenly refuse to co-operate with official telephone tapping, the Government has the safety net of a 'national security' clause, written into the privatisation law, to ensure that the taps do not run dry. Section 94 of the 1984 Telecommunications Act allows for a Secretary of State to issue BT and any other telecomms companies with such general or specific directives 'as appear to the Secretary of State to be requisite or expedient in the interests of national security'. The directive must be implemented, continues the section, irrespective of other obligations (to shareholders, for instance). Other clauses permit the Secretary to withhold the directive from Parliament 'in the interests of national security' and to reimburse the carriers for the cost of complying with the directive. The carriers are prevented from revealing the fact or substance of any such directive. Telephone tapping is most certainly considered to be 'in the interests of national security', and British Telecom, together with other telecomms companies – Mercury Communications and the Hull Telephone Department – have undoubtedly been instructed to co-operate with tapping operations where required.

Under the 1981 British Telecommunications Act, Mercury was granted permission to run a separate network to BT offering the same basic telephone, telex and data transmission services to anybody in any part of the country. Mercury was spawned, after a little prodding from the Government, by a consortium led by the Cable and Wireless group. Mercury's marketing strategy aims to entice major commercial customers away from BT by offering high-capacity and specialised services at a lower cost. The company, now wholly owned by Cable and Wireless, hopes to turn over £400 million per annum by 1988, and eventually to capture a five per cent share of the market. The logistics of tapping Mercury are fairly straightforward. Although the company has its own network, most customers are connected to this via BT's local exchanges. Tapping of Mercury's traffic can, for the most part, be done in the same way as BT's own. The remaining Mercury users are connected directly to the network with digital circuits: these require a different approach from the tappers, described in detail in Chapter 10.

BT's Chantrey House tapping unit eventually suffered the same fate of press disclosure as its Ebury Bridge Road predecessor, and the prospect of a further change of address emerged. From mid-1984, rumours circulated of possible new locations, some of them probably contrived and fed to suspected contacts of journalists in order to mislead. Recently, however, it has been established that the latest tapping centre is based on the top floor of BT's former HQ building at 2–12 Gresham Street in the City of London. The tappers occupy a suite previously used for meetings of the BT board. A special security system keeps staff based elsewhere in the building from entering this floor.

Chapter 4

Trawling

During the House of Commons debate on the Interception of Communications Bill in April 1985, Labour MP Gerry Bermingham inquired of then Home Secretary Leon Brittan, whether 'international calls will still be trawled'. Brittan's reply, as elliptical as ever, was nonetheless unusually revealing:

> I can neither confirm nor deny anything that has been said about what may or may not have been done in the past. Let me put it this way. The concept the honourable Member for St Helen's, South has in mind is broadly correct.[1]

The 'trawling' tradition in tapping is less familiar and more insidious than the procedure of hardwiring a tap against an individual line at the local exchange. The principle is that a large number of calls are intercepted on, for example, a single channel carrying groups of circuits along the same route, then put through a series of filtering stages in order to extract any traffic of possible interest. This kind of tapping originated with the British government's efforts to eavesdrop on overseas telegraph communications during the late nineteenth and early twentieth centuries. It has since been developed, by the British and others, for the monitoring of their own international telephone and telex traffic. More recently, the world's major signals intelligence (SIGINT) agencies have variously trawled through trunk calls at home, and through the domestic and overseas communications of other countries. The methods of interception and processing are explored later in the chapter, after we have looked at the origins of trawling.

The international telegraph network began in 1850, when the first submarine cable was laid across the Channel to link

Britain and France; a transatlantic telegraph cable followed six years later. From this point, the network grew in the tracks of the British empire, and contributed much to its durability. Britain maintained substantial ownership and control of the international telegraph and telephone networks into the early twentieth century. At the turn of the century, Her Majesty's Government was fully aware of the commercial and political importance of the networks under their control. They were also starting to realise the benefits that might be derived from monitoring the traffic passing through them: numerous foreign companies and even governments were frequently obliged to use British-owned cables, in the absence of any alternative, to conduct their most sensitive business. Telegrams despatched to and from Britain and its colonies were also monitored for evidence of contacts between foreign powers and their agents, sympathisers and official representatives in British territories: an early example occurred in 1899, during the Boer War, when the War Office obtained, from the Post Office, copies of all telegraph traffic between London and Cape Town, Durban, Aden and Zanzibar.[2]

During the First World War, Britain's slowly crystallising intelligence apparatus was reading every letter and telegram carried in or out of the country by the Post Office and the two private companies licensed to operate an international telegram service from Britain, Western Union and Commercial Cable. This practice – commonly known as 'vetting' (or, equally misleading, 'censorship') – could easily be justified in time of war, but after the armistice, the private telegraph companies were discreetly instructed to continue passing copies of all overseas telegrams to the British Admiralty (see Chapter 2). Although there was no legal obligation, both complied, fearing that the Government would otherwise take away their operating licences. The 'vetting' programme was inadvertently revealed just two years later, in 1920, by the president of the Western Union company, under questioning by a US Senate hearing. Each day, he explained, a convoy of Admiralty vans arrived at the company offices and removed copies of all telegrams sent ten days previously; after overnight scrutiny, the vans returned the messages on the following morning.[3] Telegram vetting thus bore more similarity to letter-opening than to tapping.

85

The British were embarrassed by the disclosure of their telegram interception operation and the subsequent diplomatic contretemps. The Government took immediate steps to ensure that, if a similar row were to break out in the future, the continuity of the intelligence operation would be guaranteed by a law compelling the telegraph companies to cooperate. The legislative vehicle was Section 4 of the 1920 Official Secrets Act, which allowed for 'a Secretary of State', under a single warrant, to demand from a telegraph company the production of

> the originals and transcripts, either *of all telegrams,* or *of telegrams of any specified class or description,* or *of telegrams sent from or addressed to any specified person or place, sent or received to or from any place outside the United Kingdom.* [emphasis added]

The wording of this clause suggests that the Government wished, if need be, to co-opt the telegraph companies into the mechanics of the intelligence process by getting them to do the initial sifting, and picking out, say, all birthday telegrams to Brazil or any message with less than five words. The intended resumption of overseas telegram trawling is implicit in this statute.

It did indeed start again, with the same, strange routine, and continued quietly and almost wholly unaltered for nearly half a century before Chapman Pincher rediscovered the operation, on behalf of the *Daily Express,* in 1967. By this time, it was an intelligence backwater, following the decline of the telegram service in favour of the telephone and telex, but its legacy was considerable. The perceived success of telegram vetting helped to establish the trawling method as a *bona fide* approach to intelligence collection. Moreover, the Official Secrets Act clause which protected the operation was still very valuable because, following a precedent set in 1880, the legal definition of a 'telegram' actually included all telecommunications, including phone calls.[4] The clause remained in force until its repeal and substitution by the Interception of Communications Act (see Chapter 6). In the meantime, it had legitimised – in the British courts, anyway – the extension of trawling from overseas telegrams to international telephone, telex and data transmissions.

One way of classifying different tapping operations is by the level of co-operation given by the carrier who handles the target calls. At one extreme are the telegram vetting programme described above, and the Tinkerbell system which was organised, implemented and, it seems, even partially financed by British Telecom. (A similar collaborative arrangement for the bulk interception of Britain's international communications will be described later in this chapter.) At the other end of the co-operation scale are a class of tapping projects of which, ideally, the carriers should be wholly unaware. These operations were originally planned by the large, well-financed Signals Intelligence combines – the UKUSA bloc and the Soviet SIGINT establishment – as methods of trawling covertly through other countries' international networks with a low risk of detection.

International telephone services developed initially during the 1890s in Britain and continental Europe, gradually producing a mesh of telephone cables connecting most major European cities. Until 1981, all Britain's international and domestic telephone services (except those in Hull) were provided by the Post Office under a government-regulated monopoly. This was the usual arrangement throughout the world, except in the United States, which left its networks in the hands of private monopolies. The organisations who operate and maintain international networks are collectively known as International Licensed Carriers (ILCs).

Clandestine trawling can obviously not be carried out at any of the exchanges serving the network under surveillance, since they are operated by the carrier, so the tap must be set up on the links between exchanges. There are a number of cable and radio transmission systems used in both trunk and international networks, but common to all of them is the use of 'multiplexing' techniques. Multiplexing is the process by which a large number of telephone conversations, text or data transmissions can be sent down the same cable or radio channel simultaneously without interfering with each other. The tap intercepts the multiplexed circuits, separates out the individual communications, and filters them, recording only those of potential value according to pre-arranged criteria.

Otherwise the design of the tapping equipment depends on the method of transmission used on the target route: cables are intrinsically more secure than radio channels, and the latter consequently attract most of the clandestine trawling effort.

The first radio systems used High Frequency (HF) signals between 3 MHz and 30 MHz which rank among the easiest targets for the SIGINT predator. In Europe, HF channels were mainly used for telegraph and, to a lesser extent, for telephone links. Further afield, until the first telephone cable was brought into service across the Atlantic in 1956, HF provided the only telephone connections to the United States for nearly thirty years (although there were a number of telegraph cables). The technical characteristics of the signals are such that they can be detected over a wide area, with fairly simple equipment.

For Britain's SIGINT personnel, most eavesdropping on commercial radio traffic was originally directed against government-to-embassy telegraph messages, until encryption methods advanced beyond the reach of the cryptanalysts in the 1950s. According to British Post Office regulations only official State communications could be encoded; ordinary commercial traffic was not, officially to prevent errors in transmission. The UKUSA SIGINT partners, with the Americans now firmly at the helm, subsequently devoted more attention to these unshrouded commercial messages (see Chapter 2).

GCHQ's main commercial High Frequency radio monitoring centre was at Hawklaw, on the east coast of Scotland. Unlike most other out-stations, it was apparently not assigned any other targets. A typical Hawklaw target, according to one inside account, was the traffic between Budapest and a selection of half a dozen other locations in Eastern Europe. Bamford and Campbell have described, in some detail, the work of Hawklaw and other HF monitoring sites in Britain and elsewhere.[5] It is not clear where, or indeed if, the transatlantic radio telephone channel was intercepted. In July 1957, Lord Waleran questioned the Government about monitoring of the International Telex Radio Service to the United States, but drew only the diversionary response that the Post Office kept copies of some messages for reference purposes when, for example, there was the possibility of a disputed bill.

The Government claimed that no copies were made of these messages, which were kept for six months in locked steel cabinets, at the Central Telegraph Office in London.[6]

High Frequency radio is still used today for public communications systems in Africa and Latin America. One of Britain's last remaining commercial HF links connects the British Telecom radio station at Portishead, near Bristol, to the Falkland Islands. Its vulnerability to interception was embarrassingly demonstrated during the Prime Minister's visit to the islands in January 1983. A radio ham managed to lock onto the circuit, and recorded a conversation between the Prime Minister's press secretary, Bernard Ingham, who was in the Falklands, and staff at 10 Downing Street.[7] However, the majority of radio transmission systems currently installed for commercial telephone networks use microwave frequencies, which carry many more calls per channel than HF links, and suffer less atmospheric interference. Several major carriers, including British Telecom, use terrestrial microwave systems for large sections of their domestic trunk networks and crossborder links to neighbouring countries. Radio hams will find the casual monitoring of microwave channels impossible but, for the determined professional eavesdropper,

> *interception of microwave signals can be done rather easily since the technical parameters of the microwave station . . . and nature of the associated multiplex equipment are public information*[8]

declared a 1976 study by the Federal Communications Commission, which regulates the American carriers. In the British Government's official rules on ministerial conduct, the section 'Propriety and Security in the Conduct of Government Business' reminds ministers that:

> *Calls from within a radius of 50 miles of London to places outside that radius and vice versa may go by [microwave] radio relay and may therefore be intercepted.*[9]

The simplest method of tapping a microwave channel, by planting a receiving antenna on, or close to, the line-of-sight path, is generally the most difficult for a foreign intelligence

89

service to carry out: the technical staff needed for such an operation must work under cover of a diplomatic or trade delegation, and their movements are subject to surveillance by local security agencies. It was believed that this was in fact the only means of intecepting microwave communications, but in fact a part of the signal can be picked up, with sufficiently sensitive equipment, from off the line-of-sight path.

British microwave tappers are at work at three sites in Ireland: in the British embassy in Dublin, where a unit is operated by GCHQ technicians attached to the SIS station; and at two centres in the North staffed by the British army's 14 Signals Regiment at Divis Mountain, near Belfast, and Clooney Park, overlooking Derry. The job of the army unit is to trawl through the two microwave trunk links across the Irish border. The equipment is probably British in design: British electronics companies, notably Plessey and Racal, provide much of UKUSA's SIGINT antennae and reception equipment under supplementary agreements on standardisation annexed to the main UKUSA treaty.

There are at least three other embassies with a permanent GCHQ presence (reduced from around fifteen in the 1950s), as well as many bases elsewhere (see Chapter 2). Diplomatic premises have been used in the past for ad hoc SIGINT projects where required. In the late 1960s, shortly after the National Liberation Front (NLF) had won control of South Yemen, a three-man GCHQ team arrived at the British embassy in Aden. According to a former GCHQ employee with knowledge of the operation,

> at the time . . . the CIA was intercepting internal telephones and we were doing military communications from within the embassy itself. From that we gleaned the entire NLF set-up and the ties with Eastern Europe and the Chinese. The operation lasted 15 months.[10]

Another tapping system, with apparently similar applications, is REPRIEVE, which the Defence Signals Division, the Australian signatory to UKUSA, installed in the late 1970s at Australian High Commissions in Port Moresby and Jakarta, capitals of Papua New Guinea and Indonesia respectively. REPRIEVE 'takes a whole room of its own and can listen to any local phone call at will', according to Australian government documents obtained by the *National Times*. The same series also disclosed that the British supplied 'reams of transcripts of phone calls made by suspected terrorists in Europe'. It is not clear how these were procured, but the Australians were not greatly impressed, according to an unidentified source:

> they're great if you want to follow the social life of Pierre the would-be terrorist in Paris, but not worth a bumper if you want something closer to home.[11]

A microwave beam transmitted from a relay tower does not simply stop on reaching the next tower but continues along the line-of-sight path away from the earth's curved surface out into space, gradually dissipating its energy through the atmosphere. In the late 1960s, the CIA began to study the possibility of using orbiting satellites to detect these very weak signals from space. The project culminated in the launch in March 1973 of the first of the RHYOLITE series of satellites. During the next five years, RHYOLITE satellites were parked in near geo-stationary orbits, which kept them at approximately 23,000 miles above a small area of the earth's surface, over the Horn of Africa and Borneo. Their targets were radar and missile signals from the Soviet Union and China, as well as microwave transmissions from these and other sources. With their receivers tuned to the standard commercial microwave frequencies, any signals within reach will be picked up. Desmond Ball, who has made a detailed study of the Australian role in US SIGINT operations, writes that:

> the coverage of the RHYOLITE 'vacuum cleaner' is so wide that communications from countries other than Russia and China would be intercepted, including those from and within Australia. According to a former CIA station chief in Australia, John Denley Walker, the intercept capability is used only against military communications: 'It is not remotely its mission to collect personal conversations; if by hazard it picked up domestic conversations, it would get no further than the responsible Australian desk officer'.[12]

France and Israel have been cited among these additional targets. The knowledge that any incidental intercepts will be passed over to the local intelligence organisation is scarcely reassuring. The arrangement in Britain, which has a closer, broader relationship with the Americans, is no doubt similar.

More advanced successors to RHYOLITE have since been put into geo-stationary orbit by the Americans. One SIGINT satellite, launched by space shuttle in January 1985, currently occupies a position over the Indian Ocean, from where it can monitor any commercial telecommunications carried by microwave or HF radio in Asia or the Soviet Union. And Britain may soon have its own SIGINT satellite, codenamed ZIRCON, parked in a similar position.

Until ZIRCON, GCHQ's interest in space technology has been concentrated on the communications carried by commercial satellites rather than on the development of its own orbiting eavesdropping platforms. The idea of a global commercial telecommunications system, using geo-stationary satellites to receive and retransmit microwave signals between distant points on earth, was perhaps the most accurate prophesy of the science fiction writer Arthur C. Clarke. Experimental work on communications satellites began in the United States in 1962. In August 1964, the International Telecommunications Satellite Organisation, INTELSAT, was formed to take control of international commercial satellite communications. The organisation now represents over 100 countries, most of them Third World states who rely on the INTELSAT system for an independent international communications network at a reasonable price: however, the heaviest users of the system are the major Western nations.

INTELSAT's world is divided into three sectors: the Atlantic, Indian and Pacific Ocean Regions, each of which is served by a handful of geo-stationary satellites. The Atlantic and Indian region satellites can be reached from British earth stations, allowing coverage of an area stretching from the western United States, through Europe, Africa and the Middle East, to Australia and the Far East. At present, British Telecom has two main earth stations, equipped with parabolic dish aerials, handling INTELSAT communications: Goonhilly Down in southern Cornwall and Madley Priors in Herefordshire.

The development of satellite communications presented new opportunities for GCHQ and NSA. The first INTELSAT probe went into operation in April 1965. Shortly before the D Notice Affair of February 1967, which served an inadvertently timely reminder that mass surveillance was a routine official activity, GCHQ despatched a group of technicians to Goonhilly Down 'to study the methods used for handling telephone traffic'.[13] The idea, which NSA was also investigating on the other side of the Atlantic, was to set up a shadow earth station in order to capture and trawl through any satellite traffic within its grasp. The concept was essentially RHYOLITE in reverse: instead of launching satellites to eavesdrop on surface communications, terrestrial monitoring posts would be used to listen to satellite transmissions.

The Post Office had chosen Goonhilly primarily for its quality of being, as trade jargon has it, 'electrically quiet' – in other words, there were few other radio transmissions in the area. This was important to facilitate reception of the feeble signals arriving at the earth station from over 20,000 miles away. For the same reason, GCHQ sought a similar environment for their shadow station to eavesdrop on the same satellites. The Ministry of Defence, co-financier of GCHQ and a substantial rural landowner, provided a cliff-top site named Cleave Camp, near the village of Bude, seventy miles from Goonhilly on the North Cornwall coastline. Not all in Whitehall were so obliging: the estimated £500,000 cost of the project drew sharp queries about its ultimate intelligence value. GCHQ chief Leonard Hooper replied that a refusal to sanction the project would put SIGINT diplomatic relations in jeopardy. The approved facility, with its compelling Atlantic panorama, was called the Composite Signals Organisation Station, Morwenstow, and employed fifty local villagers.[14]

In 1971 INTELSAT's fourth generation of satellites came into operation. Each was designed to carry two television channels, and about 3,500 telephone circuits. Morwenstow began work the following year, with two dishes measuring ninety-seven feet across. (This was also the dimension of the largest Goonhilly aerial.) Hooper jokingly christened them 'Pat' and 'Lou' in recognition of the critical lobbying support given by NSA boss Pat Carter and his deputy Louis Tordella when the Morwenstow project was in doubt.[15] The twin dishes were pointed towards the two INTELSAT craft positioned above the Atlantic. Each satellite was equipped with two sets of antennae: one for receiving the signals arriving from the commercial earth stations; the other for transmitting them back to earth. It was the downward link that interested the Morwenstow eavesdroppers.

The telecommunications satellite acts as a relay station, amplifying and retransmitting the signals which it receives, so that all earth stations within sight of it can exchange transmissions with each other. The upward links are narrow beams, of a similar width to those in ground-based microwave systems, but the downward transmissions are broad beams directed at regions on the earth's surface covering up to half the countries in the world. This arrangement means that several earth stations can send signals via the same satellite simultaneously. Each earth station within the appropriate footprint can receive every transmission from the corresponding beam, but in practice only tunes in to the channels which carry traffic addressed to it. INTELSAT assigns distinct transmission and reception frequencies to each earth station.

While the commercial earth stations only receive traffic on selected frequencies, GCHQ at Morwenstow tune in to every transmission frequency to pick up anything it can. Its two original dishes can intercept most INTELSAT Atlantic Ocean traffic bound for Africa, Europe and the Middle East, plus any transmissions to North and South America carried on the broadest beam. There is little point in using Morwenstow to monitor British international traffic, which can be done more easily elsewhere (see below). NSA has an analogous set-up in the United States: COMSAT's main east and west coast earth stations, at Etam, Virginia, and Brewster Flats in Washington State have both attracted NSA-operated shadow stations. Between them, GCHQ and NSA have complete coverage of INTELSAT's Atlantic region transmissions.

The feasibility of intercepting satellite communications intended for reception hundreds of miles away was recently demonstrated by the Dutch signals intelligence agency, the TICV:

For a long time the [Dutch] *have kept the Israeli secret service Mossad informed of Iraq's progress in producing the nuclear device. For this purpose TICV, the electronics department of the Navy Intelligence Service MARID in Amsterdam, monitored satellite communications between Iraq and Italy. Iraq obtained vital materials and components for the production of their own nuclear weapon from Italian suppliers. Jerusalem could deduce from the collections of technical data which the spying centre in Amsterdam 'caught from the air' how far Iraq had progressed with work on the bomb.*[16]

The orientation of the first two Morwenstow antennae implied that the station did not monitor communications from the Indian Ocean Region satellites, although this may have been done by a different UKUSA station. In April 1982, North Cornwall council were informed by the Government's Property Services Agency that a further three dish aerials were due to be erected.[17] By July 1986, the base had six dishes in all: three pointing towards the Atlantic Ocean satellites, and three facing east by south-east at a low elevation, consistent with monitoring the Indian Ocean satellites.

Shadow earth stations are adequate for intercepting one-way telex or data transmissions, through which much international trade is conducted, but there comes a problem in dealing with telephone or duplex (simultaneous, both-way) data traffic. The two parts of the conversation must be intercepted on different channels or, in some cases, even at different monitoring stations. Moreover, a large proportion of international communications travels via cable, including about half of the 30 million plus telephone calls made between Britain and the United States each year. An effective programme of monitoring international commercial telecommunications therefore needs more than Morwenstow and similar installations.

Cables are inherently more resistant to tapping than radio links. Consistent with their warning to staff about the dangers of microwave interception, the British Government uses cable for its most sensitive domestic communications, including those between London and GCHQ Cheltenham. Certain 'Foreign Office phone lines', installed in 1959, caused unexpected problems with Cotswold residents living near the cable routes, who complained of high-pitched humming sounds and pavements rendered unusable after being dug up to bury the cables.[18]

Cable sabotage, intended to force enemy communications onto less secure routes, had become a classic wartime strategy. In the most famous incident of this type, the first British action of the 1914–18 War was to send the Post Office cable-laying vessel *Telconia* to dig up and sever German-owned telegraph cables in the English Channel.[19] Thereafter, the Germans had to rely on cables belonging to neutral countries, notably Sweden, using circuitous routes to avoid detection or interception by the British who then controlled most of the world's cable capacity. From 1916, an American-owned cable was used to carry German diplomatic messages across the Atlantic. Unfortunately for the Kaiser, the cable passed via Britain where the Admiralty's Room 40 group monitored the traffic. Among their catches was a telegram from the German Foreign Minister, Zimmerman, to the German legation in Mexico hinting at a possible alliance between the two countries and annexation of US territory. The telegram was used by the British to help persuade the Americans to join the war, which they did. More recently, during the Arab–Israeli war of June 1973, Israeli commandos destroyed the submarine cable between Libya and Egypt, compelling them to use satellite channels. The Israelis then secured the co-operation of various European intelligence services to eavesdrop on the satellite traffic.[20]

Despite the difficulties, it is possible to tap underground and submarine cables using 'sophisticated pick-up loops . . . used in promixity to the cable to intercept bundles of communications as they pass over it'[21], according to an ex-NSA technician. These devices detect the magnetic field around the target line, caused by the current flowing through it, which can be analysed to reveal the traffic on that line. This technique was apparently used by the British during the South Atlantic war in 1982 to monitor cable-borne communications between the Argentinian invasion forces and the South American mainland. One source maintains that:

the BT cable laying ship Iris *was especially refitted in South-ampton and sent out with the Falklands Task Force to retrieve a Falkland–Argentina submarine cable from the ocean bed and fit an induction loop tap to it . . . Sensitivity to its secret role probably prompted the quick response of GCHQ in reputedly replacing BT staff overnight at Portishead* [radio station] *after it was discovered that they were playing Galtieri's phone calls over their PA system.*[22]

The trawling systems described so far do not rely on the cooperation of the tappers; indeed, attempts to solicit it could expect a firm rebuff. However, there are large-scale tapping programmes where carriers actively assist their intelligence services. One of these was exposed in 1970, when students at Copenhagen University found Denmark's international phone tapping centre, staffed by employees from the Danish tele-comms administration, in the university basement.[23] The prospect of basing a similar operation on college premises in this country is unlikely to appeal to the intelligence complex or to most British academics. Moreover, Britain's position in the international telecommunications system demands a more extensive eavesdropping operation. British Telecom currently handles approximately one million international telephone calls every day through six international exchanges linked to the Goonhilly and Madley earth stations, and to around thirty submarine cables with capacities ranging from a few hundred to over 4,000 telephone circuits. An additional pair of ex-changes switch telex and data traffic along the same routes.

All BT's international exchanges are located in London. The telephone exchanges are divided between three sites: Stag Lane, in Edgware, which houses the De Havilland and Mollison switching centres; Mondial House, in the City of London; and Keybridge House in Vauxhall. International calls dialled from Britain are transmitted through the national trunk network to one of these exchanges, depending on the region from which the call is made and the destination country. Nine-tenths of the traffic is consigned for what are termed 'Major Routes' – namely a dozen countries in Western Europe, plus the United States, Australia and Canada. Every other country is labelled as a 'Minor' or 'Intermediate' route.

Under current arrangements (which are subject to con-tinuous revision), between one-third and one-half of Britain's international telephone traffic passes through Mondial House, a concrete edifice of ziggurat (layered pyramid) design opened in 1979 on Upper Thames Street, overlooking the river. There are three exchanges here: Mondial, Thames 1 and Thames 2.

The Mondial switch carries all Minor Route traffic, including calls to and from the Soviet bloc and most Middle Eastern countries. Other countries of priority intelligence interest, including Saudi Arabia, fall into the Intermediate category; their traffic is divided between the Mondial House trio and the new Keybridge exchange. The concentration of international switching in the London area suggests that the most propitious site for an interception facility would also be in the capital.

A few minutes' walk from Mondial House, on the other side of St Paul's cathedral, is Caroone House, one of British Telecom International's many ancillary buildings. BTI rent Caroone House, at an annual cost of just over £20,000, from a religious charity, the Congregational Memorial Hall Trust, who in turn hold a 150 year lease from the Sun Life Assurance Company of Canada, the owners of the Farringdon Road site.[24] Caroone House is occupied by units from BTI's International Operations Division, IT4, which looks after the engineering aspects of the international network. Of particular interest is a group entitled IT4/NE1, with a staff of ten managers and twenty-odd technicians.

Secluded behind an electronically-controlled security door, operated with personal magnetic cards and number codes, like a 'hole-in-the-wall' cash-dispenser, the NE1 group's official brief is 'special network investigations'. What they do, explained a BT engineer familiar with their work, is to 'play with the network' in order to find answers to engineering problems which defy any orthodox solutions. The group generally works on demand from other departments using its own 'NE Private Wire Network'. However, the tardiness of NE1's work and the excessive capacity of the Private Wire Network has aroused suspicions as to exactly how the group occupies itself. Several sources have confirmed that in fact, the main function of IT4/NE1 is not special investigations, but tapping.

IT4/NE1's unchallenged access to any part of the international network for its acknowledged investigative function provides ideal cover for its eavesdropping. At the Mondial House end, the private wire network comprises a series of cables attached, like the tapping jumpers in the Tinkerbell system, to the distributions frames feeding the three switching units. Each cable is connected through a jackfield to a device

98

called a 'concentrator'. The jackfield allows different groups
of circuits to be monitored according to variations in traffic
load through the day resulting from differences in local time
across the world. NE1 have over 400 digital circuits allocated
to them, which may allow several thousand calls to be
monitored simultaneously. The intercepts are apparently not
recorded or otherwise processed at Caroone, but passed
directly to GCHQ.[25]

Another likely target of the Caroone House unit is the
transit traffic, mainly between continental Europe and North
America which, like Minor Routes, is also handled by the
Mondial House exchanges. The tapping of transit traffic is a
long-standing SIGINT practice, which takes advantage of the
fact that, by accident of geography, there are numerous pairs
of nations whose cable links necessarily pass through one or
more intermediary countries. (Moreover, some countries need
cables to others in order to gain access to particular satellites.)
In the spring of 1938, the Czech government was engaged in
feverish telephone consultations with its embassies in Paris
and London, apparently oblivious of the fact that both lines
travelled through Berlin, where the Germans were monitoring
every word, including some uncomplimentary references to
the British Prime Minister, Neville Chamberlain. (Hitler
amused himself by having these passages transcribed and sent
to the Foreign Office in London.)[26] The point about transit
access is forcefully made by an internal Foreign Office circular, 'Use of the Telephone for Communication to Posts
Abroad', written in July 1950, during a Cold War phone-
tapping epidemic in Central Europe.

*The use of the telephone is dangerous. It must be remembered
that telephone conversations to countries abroad will be monitored by the Governments of the countries through which the line
passes and that attempts to disguise the subject matter and drift
of the conversation are almost invariably unsuccessful; the
telephone is thus not suited to confidential conversations.*[27]

Not all the traffic passing through the British Telecom
network is necessarily trawled by British intelligence themselves, given the limits on their SIGINT resources. GCHQ
apparently receives some of this material from NSA. One of

the functions of the NSA station at Menwith Hill, near Harrogate in Yorkshire, seems to be monitoring a proportion of international communications passing through Britain.

According to a detailed account of the Menwith Hill monitoring operation published by the *New Statesman*, a set of one-way cables, with a total capacity apparently in excess of 5,000 telephone circuits, carry communications traffic into the complex from BT's microwave network. In response, the Ministry of Defence delivered what they themselves described as a 'limited and highly specific denial':

> *The Ministry stated that Menwith Hill did not intercept 'transatlantic incoming and outgoing calls'; nor did it intercept British domestic calls. The interception of traffic to and from Europe, within Europe, or going through Britain was, in this instance, virtually admitted by non-denial.*[28]

NSA may or may not be involved in tapping British domestic traffic from Menwith Hill; the station has other functions and, according to one former NSA employee, 'the Brits do most of the commercial voice stuff'[29] in Western Europe. In summary, the combined coverage of the three identified interception facilities – Morwenstow, Caroone House and Menwith Hill – is a large proportion of the phone calls, telex messages and computer data transmissions going into, out of and through Britain; and a large proportion of INTELSAT traffic bound for other countries. The value of the system, however, depends on how efficiently GCHQ and NSA are able to sort through this mountain of intercepts, especially as the contents of many communications carried on international public networks are trivial or irrelevant. It is this processing function with which the rest of this chapter is concerned.

*

Back in 1967, in a vain effort to forestall publication of Chapman Pincher's story on telegram vetting, Leslie Lohan, a civil servant from the Ministry of Defence, took the journalist, in the time-honoured manner, out to lunch. During the meal,

Lohan elaborated on the paramount importance of telegram vetting. Pincher writes:

> *he explained that cables* [i.e. telegrams] *were vetted by the security authorities in the hope of establishing a 'pattern' of messages which might lead to information of security interest. He said that since a foreign agent or person inimical to the State would not use the same cable office but would keep moving about, it was essential for all the cables to be available.*[30]

The system, under which squads of intelligence clerks ploughed through vanloads of telegrams in search of some elusive 'pattern', was based on the study of externals described in Chapter 2. However, manual sorting was by then outmoded: four years earlier, NSA had started to use computers to trawl through telegram and telex transmissions (but not phone calls), using a custom-built IBM computer system known as HARVEST. This comprised a special purpose processor, high-speed memory and a very fast tape system. The tape system, wrote a trade magazine in 1980, 'was particularly spectacular; in fact its performance rivals what many commercially available systems achieve today'.[31] That was nearly twenty years after the first use of HARVEST – aeons by the standards of the computing industry.

The American carriers had recently installed their own, less sophisticated computers to record all their text traffic on magnetic tapes, so NSA could now simply arrange to obtain copies of these tapes and run them through HARVEST. Each day couriers arrived by plane from NSA headquarters, picked up the tapes, took them back to Fort Meade to be copied, and returned them to the carriers within twenty-four hours.

Once copied, the telegram tapes obtained from the carriers 'would be run through HARVEST, which could be programmed to "kick out" any telegram containing a certain word, phrase, name, location, sender or addressee, or any combination'.[32] The system, which was installed at Fort Meade and, in a later version, at Menwith Hill, ran for fourteen years before being replaced by a Cray system.

The HARVEST processor was employed in one of NSA's most notorious programmes codenamed MINARET, which between 1967 and 1973 gathered intelligence on American citizens, specifically political radicals, on behalf of other Federal agencies. This was the first operation in the history of the NSA whose primary targets were American nationals. A significant feature of MINARET was the participation of GCHQ, as the report of the US Justice Department team, set up to investigate the programme, illustrates:

> *MINARET intelligence, except one category of international voice communications involving narcotics, was obtained incidentally in the course of NSA's interception of aural and nonaural (e.g. telex) international communications and the receipt of GCHQ-acquired telex and ILC cable traffic.*[33]

To run MINARET, NSA and GCHQ were equipped with 'watch lists' of names for which to look out. Any traffic to, from or simply mentioning a name on the list was picked out. Actress Jane Fonda, black activists Martin Luther King and Eldridge Cleaver, and the singer Joan Baez all graduated on to the list. The subsequent exposure of MINARET was a major embarrassment to NSA and led to the passage of legislation limiting some of its activities (see Chapter 7). Nevertheless, joint operations between NSA and GCHQ, directed against international commercial traffic, have continued. Late in 1984 an investigation into arms smuggling between the United States and Iran, via Britain, was successfully concluded after months of surveillance of transatlantic phone calls. The leader of the smuggling ring, Primitivo Cayabyab, and his associates in Europe and America were arrested.[34] Elsewhere in UKU-SA, the Defence Signals Division – Australia's signals intelligence agency – eavesdropped on opponents of the Canberra Government's policy on Indonesia.[35] Among names of GCHQ's watch list is said to be the Scottish trade unionist Jimmy Milne.[36] The comment of a former GCHQ employee, Dennis Mitchell, hinting darkly at 'excesses that would outrage the British public if they were allowed to know about them'[37], suggests MINARET has crossed the Atlantic.

At NSA, HARVEST has since been replaced by an extremely powerful 'supercomputer' manufactured by the Minnesota-based corporation Cray Research. GCHQ has also acquired a Cray computer which, according to one source, has a similar purpose: to search for and retrieve items from GCHQ's vast database of intercepted communications. The British could not actually afford to buy the Cray, according to a former NSA employee, so the Americans provided it on loan complete with support staff. GCHQ's computer engineers were thrilled when it arrived a few years ago.

Even with the power of a Cray machine, a computer search through intercepted telephone communications is a monumental, possibly insurmountable task, due to the complexity of speech signals in comparison with the elementary structure of telex and data communications. Some telephone calls are manually transcribed and stored on microfiche. However, there are a number of external characteristics of telephone calls where computers can be used to choose those of likely interest. *Questions of Procedure for Ministers*, undoubtedly drawing on information from GCHQ, notes that:

> *interception may be facilitated by the comparative ease with which calls may be selected, i.e. calls over private circuits, calls to identified numbers of intelligence interest and those calls where a scrambler is used.*[38]

GCHQ is equipped with Tandem computers, especially designed for processing communications, which can be programmed to sort through ILC intercepts according to the criteria cited above. Taking these in reverse order, modern scrambling techniques are explored in Chapter 10, while methods of selecting calls according to destination are described in detail in Chapter 9. A private circuit is an exclusive connection, rented from British Telecom (or other carriers), which links two specific locations: a pair of company offices, say, in London and Manchester. British Telecom guarantees that a circuit is available at *any* time for communication between these two sites. Companies and government departments prefer private circuits to the public network because they are connected so as to avoid local exchange equipment where most faults occur; they are also better suited for carrying computer data, and may, in some cases, be cheaper. The key technical feature of a private circuit is that it is a *facility*, and not necessarily a physical entity. Private circuit

103

traffic between London and Manchester, for example, may be carried over the same trunk routes as public calls. The difference is that private circuit calls are not switched. For the eavesdropper trawling through a high-capacity channel, extracting the private circuit traffic, which is invariably of a commercial or official nature, is a priority. A special set of electronic signals are needed to identify private circuit traffic to the exchanges; this also allows the tappers to isolate these calls from the rest.

The advice paper makes no mention of two further methods of selecting calls: from the content of the conversation, and the identity of one or both of the speakers. Both techniques demand computer speech recognition techniques which have only recently been developed.

There is a high-technology myth of telephone tapping to match the traditional folklore of strange noises, 'men-with headphones', playbacks and the rest. Replacing the 'men-with-head-phones', in this version, are 'men-with-teleprinters' who sit and read transcripts of telephone conversations which have been generated by computer, directly from a phone tap.

Although speech recognition technology is available, Britain's tappers are unlikely, on grounds of cost alone, to have committed themselves to a system of full automatic transcription for tapped telephone conversations. The main reason is that vast computing power is needed for handling speech signals – one second of speech converted into computer code (binary) is equivalent to a telex message of roughly 1,000 words – and automatic recognition demands very complex processing techniques which put additional demands on the computer's resources. Also, telephone speech is subject to particular distortions during transmission which render it difficult to analyse both continuously and accurately. Finally, the intelligence yield from a recording may far exceed that from a transcript, especially if the conversation is conducted in opaque terms. The South African intelligence services, for example, use extensive voice recordings to assess individual personalities, moods and style, in a form of involuntary polygraph testing:

a person for example who speaks in code will not necessarily reveal facts but he or she will reveal – through how they talk,

104

whether or not they are excited – that something different is happening. Careful analysis will often reveal what it is.[39] [emphasis in original]

Intelligence may suffer then, if recordings are dispensed with entirely. However, automatic speech processing techniques can be used to improve the efficiency of tapping by searching electronically through a large volume of intercepted communications, selecting those worth recording for subsequent, detailed analysis, and ignoring the rest. Two methods are favoured: *voice recognition*, which seeks to identify a particular speaker, rather than what is being said; and *keyword recognition*, which registers the occurrence of a particular word in conversation, irrespective of who says it.

The development of speech processing technology, especially recognition, has been slow. 'It's a scientific Gordian knot'[40], said one American specialist, which draws on 'chip design, signal processing, acoustic-phonetics, natural language theory, linguistics, mathematics of stochastic (probability) processes, and computer science techniques'. A leading British researcher, in a less expansive frame of mind, compared speech recognition with trying to put toothpaste back into a tube.[41] The commercial potential of speech processing is now apparent from the projected growth of the market – $1 billion world-wide by 1990 is a conservative estimate[42] – and the systems needed to realise that potential are no longer technological mirages. Most currently available speech processing systems have to be made familiar with the voice of each potential user, who must pronounce examples of every word that the system will be required to recognise; when the system is put into use, the words must be spoken in isolation. Nevertheless, these rather primitive systems have applications in warehouse stocktaking and security control. In principle, every computer function could be executed through voice commands, rather than through a keyboard or other form of input. The next few years may see the introduction of voice-operated typewriters and word processors.

In Britain, commercial research into speech processing was minimal until the 1980s. Since 1985, the Alvey Directorate, which administers a programme of government funding for information systems research, has sponsored a number of computer speech projects. One of these is the design of an automated inquiry service which recognises and responds to telephone requests about railway timetables; the participants are British Telecom, Cambridge University and the computer systems group Logica, whose LOGOS speech recognition unit has been adopted for the proposed system. Promotional literature for LOGOS declared it to be 'a significant technological advance' over existing word recognition systems. Equally significant was one of the reasons for the advance. LOGOS had been designed by Logica under contract from, and based on research by, a little-known appendage of GCHQ's Directorate of Communications Security, called the Joint Speech Research Unit (JSRU).

JSRU has been in the speech processing field since the Second World War. Before suffering two rehousings in fairly quick succession, its whole life had been spent at GCHQ's former headquarters at Eastcote in Middlesex. In the late 1970s, it took up premises in a newly-constructed facility in GCHQ's Benhall complex on the western outskirts of Cheltenham. After experiencing staff problems, partly caused by the ban on trade union representation, JSRU was removed from GCHQ auspices altogether and put under the wing of the Royal Signals and Radar Establishment, at Malvern in Worcestershire. The Malvern establishment has its own Automatic Speech Recognition Section, which is participating in another Alvey speech project concerned with the Chinese language.

Between 1972 and 1978, the Joint Speech Research Unit carried out a series of experiments to develop an automatic method for identifying individual speakers, regardless of what they might be saying. The objectives and likely application of this search were outlined at a 1977 scientific conference by JSRU technicians John Bridle and John Yates, and Melvyn Hunt, who was seconded to the Unit from the Canadian National Research Council (the Canadian signatory to the UKUSA SIGINT treaties).

Such a facility might be useful . . . in the early stages of a police investigation where a telephoned message is to be compared with the recorded voices of a large number of suspects. The requirements, then, are that the system should be text independent and that as far as possible it should work on speech that has been

106

degraded by transmission over communications channels such as the telephone. Satisfying these requirements entails some disadvantage in terms of accuracy . . . We are aiming for a system that would take as input a twenty-second sample of telephone quality speech from an unknown speaker. The output would be a list of the five or ten per cent of speakers known to the system whose voices are most similar to that of the unknown speaker.[43]

In 1983 Hunt recounted further details of the project, explaining that

the particular concern here is with speech transmitted over the public telephone network using conventional handsets . . . We have assumed that the individuals in the group thought to contain the unknown speaker (the reference group) cannot be expected to co-operate in reproducing the text used by the unknown speaker, hence the need for a text independent method. We have aimed the work at situations where the reference group is so large that identification by human listening would be impracticable with the idea that the automatic method would be used to reduce the reference group to a smaller group which could then be subjected to further scrutiny.[44]

Given JSRU's affiliation, the expression of a special interest in telephone speech, the concession on accuracy, and the acknowledgement of speakers' probable lack of co-operation are wholly consistent with the development of a system designed to sift a large volume of telephone intercepts according to the likely identities of speakers. Such a system could, for example, be used to trawl out all international calls made from any telephone by a particular political activist.

JSRU's recognition method used a mathematical technique called 'cepstrum analysis' to produce a 'voice print' of thirty odd numbers for each speaker. (The cepstrum is a mathematical function with useful analytical properties but no direct relation to any physical quantity.) These quantities were related to the vibration frequency of the vocal chords, known as the 'pitch', and to the frequencies which were most prominent in the utterance of a particular sound, which are called 'formants'. For example, each person has one set of formants for the vowel 'A', and another set for the vowel 'I';

both are unique to that person. On the basis of earlier research, JSRU believed that the pitch was particularly suitable for identifying a telephone speaker because its value was not altered significantly by telephone line distortion.

Staff from the police technical laboratories, at Sandridge near St Albans, and from the Meteorological Office, headquarters of the nation's weather forecasters, were enlisted to supply speech extracts of around twenty seconds in length under a variety of circumstances. The system, centred on a standard piece of speech processing equipment called a 'vocoder', calculated fifty times per second estimates of the pitch value and of an additional set of parameters called 'cepstrum coefficients'. The pitch and cepstrum data were used to compile JSRU's thirty-number voice print. Recognition was simply a matter of finding which of the stored voice prints best matched the print obtained from the extract under test.

JSRU first took radio recordings of weather forecasts as raw material and managed to produce 90% correct recognition at the first attempt, with 99% success at the first two attempts. The same methods were then applied to telephone speech, using extracts from calls made in public phone boxes. But when the researchers compared two extracts from two phone calls made from different telephones by the same speaker, first time recognition fell to around 30%; and a more subtle measurement based on the accuracy of a short-list of possible speakers also showed a disappointing performance. The outcome, according to Melvyn Hunt, was 'unacceptably poor'.[45]

A study of call box results showed that the major problem was the variation in the quality of different telephone circuits; and if speaker identification depended on the state of the phone line, it could hardly be exploited as a tool of tapping. Nevertheless, the cepstrum method was a proven method of distinguishing between individual voices; in any case, JSRU is most unlikely to have abandoned its carefully formulated objective. American research suggests that the problem of variations in line quality was overcome by building statistical descriptions of them into the voice recognition model. Moreover, other sources contend that scientists from R18, the speech processing division of British Telecom's research laboratories at Martlesham in Suffolk – the same group engaged in the Alvey railway inquiry project – have achieved recognition rates of 80% on telephone speech. They add that Marconi Communications Systems, located in nearby Chelmsford, have subsequently been commissioned, apparently at the instigation of MI5, to produce further increases.

Picking out key words from telephone speech, no matter who utters them, is a more intractable theoretical problem than even voice recognition; nevertheless, here also JSRU made significant headway during the mid-1970s. The main difficulty, as described by John Bridle, now head of JSRU, is that

> *two utterances of the same word have different time-structures because of differences in pronunciation: some parts of the word become longer, others shorter, to varying extents.*[45]

In JSRU's system, each key word is stored in computer memory as a 'template' consisting of a set of parameters relating to the formant values for each frame in a spoken example of that word. Before a test word can be compared with any template, the time-structures must be aligned, in a process rather like matching up two sets of markings made on a pair of elastic bands.

The 'time-warp' problem, as it has become known, illustrates why recognition of an *isolated* word is simpler than that of a specific word in a piece of continuous speech. In the former case, the beginning and end of the test word are compared with the corresponding frames in the stored templates. Those templates which show no similarity at the extremities can be rejected immediately. If the extremities do coincide, a technique called 'dynamic programming' is used to measure the similarity between test and template words for various frame alignments. The system registers recognition when the similarity measure exceeds a given threshold.

For a *continuous* speech extract, the situation is more complicated. There are generally no well-defined boundaries in the speech signal separating one word from the next: the apparent demarcation between successive words, through which people understand conversation, is a figment of cerebral activity. So different portions of the whole extract have to be successively compared against each word template to find a passable similarity. JSRU have negotiated this hurdle with a series of elaborate mathematical mechanisms. One of the most advanced is the ZIP algorithm. JSRU papers say that

ZIP has been used to align sentences and much longer speech utterances successfully. These have included passages of about one minute of speech from two speakers. Several short sentences of synthetic and natural speech have also been correctly aligned.[47]

The matching of synthetic and natural speech mentioned above is especially important, since a speaker-independent system must use artificial, 'average' models of each key word to make up its reference templates.

Though cheaper and faster than full automatic transcription, the use of key word systems is no less governed by financial considerations. An NSA employee, interviewed in 1980, said that the agency was capable of performing key word analysis on telephone conversations, but that

this technique is not in widespread use on oral communications, because there are other processes that will allow them to zero in on conversations of interest. They can do it, but it requires a great deal of expense and computer time . . . it is generally not cost-effective to screen oral communications by automatic electronic analysis.[48]

In the 1980s, the balance of cost-effectiveness has shifted rapidly in favour of automation. The American Defense Department now uses a key word system to analyse the outpourings of the world's radio and television stations, and finds it cheaper than the old system of recording everything and detailing intelligence analysts to plough through it. It appears, moreover, that full automatic transcription systems are in operation with the US National Security Agency. A former NSA official has described a Cray Research system, installed at NSA's base at Chicksands in Bedfordshire during the early 1980s, which automatically descrambles intercepts of Soviet air force radio traffic and transcribes them into Russian text.[49]

In Britain GCHQ is believed to have installed voice and

word recognition equipment in the Tinkerbell domestic tapping centre. This does not necessarily imply that Tinkerbell's descendents are engaged in trawling, although there are unconfirmed reports from within the electronics industry that a tapping operation has recently been established in the London area to sweep through tens of thousands of trunk circuits. During the 1984/85 coal strike, a local BT engineer told one group of miners that their phone calls were being analysed for key words. The engineer advised them to 'guess at the trigger words and use them in as random a way as possible'.[50] The periodical *Private Eye* later claimed that the miners' dispute had actually overloaded MI5's tapping system. The tapping of 'Union officials in every lodge and NUM Branch', together with the multitude of support groups throughout the country, caused an 'information mountain'. Even words like 'picket' triggered the system; tape recorders were running continously, and one morning the whole operation simply ground to a halt when all the tapes ran out.[51]

Since then, according to one BT source, Tinkerbell has concentrated on voice recognition to pick out calls of interest. This is likely to be more productive than key word recognition: targets of tapping are frequently circumspect in what they say on the phone, but the presence of a particular speaker cannot be disguised – false accents will not fool the system.

The use of trawling systems and automated selection methods, like voice and speech recognition, on domestic telecomms, poses an appalling threat to rights of privacy and appears to be illegal, although trawling is lawful on international lines. The development of British tapping laws and regulations is the subject of the next two chapters.

Chapter 5

Tapping, Parliament, and the Law

'The origin of the authority of the Executive to intercept communications is obscure.'[1] With these words, the 1957 Birkett Committee began its main report. They emphasise, in the restrained way of Privy Councillors, that, until the 1985 Interception of Communications Bill was forced upon an unwilling Conservative government by the European Court of Human Rights, there was no precise legal basis for State tapping of telephones. The practice was justified by successive governments of all parties as a Royal Prerogative, derived from an ancient right of the Crown to open any letters carried by the Royal Mail.

Mail opening was indeed an Executive pastime with a long tradition. It was mentioned in the 1657 law which first gave the state a monopoly of postal delivery. This would, the decree said, enable the Government to

> . . . *discover and prevent many dangerous and wicked Designs, which have been, and are daily continued against the peace and welfare of this Commonwealth.*[2]

It is strange that this, a Cromwellian law, should thus be the first to refer, however obliquely, to the practice of interception which was to be claimed as a Royal prerogative. However, neither this ordinance, nor the Proclamation six years later, which gave to 'the Secretary of State' the sole right to authorise letter opening, actually made legal the practice itself.[3] Neither did the Post Office Acts of 1711, 1837, 1908, 1953, or 1969. All these referred to the practice of interception and confirmed the authorising powers of the Secretary of State, but did not formally legitimise the activity they tacitly sanctioned.

112

The first major Parliamentary investigation of mail opening was launched in 1844. This followed a public scandal over a warrant signed by the Home Secretary, Sir James Graham, to open the letters of Joseph Mazzini, the Italian liberal revolutionary. Two wholly secret Committees, of the House of Lords and the House of Commons, were set up to enquire into the state of the law regarding the interception of communications. Both committees, however, refrained from any discussion of the source of the authority to open letters. The Lords Committee reported that they had

. . . not thought it necessary to attempt to define the Grounds upon which the Government has exercised the Power afforded by public Conveyance of letters of obtaining such Information as may be thought beneficial for the Public Service; it seems sufficient for the present purpose to state, that the exercise of this Power can be traced from the earliest Institutions in this country for the Conveyance of Letters.[4]

And there matters rested. In later years, when pressed in the House, ministers repeated that the power to open letters, read telegrams, and tap telephones was derived from a Crown Prerogative which had been exercised from the earliest times. The strange thing about this particular prerogative, as the Birkett Committee remarked in 1957, was that it went unmentioned by any of the standard Constitutional authorities. Neither Blackstone's *Commentaries*, nor Tasswell Langmead's *Constitutional History* talk of any such a prerogative. According to a writer on the constitution in the 1950s, if the authority to tap existed at all, 'the power must have been vested in the Sovereign prior to the beginning of legal memory'.[5]

The legal Commentators agree, however, that any authority to tap telephones must derive, by analogy, from this supposed prerogative to open letters. They also agree that this extension of the prerogative to the new communications technologies of telegraph, telephone and telex occurred from the moment each new medium was invented. However, unlike the seventeenth-century Ordinance granting the state a postal monopoly, the Act which established a national telecomms monopoly did not refer, even in passing, to interception. Moreover, whatever the legal basis of telephone tapping, until

1937 it was simply performed by the Post Office at the request of the police or security services, neither of which required ministerial sanction. Again, this differed from the procedures for mail opening which, since 1663, had needed authorisation by a Secretary of State.

The Post Office apparently believed that their authority to tap phones on request lay, not in any Royal Prerogative to intercept all communications, but in a right of any telephone company to operate its system as it thought fit, within the law. And there was certainly no law *against* tapping, whether by the State or anyone else. In 1937, this glaring contradiction, between the procedures for telephone tapping and those for letter opening, came to the notice of the Home Secretary, who ruled that his power to authorise the opening of letters (which, at that stage, rested in the 1908 Post Office Act), should henceforth apply to phone taps as well.

These legal anomalies underline the bald truth that successive governments paid little attention to the legality of their snooping operations, until these activities were brought into the public eye. For many years, this just did not happen. The police and security services were always careful to use tapping for intelligence gathering only, rather than using the material as evidence, so the matter never surfaced in court. During the Second World War, rumours of tapping were rife; but, in the absence of information, public concern over the issue was not strong enough to worry the Government, until the mid 1950s.

Before then, Parliamentary Questions on the subject of tapping were met with a blanket denial. In 1947, Sir Waldron Smithers, Conservative MP for Orpington, told the Postmaster General, who was responsible for the telephone system as head of the Post Office, that, 'There is a widespread feeling that tapping and monitoring goes on', and asked for 'an assurance that there is no tapping of calls on a political basis'.[6] The Postmaster General, Mr Wilfred Paling, replied that

Officers of the Post Office are strictly forbidden to listen in to telephone conversations except in so far as may be necessary for the efficient performance of their duties.[7]

He denied that any form of tapping went on at all except for routine service monitoring, to ensure the efficiency of the telephone system. Mr Paling repeated his assurances later that year,[8] and they were echoed by his colleague at the Board of Trade, one Harold Wilson MP, after accusations that officers of the Board had used material from telephone taps during the questioning of some Manchester businessmen suspected of evading trade regulations.[9]

Neither the Postmaster General nor the Secretary of the Board of Trade were intentionally lying. They simply knew nothing about the tapping that was going on, which was the responsibility of the Home and Foreign Secretaries, together with the ministers responsible for Scotland and Northern Ireland. Clearly, however, the Government could not avoid awkward questions for ever.

The first real signs of public anxiety surfaced in 1952, after a number of Borough Councillors from Slough, in Berkshire, paid a visit to their local telephone exchange. The local worthies were shown around by a fellow councillor, who happened to work at the exchange. The trip included a demonstration of how phones were tapped, either by a police officer sitting next to the switchboard operator with a parallel plug to listen in to a particular call, or by a permanent hardwired link to the subscriber's telephone line, which went out from behind the switchboard to 'secret premises'.

The visit was reported by the local press, and the story was quickly taken up by Fleet Street. A long article which appeared in the *Sunday Pictorial* of 30 March 1952 not only described in some detail the process of tapping, but also published allegations by two MPs that their phones were being tapped by MI5. The scandal that followed prompted a series of questions in the House by the Labour MP, Sydney Silverman. This finally produced some information from the Government. The Home Secretary, Sir David Maxwell Fyfe, told Mr Silverman that the power to tap telephones rested with 'The Secretary of State', who exercised it only 'in exceptional circumstances'. Asked under what authority he exercised this power, Sir David replied

It is a power which has been used by every government, of whatever political persuasion, since the telephone was invented, and is a Prerogative power.[10]

The revelations of 1952, however, were as nothing compared with the embarrassment that hit the Government four years later, when the Marrinan case hit the news stands. It was this incident which led to the Birkett Committee's investigation of the Government's right to intercept and transcribe its citizens' communications.[11]

The trouble arose when the Metropolitan Police tapped the telephone of a gangster, Billy Hill, known by the popular press of the day as 'The King of the Underworld'. The tapping was authorised by the Home Secretary, and, as usual, was not mentioned in court when Hill was tried in 1956. However, the prosecution evidently had access to transcripts of phone conversations between Hill and his barrister, Patrick Marrinan. During the course of the trial, accusations were made to the effect that Marrinan had obstructed the course of justice. Once the proceedings were over, the Prosecution Counsel, Mr R.E. Seaton, wrote to the Attorney General about Hill's lawyer, indicating that the police held transcripts of conversations between Marrinan, his client's solicitor, and Hill himself, which showed professional misconduct by the former.

The Attorney General informed Sir Hartley Shawcross, a former Labour MP, but, by then, the head of the Bar Council, the legal profession's combined trade union and self-regulating disciplinary body. The Bar Council proceeded to write to Metropolitan Police Assistant Commissioner Jackson, in charge of the CID, requesting the transcripts. He obligingly showed the conversations between Marrinan and Hill both to Sir Hartley and to the Secretary of the Bar Council, but refused their request to allow them to copy the intercepted material to the authorities at Lincoln's Inn (to which Marrinan belonged), unless they first obtained the permission of the Home Secretary.

That post was held by Viscount Tenby, who agreed to the request, and the content of the phone taps was duly shown to the whole Bar Council, to the Benchers of Lincoln's Inn, and even to Patrick Marrinan himself. The latter was eventually disbarred, and left the country, but not before his case had become a *cause célèbre* which opened to debate the whole question of tapping.

It was Marcus Lipton, Marrinan's MP and the Labour

Member for Brixton, who first rose, at *Question Time* on the morning of 6 June 1957, to question the propriety of handing out such information to private bodies such as the Bar Council. By this time, Viscount Tenby had given way as Home Secretary to R.A. ('Rab') Butler, who, therefore, had the uncomfortable task of justifying his predecessor's decision. Part of the ensuing dialogue went as follows:

Mr Lipton: Is it not a monstrous state of affairs that a telephone conversation between a barrister and his instructing solicitor should be intercepted, transcribed, and transmitted to the Bar Council and to the Benchers of Lincoln's Inn, by someone acting under the authority of the Home Secretary? Are we now living in a police state?

Mr Butler: The answer to the last part of the question is that the Secretary of State only acts in this way when he realises that the public interest necessitates such action. I will give an undertaking to the House that this action will never be used except in the interests of public order. I would like to add that it is of the highest importance that persons concerned in the administration of justice should not be associated with criminals in their criminal capacity. Because of these considerations, it was thought right to assist the Bar Council in their investigations of allegations of this nature.[12]

Pressed the following day by both the Leader of the Opposition, Hugh Gaitskell, and the Liberal leader, Jo Grimond, Butler replied that the passing-on of telephone tap information to a non-official body was exceptional, and would not be construed as a precedent. The Opposition leaders both pointed out that the Bar's disciplinary proceedings against Marrinan involved neither considerations of national security, nor serious criminal activity. Butler replied:

It is the settled policy that such information is not disclosed to persons outside the public service. I have said that there were

117

exceptional circumstances in this case . . . The power [to tap phones] *is used to detect serious crime and would never be used for prying into confidential communications between an accused person and his legal advisor. I can say no more about this case.*[13]

But say more he did. The House entered the Whitsun recess the next day, and the next opportunity to question the Home Secretary did not occur for three weeks. By then, no fewer than eight MPs had questions on the Order Paper. Mr Butler's stonewalling tactics had collapsed, and he announced that he and the Prime Minister, Harold Macmillan, would '. . . meet the Leader of the Opposition and the Leader of the Liberal party this evening to discuss how certain aspects of this matter could best be handled in future'.[14] The next day, Downing Street announced that a committee of three Privy Councillors was to be set up, under the Chairmanship of Sir Norman Birkett.

Birkett had been one of the century's greatest criminal lawyers, and had defended many of the famous murder cases of the inter-war years. Sir Patrick Hastings, a former Attorney General, once said of him,

If it had ever been my lot to decide to cut up a lady in small pieces and put her in an unwanted suitcase, I should without hesitation have placed my future in Norman Birkett's hands. He would have satisfied the jury: (a) that I was not there; (b) that I had not cut up the lady; and (c) that if I had, she thoroughly deserved it anyway.[15]

One cannot, of course, be sure that it was this ability to help those wanting to get away with murder which commended Sir Norman to the Government in 1957. He had also been an MP, and a High Court judge, in which capacity he had sat as Britain's representative on the Nuremburg tribunal, which tried Nazi war criminals. He had retired from the Bench as Lord Chief Justice Birkett at the end of 1956. Birkett's terms of reference for his new job were:

To consider and report on the exercise by the Secretary of State of the Executive Power to intercept communications, and, in

118

*particular, under what authority, to what extent, and for what
purposes this power has been exercised, and to what use
information obtained by such means should properly be used or
disclosed.*[16]

Apart from Sir Norman himself, the Birkett Committee
consisted of Lord Monckton, another lawyer and former
Minister of Defence, and Patrick Gordon Walker MP, Labour
Member for Smethwick and a former Foreign Office Minister
(later to become Foreign Secretary, and thus to authorise his
own taps).

These eminent national figures were being asked to report
in an atmosphere of considerable public concern. Fleet Street
was in an uproar about phone tapping. Even *The Times* had
come out wholly against the practice of tapping, in two
thunderous editorials entitled 'An Odious Practice' and 'Still
Odious'. The latter commented on the choice of Birkett and
his team:

> *They have been men in authority. The necessity of certain
> aspects of the State being satisfactorily administered may seem to
> them to be greater than the need to give every citizen his full
> rights, liberties, and privacy . . . It will not really be enough for
> the Privy Councillors to say that telephone tapping is all right.*[17]

Further pressure on the Committee's deliberations was
applied by a number of motions at that summer's trades union
conferences, as well as by a whole series of parliamentary
questions throughout the period that Birkett's Committee was
in session. The questions in the Commons covered the Hill
case, tapping in general, and the progress of the work of the
Committee itself, which was left in no doubt of the interest of
MPs in its deliberations.

Birkett's final Report is dated 18 September 1957, but it
was not, in fact, released for a further six weeks, while officials
of the intelligence services argued for the deletion of several
sections. It had already been decided not to publish any of the
detailed evidence put to the Committee, but Macmillan
apparently insisted that the Report itself should be published
in full.

The Birkett Report extends to forty-three pages, including

appendices and a dissenting Report by Gordon Walker. It remains the most extensive official source of information about telephone tapping, and lays down procedures for issuing warrants that have remained largely the same down to the present day. The Privy Councillors summarized their findings in the Introduction. As *The Times* had anticipated, it came down in favour of tapping:

> *The use of the power* [to intercept communications] *has been effective in detecting major criminals and preventing injury to national security . . .* [it] *should be allowed to continue, under the same strict rules and supervision . . . The criminal and the wrongdoer should not be allowed to use services provided by the State for wrongful purposes quite unimpeded . . . The interference with the privacy of the ordinary law-abiding citizen or with his individual liberty is infinitesimal, and only arises as an inevitable incident of intercepting the communications of some wrongdoer. It has produced no harmful consequences.*[18]

The value of the Birkett Report, however, lay, not in its somewhat anodyne conclusions, but in what it revealed (for the first time) about official attitudes to tapping policy and practice in the UK. At the same time, the picture painted by the Report is seriously incomplete. It completely ignores the tapping of calls to and from overseas destinations, and any other taps authorised by the Foreign Secretary. The report even claims that '. . . it is today the invariable practice that the interception of communications is carried out only on the authority of these two' – i.e. the Home and Scottish Secretaries.[19] This was untrue, and it may be wondered whether the members of the Committee were informed about GCHQ's tapping operations, or even the existence of the Foreign Secretary's taps.

The Committee was just as coy on the question of the *legality* of phone tapping. It had heard two arguments on the source of the State's right to intercept. One was based on a line in the 1868 Telegraph Act, which instructed the Postmaster General to issue regulations covering the release of the content of telegrams. In fact, no such regulations had ever been issued, and Birkett was profoundly unconvinced by this line of argument. He preferred the second approach; the 'ancient

Royal Prerogative' line discussed earlier. Even in this case, the Report was tentative in its support:

> *We favour the view that* [the right to intercept communications] *rests on the power plainly recognised by the Post Office statutes as existing before the enactment of the statutes, by whatever name the power is described.*
>
> *We are therefore of the opinion that the state of the law might fairly be expressed in this way:*
>
> *(a) The power to intercept letters has been exercised from earliest times, and has been recognised in successive Acts of Parliament.*
>
> *(b) This power extends to telegrams.*
>
> *(c) It is difficult to resist the view that if there is a lawful power to intercept . . . letters and telegrams, then it is wide enough to cover telephone communications as well.*[20]

As none of the Acts which 'recognised' the power to tap actually made it *legal*, Birkett's wording enabled the Committee to avoid the crucial question of whether the Government was acting within the law by intercepting communications, and, if it was, which law? In a sense, it did not matter; there was certainly no law *prohibiting* tapping, and Post Office employees were exempted from prosecution for connecting taps by the Crown Proceedings Act of 1947.

The Privy Councillors were rather more forthcoming about the arrangements for obtaining warrants to tap phones. Fourteen authorities, including the Post Office Investigation Branch, the Port of London Authority, and the Ministry of Food, had been granted warrants to tap by the Home Secretary in the period between 1937 and 1956. The major customers of warrants, though, were as ever, the Metropolitan Police, the Customs authorities, and MI5. Procedures were such, Birkett said, that, 'there are likely to be very few applications that need to be rejected' by the Secretary of State.[21] The Committee did, however, propose a few administrative changes in the warrant system.

The regulations laid down three conditions which had to be met before the police or customs could obtain a warrant to tap.

(a) The offence must be really serious.

121

(b) Normal methods of investigation must have been tried and failed, or must from the nature of things be unlikely to succeed if tried.
(c) There must be good reason to think that an interception would result in a conviction.[22]

The Report went on to claim a high conviction rate for both police and Customs' taps.

Such factors as measurable success rates did not concern the security service. According to the Committee:

Besides securing convictions, the security service has the duty to keep up to date its information covering espionage and subversion [and therefore] . . . *less stress is laid on the need to secure convictions.*[23]

Such 'political' tapping needed to meet only two conditions before a warrant would be forthcoming: firstly there must be a major subversive or espionage activity that is likely to injure the national interest, and secondly the material likely to be obtained by the interception must be of direct use in compiling the information that is necessary to the Security Service in carrying out the tasks laid upon it by the State.

The report was, unsurprisingly, vague about the nature of these tasks, and about the definition of 'major subversive activity'. However, at the time, 'subversive' was almost exclusively applied to the activities of the Communist Party, and Birkett did mention that tapping had led to 'the detection of Communists operating secretly in the civil service.'[24]

Birkett concluded that both the apparently strict rules applied to the police, and the somewhat vague principles upon which MI5 tapped, were sufficiently effective safeguards against the misuse of the power to tap. It is difficult to agree. Although applications from the police and Customs are first submitted to Home Office officials, and then to a Permanent Under-Secretary, before going up to the Minister, critics have often suggested that it is, in practice, very difficult for such civil servants to challenge the operational assessments of the police. This argument applies still more strongly in the case of the Security Service.

The Birkett Report also published, for the first time, the

numbers of warrants that had been issued by the Home and Scottish Secretaries over the preceding two decades. The figure had risen from seventeen telephone warrants in 1937, to a peak of 242 in 1956, but even the Committee conceded that this was not an accurate guide to the number of phones tapped, especially as 'a single warrant has been issued in the past to cover a number of names'.[25] Birkett recommended that, in future, this practice should cease, and each warrant should specify only one name or telephone number.

The Report said very little on the subject of unauthorised tapping, and what it did say gives little ground for confidence.

All the evidence we heard was to the effect that there is, and has been, no tapping of telephones by unauthorised persons in this country . . . However, there can be no certainty that unauthorised tapping does not occur . . . In these circumstances, Parliament may wish to render the unauthorised tapping of a telephone line an offence.[26]

Parliament did not so wish, until another quarter century had elapsed, and tapping had once again become an item of public concern. On the Marrinan case itself, the Birkett report delivered a very quiet rebuke. Sir Norman, Lord Monckton, and Mr Gordon Walker said that 'there can be no doubt that the decisions of Sir Hartley Shawcross and Viscount Tenby were wholly governed by considerations of the public interest'[27] and stressed that they were '. . . anxious not to use language which might imply that the decision of Viscount Tenby was unreasonable'.[28] They concluded, however, 'The decision of the then Secretary of State to make transcripts of intercepted telephone conversations available to the Bar Council and the Benchers of Lincoln's Inn was a mistaken decision',[29] and recommended that, in future, '. . . there should be no disclosure of the information obtained on public grounds, by the exercise of this great power, to private individuals or private bodies or domestic tribunals of any kind whatsoever'.[30]

The Committee recommended that tapping for reasons of national security or the detection of serious crime should continue, subject to the safeguards already existing, and those recommended by the report itself. Patrick Gordon Walker, however, issued a caveat to the majority recommendations, in the form of a 'Reservation' appended to the main report. His argument was that the use of phone taps by the Security Service should continue unimpeded, but in criminal cases resort to these methods should cease almost entirely, on the grounds that 'public repugnance' towards tapping might cause a loss of confidence in the police.[31]

The historian of the 1945–51 Labour Government Kenneth O. Morgan, has described Gordon Walker as 'perhaps the most Right Wing member of the entire administration'.[32] However, as the sole Labour Party member of the Birkett Committee, his support for tapping only 'subversives', terrorists, and spies merely echoed the attitudes of trades union leaders at that summer's round of conferences. In the wake of the Marrinan case, the Post Office Engineering Union Conference in June 1957 passed a resolution deploring the passing-on of intercept material to the Bar Council. The General Secretary, Charles Smith, told delegates that he 'did not think they could deny that such methods might be regarded as legitimate in cases involving the highest degree of security',[33] but not ordinary 'serious crime'. Three months later, the TUC remitted a motion proposed by Smith, in which he suggested that tapping should be confined to 'cases of the highest degree of security, or cases in which the telephone conversation itself constitutes the offence' (eg obscene or malicious calls).[34] Gordon Walker's approval of tapping 'subversives', but not criminals, thus reflected the official Labour movement line of the period.

Public concern is a fickle creature, especially when it is not over-stimulated by its representatives in Parliament, nor by the news media. By the time the Report was finally issued, with the Prime Minister's assurance that its recommendations had been accepted, the tapping scandals that had arisen in the wake of the Marrinan case had vanished from the headlines, and, seemingly, from the minds of MPs. Even Gordon Walker's minority report went undefended by the members of his own party. It was left to the Liberal leader, Jo Grimond, a whole five months after the Report was issued, to ask the Home Secretary whether any of the Labour member's recommendations had been implemented by the Government. They had not.

124

The key to Labour's silence is to be found in a reply given by Butler, as Home Secretary, to Gaitskell, back in July 1957, before the Report was issued. Asked whether a full debate would follow publication, Butler replied that this point '. . . should be discussed through the usual channels'.[35] This phrase was repeated by the Prime Minister, Macmillan, on the day the Report was published, after Marcus Lipton MP had complained about the lack of time to consider the Committee's work. To Parliamentologists, 'the Usual Channels' is the codename for the civil servant whose job it is to mediate between the whips' offices of the two main parties. The clear implication, to those skilled in such arcane mattes, is that the Conservative and Labour leaders had arranged for the Birkett Report to be greeted with a deafening silence. Not a single Labour MP asked one question about the content of, or the omissions in, the Report. This is clearly a tribute, not just to the power of the contemporary whipping system, but to the strength of the desire of both leaderships for abstainance from comment. One can only speculate as to whether such a silence was the price paid for the withdrawal of the intelligence establishment's objections to publication. At any rate, the episode reflects little credit on Parliament as a watchdog of the citizen's interests and liberties.

The press did little better. With the release of the Report, *The Times* decided that tapping was, by and large, a good deal less odious than it had thought six months previously. On publication day, the paper editoralised:

> *When the issue was raised in June, the public's instinctive distrust of the business was fed by the imagination, which in the almost total absence of facts, was the only faculty that could supply the details . . . On the whole, however, the Privy Councillors' revelations should allay the worst fears . . . On the showing of the report, the information obtained by these methods is very rarely misused.*[36]

The Times disagreed with Birkett in just two respects; firstly in going along with Gordon Walker's reservations about the tapping of those suspected of 'serious crime', and, secondly, in calling for the annual publication of the number of warrants issued, contrary to Birkett's advice.

125

This time, it was left to the *Daily Express* to call the practice of tapping 'odious', in an editorial entitled 'The Tyrant's Way'.[37] However, this, too, was concerned purely about the tapping of suspected criminals, and exempted 'national security' cases from its general strictures. It is almost as if there was an orchestrated silence on the question of the tapping of those deemed subversive, which, at this time, everybody understood to mean members of the Communist Party.

Another issue on which the media (and Parliament) were silent was that of the legality of intercepting communications. Once again, it was left to Jo Grimond to voice any concern. In a New Year speech released to the press on the last day of 1959, he declared plainly that 'tapping is odious and should be illegal'.[38] The next morning the papers carried the New Year's Honours List. It was headed by the name of Sir Norman Birkett, who had been rewarded for his services to the State with a barony. The new Lord Birkett of Ulveston chose as his motto *Lex Mea Lux* – The Law Is My Light.[39] Parliament remained unwilling to legislate on tapping.

Moreover, back in late 1959, events had occurred which were to cast doubt on the effectiveness of Birkett's recommendations, even as regards the very *raison d'être* of the Committee – the Marrinan case. On Thursday 3 December, Patrick Gordon Walker moved an adjournment motion criticising the Government for allowing the interception of a phone call without a warrant and disclosing the taped material to a professional tribunal – this time the General Medical Council.

On this occasion, it was a Doctor Fox who was the subject of investigation. The police had taped a call between the Reading GP and a woman who had arranged for the police to record the conversation from an extension in her house. She later gave evidence to a disciplinary tribunal of the General Medical Council, and told them of the tape. The GMC, although a private body, possessed powers of subpoena, and was able to issue an order for the police to produce the intercept material. The upshot was, as *The Times* suggestively, if vaguely, put it, that Dr Fox was struck off the register of qualified practitioners for 'infamous conduct in a professional respect (which was not of a criminal nature)'.[40]

The Government claimed, in response to Gordon Walker's allegations, that no warrant was required in this case, because one of the participants in the call had given her permission for the interception. Thus it was not a 'tap' as such, and not covered by the recommendations of the Birkett Committee. For the same reason, Butler maintained that the material could legitimately be disclosed to the GMC. Questioned about the frequency with which the police used this method of listening to phone calls, Butler replied:

> *I think that anybody in the important and heavily responsible position I hold would not be able to cross his heart and say that there had never been listening either on an extension or anything else in the whole course and range of police activities, especially in criminal investigations. What I do say is that, after inquiry and having consulted my inspectors, I find this to be a most exceptional procedure.* [41]

At this last phrase, memories of Marrinan must have stirred uneasily in the minds of at least some MPs, but at the time Parliament (and the press) accepted the Home Secretary's explanation. The nation was preparing for Christmas.

The sixties, belying its reputation as a turbulent decade, saw less parliamentary and media concern about tapping than the previous ten years. How well this mirrored the public's own view is disputable. Certainly, among anti-establishment groups (for example the nuclear disarmament movement or militant trades unionists) there was considerable awareness of the practice of interception. The silent majority, as usual, was largely silent; though when the *Sun* published a page of readers' letters on the subject of telephone taps, the majority of correspondents were against the use of such measures in any circumstances.

The one major scandal that was unearthed by the press in the sixties concerned the interception of international communications. The story, briefly mentioned in Chapter 4, was broken by Chapman Pincher in the *Daily Express*, which ignored a 'D Notice' requesting it not to print anything on the subject. The article itself said, correctly, that all overseas telegrams were read by the security authorities, under a class of warrant unmentioned in the Birkett Report, issued under Section 4 of the 1920 Official Secrets Act; the *Express* story did not mention that the same procedure applies to letters and telephone calls to or from overseas, as well. In fact, the content of Pincher's story was largely ignored, as the rest of the media concentrated on the Government's attempt to censor the story, in what became known as the 'D Notice Affair'.

Throughout the sixties and seventies, Parliamentary Questions about tapping were met with the standard response that procedures were as laid down in the Birkett Report. Questions about the number of warrants being issued were countered by a polite refusal, citing Birkett's conclusions that such a disclosure would harm the public interest. This peaceful scenario hid a doubling of the number of warrants, from an average of 130 per annum in the period covered by Birkett (1937–1956), to an average of 279 per annum over the sixties.

The one question that did engage the eager attentions of Parliament was very close to home; the tapping of MPs. Here the sixties saw an innovation in the tapping regulations. The Birkett Committee had concluded that parliamentary privilege did not extend to a general immunity from official interception:

A Member of Parliament is not to be distinguished from an ordinary member of the public, so far as the interception of communications is concerned, unless the communications were held to be in connection with a parliamentary proceeding . . . It is difficult to imagine the circumstances in which a telephone conversation might be held to be related to a proceeding in Parliament.[42]

In November 1966, under Harold Wilson's Labour Government, MPs began to express concern that their calls might be being tapped, following the tabling of a question to the Home Secretary, Roy Jenkins. Russell Kerr, Labour MP for Feltham, wanted to know how many warrants against MPs' telephones he had granted. Opposition Members, such as Sir Tufton Beamish, joined in with the opportunity to criticise the Government. The critics were outflanked however, when Wilson, with characteristic flair, announced that he had banned the tapping of MPs' phones on assuming office in 1964. He went on to sidestep a question from Tom Driberg MP on whether it had been the practice to tap Members'

128

phones before 1964, but managed to leave the impression that such things might possibly have been done under the Tories. The Conservative front bench responded with what *The Times* called an 'uncomfortable silence'. Later, the paper remarked, 'they were not very happy with themselves'.[43]

Wilson himself may have felt pleased with his *coup de théâtre* at Question Time, but matters were not to rest there. Within days, peers were demanding the same immunity. So, not to be outdone, were the legal profession. Wider demands, such as for legislation against what was termed 'free-enterprise tapping', followed in the wake of the interest generated by Wilson's statement. The Government was able to assure their Lordships' House that they, too, would henceforth be immune from official snooping. No such offer was made to the lawyers, nor was anything done about unauthorised tapping. An irate socialist complained in *The Times*:

> *A discrimination that was dubious thus becomes an absolute scandal. There are many peers who never set foot in their House for months on end, but who are now to be thus favoured for no other reason than their possession of the prefix 'Lord'.*
>
> *Was it in order to increase aristocratic privilege that millions voted Labour at the last election?*[44]

The introduction of parliamentary immunity remained Labour's sole attempt to improve upon the tapping procedures laid down by Birkett. Since 1966, successive governments have maintained that Wilson's ruling remains in force, while, in practice, they have watered it down. In 1970, Prime Minister Edward Heath promised that MPs were immune, then added in his last sentence, 'I stated this principle with only this proviso – that security of the state must be preserved'.[45] And ironically, in 1977, Wilson personally was to call for an enquiry into allegations that he himself had been the subject of surveillance by the Security Service while he was Prime Minister.

It was the question of tapping MPs which finally led, in 1973, to the voicing of parliamentary concern over the rise in the number of warrants being taken out against less privileged folk. The events began in November, 1972. By this stage, Edward Heath's Conservative Government was in power, and in trouble. Amongst other tribulations, someone had leaked a secret Department of the Environment report on proposed British Rail line closures to a respected trade paper, the *Railway Gazette*. Police raided the office of its editor, Mr Richard Hope, and at about the same time, he and his wife began to notice their home phone doing strange things. It kept ringing, but when they went to answer it, there was only silence at the other end. The Hopes shared a party line with some neighbours, who observed the same phenomenon. By 1 December, Mr Hope had had enough. That afternoon, he received a call from Les Huckfield, the Labour MP, and told the Member for Nuneaton that he believed his phone to be tapped. The moment Hope mentioned the interception, both men experienced the line going dead for about three seconds.

An outraged Huckfield, believing that both he and Hope might be tapped, raised a number of questions in the House, and, by 18 December, the matter began to develop into a full-scale parliamentary row. Harold Wilson (whose whole career seems strangely intertwined with the history of tapping) took the opportunity to call for editors of newspapers and magazines to be added to MPs and peers in the select list of those 'immune' from official tapping.

This time, the issue did not vanish over Christmas, and matters came to a head in February 1973, when the press began to speculate about the number of people being tapped. The figure of 1,250 warrants was quoted for 1972, a sum so far above what had been instanced by Birkett that MPs became seriously concerned. Alex Lyon MP took the opportunity of an adjournment debate to ask the Home Secretary, Mark Carlisle, whether this figure was correct, and to raise yet again the question of the publication of the number of warrants issued. Lyon claimed that an increasing number of organisations (he cited Anti-Apartheid groups) had complained to him of Security Service tapping. The Home Secretary called the figure of 1,250 warrants 'ludicrously high', but followed his predecessors in refusing to state the official figures, citing Birkett's recommendation against such disclosures. He also refused either to confirm or deny that Mr Hope's phone had been tapped.

It was nearly midnight when Lyon, presumably still concerned over the welfare of British opponents of the South African regime, asked whether:

> . . . in defining 'security', the phrase is ever used to cover the security of any state apart from our own?

Carlisle's reply was cut off by the Deputy Speaker in mid-sentence, and the House was adjourned. All the Secretary of State managed to say was:

> At this moment I can only reply to that by the definition of security as laid down by the Birkett Committee and assure the Honourable Gentleman that these terms are scrupulously abided by. As I have made absolutely clear, this is a matter for the Secretary of State, and I think I must stick to what I have said, that security is defined entirely —.[46]

With these unenlightening words ended the last parliamentary debate on the subject of tapping, until the events of the Malone case in 1979. This story will be told in the next chapter.

If the British legislature spent much of the sixties and seventies avoiding the subject, the judiciary were happy to continue the evolution of tapping law. Not that they got the chance very often. In 1968, the Court of Appeal determined that material from unofficial taps was admissible in court. The case, appealingly called *Regina v. Sin*, involved an attempt to hide adultery in a divorce case. This 'conspiracy to pervert the course of justice' was revealed by recordings from a tap put on the erring husband's phone by a private detective employed by his wife.

The court ruled that the assurances in the Birkett Report were irrelevant in this case, because:

> Those assurances . . . had been given by the Crown in relation to conduct by the Crown in respect of action taken by the police, security forces and the like. There was no suggestion that the Crown could bind other people not to tap telephones or make use of recordings so obtained.[47]

If this appeared to give *carte blanche* to the freelance

131

snooper, this impression was briefly dispelled in 1974, when, for the first time, someone was successfully prosecuted for unauthorised interception. Leeds Crown Court fined a private detective £500 for tapping the telephone of a client's wife during a divorce case. The private eye, Graham Blackburn, was an ex-policeman who had hardwired a link from a distribution cabinet outside the wife's house, in order to obtain evidence of adultery. The crude intercept led to a garden shed belonging to a friend of Blackburn's, where the latter was discovered by a Post Office engineer. The Leeds judge, Mr Justice Nield, accepted Blackburn's plea of not guilty to conspiracy charges and theft of Post Office electricity, but he did plead guilty to conspiracy to effect a public mischief. However, a few months later, the House of Lords, in the case of *DPP v. Withers*, in November 1974 ruled that no such offence existed. Private enterprise tapping was once again on the road.

By the late seventies, there was widespread cynicism on the subject of tapping. Governments continued to profess strict adherence to Birkett, but they were widely disbelieved, while informed journalists persisted in suggesting that far more phones were being tapped than before. It took a scandal the size of the Marrinan affair, and interference by an international court, before a Prime Minister finally agreed to introduce legislation on tapping. These events are the subject of our next chapter.

Chapter 6

Tapping Law in the 1980s

On 22 March 1977, a police unit arrived at the home of James Malone, a London antique dealer suspected of handling stolen property. The house, in the Vauxhall district of South London, was searched and a large number of items removed: the police later claimed that these were some of the proceeds from no less than thirty-three separate burglaries. Following this raid Malone was charged with several offences and committed for trial, along with five other defendants, at Newington Causeway Crown Court. The trial, which began on 5 June 1978, ended ten weeks later with the jury acquitting Malone on some charges while failing to agree on the others. At the subsequent retrial the following spring, the jury again failed to reach a verdict on the outstanding charges. The case was then dropped.

Halfway through the first trial, on 18 July, Malone's lawyers asked to examine the notes made by the police officer in charge of the case, Detective Sergeant Ware. This is normal court practice. On this occasion, however, the defence were in for a surprise. For one page of Detective Sergeant Ware's notebook contained details of a conversation in which Malone was one of the participants, and a note indicating that the information was derived from a telephone tap. This improbable turn of events spawned a chain of litigation lasting six years which culminated in the Government being compelled to introduce legislation to deal with tapping.

The immediate consequence of Ware's unfortunate gaffe was a rare official admission that a tap had actually taken place. 'In the circumstances I am authorised to say that there was such an interception carried out on the authority of the Secretary of State's warrant'[1], announced the leading counsel for the Crown. True to precedent, the information supplied

133

was confined to an absolute minimum. Attorney General Sir Michael Havers later told the European Court of Human Rights that the Government admitted only: 'that there was an interception of a communication . . . but *not* that this interception was effected by tapping his own telephone line' [emphasis in original].[2]

Disclosure of further details would, the Government claimed,

frustrate the purpose of telephone interceptions and might also serve to identify other sources of police information, particularly police informants.[3]

There is some evidence that the tap was in fact fitted on Malone's line. Towards the end of September 1978, a month after the first trial was completed, Malone contacted his local telephone exchange and asked for any tap to be removed. The GPO's (and now British Telecom's) standard response is to refer the caller to the Home Office, which is nominally responsible for domestic telephone tapping. On this occasion, however, the inquiry was passed up the GPO bureaucracy as far as a Mr Prior, described as 'a senior executive'. Prior subsequently came back to Malone and announced that he had been authorised to remove the tap.[4]

In any event, Malone was armed with incontrovertible evidence of a tap, and set out to challenge its legality. On 17 October 1978, he issued a writ against the Metropolitan Police Commissioner to secure the following: an injunction preventing further tapping; a court order requiring that any transcripts, tapes or other material based on intercepted conversations be handed over to him or destroyed; and finally an appropriate sum in damages. The application was heard in the High Court's Chancery Division by the Vice-Chancellor, Sir Robert Megarry, in the last week of January 1979. Early on in the eight-day hearing, most of which was devoted to intricate legal dispute, the writ was dropped on Megarry's advice and the motion altered to a simple request for a ruling on the legal status of telephone tapping.

Malone's counsel, Colin Ross-Munro QC, put forward three principal arguments: that telephone subscribers had rights of privacy and property over their conversations; secondly, that tapping breached the European Convention on Human

134

Rights; thirdly, that tapping was unlawful because there was no statute specifically authorising it.

Megarry delivered his judgement on 28 February. It consumed some 20,000 words and took two hours to read. He rejected Ross-Munro's submission in its entirety but made clear his view that the absence of any legal safeguards was a serious deficiency which should be urgently rectified. 'It is plain that telephone tapping is a subject which cries out for legislation',[5] was his widely-quoted pronouncement, one which was studiously ignored by both the Labour Government of the day and their Conservative successors.

In spite of the length of his judgement, Megarry dealt clinically with Ross-Munro's three-pronged attack. 'I do not see how words being transmitted by electrical impulses could . . . be said to be the subject matter of property',[6] he ruled, dismissing right of property. The related privacy argument also fell because the concept is not defined in English law. Turning to the European Convention, Megarry simply pointed out that it was not enforceable in English courts. Lastly, the notion that tapping was illegal just because there was nothing to render it licit was an utter anathema: 'England is not a country where everything is forbidden except what is expressly permitted',[7] he said, using a peculiar analogy between telephone tapping and cigarette smoking (which he described as an objectionable, though not unlawful invasion of the privacy of non-smokers).

An interesting side-show at the hearing, which took up much of the third and fourth days, was Malone's effort to subpoena the Post Office to produce the warrant for the tap in court. Both the police barristers and the Solicitor General (who was appearing in court to argue the Government's case) contested the subpoena. The Solicitor General, Peter Archer, arranged for a copy of the warrant to be brought to court where it lay, like some sacred scroll, untouched upon Megarry's bench inside a sealed envelope. Archer had offered to show the warrant to Ross-Munro, but only on condition that it was not shown to his client, Malone. The police team argued that the production of the warrant had no relevance to the case and the subpoena application should therefore be dismissed. It was. Thwarted by the British courts, Malone decided to take his case to Europe.

The 1950 European Convention on Human Rights was among the first products of the Western European movement which emerged after the Second World War. The United Kingdom ratified the Convention in November 1951 but withheld the right of individual petition until 1965 because it was thought that people from the colonies would exploit it.

Under Article 25 of the Convention, a plaintiff who believes that her or his rights, as defined by the Convention, have been contravened may submit a complaint to the *European Commission of Human Rights*, a body associated with the Council of Europe and composed of lawyers from signatory states. The Commission's first task is to decide whether the case is admissible. Of the 2,500 or so annual applications, over three-quarters are rejected immediately, usually for technical reasons.

Once a case is declared admissible, the Commission is required under Article 28(b) of the Convention to try to bring about a settlement of the dispute. In the Malone case, the Commission concluded that 'in the light of the parties' reaction . . . there is no basis on which such a settlement can be reached'.[8] Their next move was to implement procedures laid down by Article 31 which, in the absence of an agreement, demands the production of a report:

1. to establish the facts; and
2. to state an opinion as to whether the facts found disclose a breach by the respondent Government of its obligations under the Convention.

By any standards, the wheels of European justice grind with extraordinary sluggishness. The members of the Commission work only part-time, meeting for just five fortnight-long sessions every year. The Malone case was declared admissible on 13 July 1981, but nearly eighteen months had passed before the Commission completed its report in December 1982.

Malone's submission alleged that the interception of conversations violated the Convention's Article 8, which reads:

1. Everyone has a right to respect for his private and family life, his home and his correspondence.
2. There shall be no interference by a public authority with the

136

exercise of this right except such as is in accordance with the law *and is necessary in a democratic society in the interests of national security, public safety or the economic wellbeing of the country, for the prevention of disorder or crime, for the protection of health or morals, or for the protection of the rights and freedoms of others.* [emphasis added]

Correspondence, in this context, includes telephone messages.

Malone's case, and the subsequent argument, centred on interpretation of the emphasised phrase. Malone's legal representative, led once again by Colin Ross-Munro QC, claimed that neither the interception nor the metering could have taken place 'in accordance with the law' because there was no clearly defined relevant law. They further maintained that there was no redress for this apparent breach of Article 8, which in itself constituted a breach of the Convention under Article 13:

Everyone whose rights and freedoms as set forth in this Convention are violated shall have an effective remedy before a national authority notwithstanding that the violation has been committed by persons acting in an official capacity.

The British Government fielded a nine-strong team led by the Attorney General, Sir Michael Havers, to reply to Malone's submission. Their defence relied primarily on Section 80 of the 1969 Post Office Act, which placed on the Post Office

a requirement to do what is necessary to inform designated persons holding office under the Crown concerning matters . . . transmitted or in the course of transmission . . . by the Post Office.

In the case of telephone taps, this meant that if the Government asked for one, the Post Office was obliged to fit it.

Turning to the claim under Article 13, the Government insisted that any redress should be limited to the need for secrecy, citing the Klass judgement (see Chapter 7) as precedent, but maintained that it was nevertheless available in the

137

form of court injunctions, complaints against the police, or an appeal to the Secretary of State.

On two of the three counts, the Commission came down on Malone's side. They dismissed the Government's appeal to the 1969 Post Office Act.

> *It does not . . . appear to the Commission that Section 80 limits in any way the circumstances in which interceptions may be carried out. It only limits the circumstances in which the Post Office may be required to carry them out . . .*
>
> *Section 80 . . . does not regulate either the purpose for which warrants may be issued or their content or duration in the manner contended by the Government. In any event it fails to do so with any reasonable degree of clarity.*[9]

By a majority of eleven votes to nil, the Government was found to be in breach of Article 8 regarding the phone tap; and by ten votes to one to have broken Article 13. There was one abstention in each case.

The Commission's report, it should be stressed, was in no sense legally binding on the British Government: it merely expressed an opinion. However, the Commission decided to refer the case to the *European Court of Human Rights* which, under international law, could oblige the Government to correct any deficiencies which the Court identified in British domestic law. The Court's powers in this respect were formally accepted by the Government in a declaration to the Council of Europe in 1966 which has been renewed and is still in force. Since the Court's judgements had historically tended to take the same line as the Commission, the latter's conclusions were a significant breakthrough for Malone.

While Malone's slow fuse burned away in Strasbourg, a succession of events kept the Government on the defensive over tapping at home. A review of telephone tapping had been initiated by Home Secretary Merlyn Rees immediately after the Megarry judgement and continued under his Conservative successor, William Whitelaw. Yet with no official pronouncement after nearly a year, it seemed that the Government was content to adopt the inert posture of its predecessors. The *New Statesman* then delivered a rude shock at the beginning of February 1980 with its article describing the Tinkerbell system. Amid much clamour over the details of the piece, Whitelaw promised a statement before Easter.

April Fool's Day was chosen for delivery of the statement and the simultaneous publication of a new White Paper, *The Interception of Communications in Great Britain*. Northern Ireland was excluded. At first glance, it was simply an eight-page *précis* of the Birkett Report. Only the police, Customs and Excise and MI5 were discussed by the White Paper which declared that, as before, their taps required a warrant. The formal conditions of issue remained 'the detection of serious crime and the safeguarding of the security of the nation'.[10] Turning to the particulars of warrants, the White Paper maintained that 'although since 1957 certain practical adjustments have been made in the detailed procedures, the essential features of Birkett are closely followed'.[11]

Whitelaw's statement to Parliament concentrated on the control of tapping. Although some lobby journalists believed that Whitelaw supported legislation, the Home Secretary deployed the familiar argument that recourse to the courts would inevitably hinder tapping as a tool of investigation.

The Government aimed to defuse criticism of tapping controls by arranging for independent scrutiny by a figure of unassailable impartiality. Whitelaw duly announced the appointment of a Judicial Monitor with the following terms of reference:

> to review on a continuing basis the purposes, procedures, conditions and safeguards governing the interception of communications on behalf of the police, HM Customs and Excise and the Security Service . . . and to report to the Prime Minister.[12]

The appointment was delayed, without apparent cause, for two months, suggesting to a sceptical Post Office Engineering Union that 'the proposal was something of an afterthought, a last-minute effort to head off political concern',[13] particularly as the White Paper made no mention of it. It seemed, in part, to be an example of what Harold Macmillan once called the 'principle of Albert and the Lion . . . the public will feel that something is being inquired into'.[14]

The choice of Lord Diplock as Judicial Monitor, confirmed

139

on 4 June 1980, was in some respects an obvious one. Since 1971 he had been a member of the Security Commission, which investigates apparent breaches of official security, becoming its head six years later. He was therefore familiar with the inner workings of the nation's intelligence machinery. Outside the Government, it was widely felt that Diplock's experience was a drawback, because it nurtured an unhealthy intimacy with the intelligence community. Diplock was also renowned for his pronounced right-wing opinions. He is best remembered today for proposing the establishment of the juryless courts, which bear his name, for trying terrorist cases in Northern Ireland. His alleged racism and antipathy to trades unionism compounded doubts about his neutrality and commitment to civil liberties. Personalities aside, there was some concern that the principle of co-opting the judiciary into an essentially political function on behalf of the executive compromised the former's independence; a committee of Privy Councillors was proposed as an alternative.

Home Secretary Whitelaw rejected these criticisms. Diplock, he said, 'is held in very high regard. His independence and integrity are beyond question'.[15] The judge himself presented a rather different motivation:

> as holder of the position of Chairman of the Security Commission I am qualified to be the recipient of information which falls even into the 'top secret' class. This, indeed, formed the principal reason why I felt it to be my duty to accept the task.[16]

Diplock's first report to the Prime Minister, Whitelaw promised, would examine existing measures and would be made public. All subsequent reports would remain secret, although Whitelaw agreed to inform MPs of general findings and any alterations in policy or practice.

The first report was delivered at the beginning of March 1981. In it Diplock diagnosed perfect health in the nation's tapping procedures on the basis of a detailed study of documents and discussion with officers concerned in a number of randomly selected cases from each agency. This conclusion appeared to critics as confirmation of their earlier objections. *The Times* raised a bemused eyebrow, describing the report as 'a curious document'.

140

*Did he check five cases at random, or fifty? If his conclusions,
totally favourable to tapping authorities, are to convince, more
information is required about his methods.*[17]

No more information was forthcoming. Yet even that which
was provided was not entirely accurate. 'The Birkett Report',
Diplock claimed, 'recommended some modifications of the
then existing practice. All of these were subsequently adopted
and have been followed ever since'.[18] This is not true. Birkett
recommended that the specifications of each warrant be
confined to a single person and a single address or telephone
number, but the 1980 White Paper stated that:

*Occasionally a target of interception uses or operates from more
than one address or telephone number. In those cases all
addresses or numbers covered are set out in the warrant.*[19]

Diplock completed one further report before his retirement,
aged seventy-five, in the summer of 1982. Its contents were
not disclosed, other than one alteration to the conditions for
issue of warrants, which expanded the definition of serious
crime, this time to encompass cases where very large amounts
of money are involved.[20] Diplock was replaced as head of the
Security Commission by Lord Bridge, described by liberals as
'another Diplock'.[21] Bridge in turn retired after a three-year
stint, to be succeeded by Lord Griffiths.

Diplock's first report was published in March 1981, shortly
after another official tome which also, within a much wider
remit, discussed electronic surveillance. The Royal Commission on Criminal Procedure, examined *inter alia* police intelligence gathering techniques, including phone tapping. Compared with the prevailing official wisdom, its conclusions were
revolutionary:

*the use of surveillance devices by the police (including the
interception of letters and telephone communications) should be
regulated by statute. The specific practices subject to regulation
should be set out in secondary legislation to enable new
techniques to be incorporated as they are developed. Each
occasion for the use of a device should require specific authority,
in the form of a warrant from a magistrate.*[22]

141

The suggested criteria were very similar to the existing measures for phone tap warrants described by the 1980 White Paper. On the other hand, the idea of application to a magistrate was to regulate surveillance warrants in the same way as search warrants, aiming towards a comprehensive and homogenous system of control for all invasions of personal privacy. Another recommendation from the Royal Commission concerned redress:

> *unless judicial authority to the contrary is obtained, the person subject to the surveillance should be told of the surveillance after the event . . . By* [this] *means, it should be possible for the justification of the surveillance to be challenged.*

Many of the report's recommendations were implemented, but none of them had anything to do with tapping.

Meanwhile, efforts to introduce specific tapping legislation continued. Amendments for this purpose were put forward on three separate occasions, during Parliamentary consideration of the 1981 British Telecommunications Bill. The chief architect of these amendments was John McWilliam, a Labour MP and former telephone engineer sponsored by the Post Office Engineering Union. The Union's interest in tapping had grown sharply as the subject assumed a recurrent position on the political agenda during the early 1980s, and it subsequently took on a major role within the Malone camp at Strasbourg.

All three amendments were rejected by the Government, despite drawing support from a number of MPs on the libertarian right of the Conservative Party. Another unsuccessful attempt to bring in legislation was made during the 1983 debate on the sale of British Telecom. This privatisation Bill fell foul of an overcrowded timetable, but after reintroduction in the following session the Opposition managed to push through an amendment on 21 February 1984 in the House of Lords during the Committee stage, the point at which draft legislation is considered in the closest detail.

The contents of the amendment, 'Clause 46' as it was known during its short lifespan, were deliberately unspectacular. Tapping, it suggested, should be illegal unless conducted under warrant, with conditions of issue and subsequent procedures which were copied directly from the 1980 White Paper. Since these arrangements were already in operation and apparently functioning perfectly (nothing to the contrary had been heard from the Judicial Monitor), there could be no harm, reasoned the Opposition, in giving them force of law. The timing of 'Clause 46' was poignant: only the previous day, both sides in the Malone case had made their final submission to the European Court of Human Rights. So in addition to the usual objections, Lord Mackay, leading for the Government, exploited the impending judgement of the European Court in claiming that it was:

> not an appropriate time at which to attempt to deal with this matter in legislation, when there is a case pending which is absolutely germane to it.[23]

Although they did not mention it, the Government would have realised that 'Clause 46' was too narrow to allow all their tapping operations – especially those carried out in Northern Ireland and by GCHQ – and thus would have preferred to wait for the European Court ruling. Somewhat to their chagrin, the amendment was passed by a margin of seventeen votes: the natural Conservative majority in the Upper House was overwhelmed for once by the combined forces of Labour, Alliance and independent peers.

The Government could, of course, have disposed of 'Clause 46' with no difficulty, by using its substantial majority in the House of Commons. Instead, bearing in mind the virtual certainty of defeat in Strasbourg, the Leader of the House and former Home Secretary Lord Whitelaw chose to ask for a withdrawal of the clause by the Lords in exchange for an assurance that the Government would bring forward legislation in the next session of Parliament. Whitelaw made a point of saying that this undertaking 'is in no way dependent on the outcome of the Malone case'. Having made their own point, the Lords agreed.[24]

On 2 August 1984, shortly after the fifth anniversary of Malone's original application to the European Commission, the European Court of Human Rights issued its judgement. The major findings of the Court concurred with those of the Commission delivered in December 1982. In the first place, the law covering interception was 'obscure and open to differing interpretations'[25] because of the uncertain distinction between statutory provisions and executive discretion. Secondly, there were no adequate guarantees against abuse of the existing procedures. Police tapping (the Court was careful to confine itself to the one agency) was therefore not conducted 'in accordance with the law' nor was it 'necessary in a democratic society'. Both decisions were reached by unanimous verdicts in favour of Article 8 violation. The Court did not bother with ruling on a possible Article 13 violation through the lack of domestic remedy, much to the chagrin of two of the eighteen judges who accused the Court of evading a complex problem of interpretation.

The Home Office spent the next six months preparing legislation to conform with the European Court ruling. There were two main tasks for the drafters: to construct a coherent legal framework around all tapping operations, and to design a remedial mechanism to cope with any future cases like Malone's. A White Paper outlining the Government's proposals was published and debated on 7 February 1985.[26] A week later, the measures outlined by the White Paper were, with minimal revision, laid before Parliament as the 'Interception of Communications Bill'. By the time the debate began in the middle of March, the atmosphere had been sharpened by the timely screening of the television documentary *MI5's Official Secrets*.

The twelve clauses and two schedules of the Bill were debated over five and a half months and squeezed into the Statute Book on 25 July 1985 just before the summer recess. The Government had little difficulty managing the Bill's passage through the Commons, while this time the Lords confined themselves to tinkering and polishing. The Bill's main objective was the definition of criteria and procedures for lawful phone tapping. The drafting required simply writing these into law as exceptions to some general offence. The final statute retains this format.

The opening section of the Interception of Communications Act creates a crime of 'intentional interception', punishable by a maximum of two years' imprisonment and a £2,000 fine, and deals with various technical immunities. Interception by carriers is allowed for network control, which for British

144

Telecom includes Service Observation and routine operator checks on lines occupied for long periods, and for protection of radio telecomms traffic from interference. Interception can also be conducted legally with the consent of one participant. (Connection into a crossed line is unintentional and so not liable to prosecution.) The remainder of Section 1 formally exempts official interception from prosecution provided that the Government and its agencies adhere to a set of administrative practices which are derived, naturally enough, from the old warrant system.

In the domestic arena, the warrant machinery described by the 1980 White Paper was transplanted into the Bill *en bloc* and survived the transition into law virtually intact; some minor alterations had a slight loosening effect in favour of the authorities. Prevention and detection of 'serious crime', using the extended Diplock definition of 1982, remained the criterion of issue to the police and to Customs and Excise. 'Interests of national security' now suffice for an MI5 warrant. The 1980 precondition that 'normal methods of investigation' must have failed or be likely to fail, which applied to all three agencies, is retained in a diluted form: the availability of 'other means' need only be 'taken into account' by the Secretary of State who studies an application.

No individual agency or Secretary of State is mentioned by title in any part of the Act. At present, the ministers who issue warrants are those in charge of the Home, Foreign, Scottish and Northern Ireland Offices, but there is nothing in law to prevent any other Secretary of State from doing so – the Birkett Report illustrated several warrants of the past whose origins now seem rather peculiar. The most likely alternative sources are the Chancellor of the Exchequer, the Defence and Trade Secretaries; it is even possible that the Prime Minister might indulge.

Emergency measures to ensure urgent taps can be authorised in the absence of the concerned Secretary of State were altered by the Bill. Five years previously, an absent minister could telephone approval to his Permanent Secretary (the department's senior civil servant) for an unwarranted tap to be fitted. A warrant would have to be issued 'at the earliest possible time thereafter'.[27] Since taps with no warrant were being made illegal, the rules were changed to allow a civil servant from one of the top three grades to authorise a warrant on the Secretary of State's behalf for a period of two working days.[28]

The lifetimes for various warrants were little changed, despite the Bill's attempt to set a six-month standard period for all first issues and renewals. A Lords amendment brought the initial period back down to two months. Renewal periods were fixed at one month for crime-related warrants and at six months for 'national security' warrants. The conditions for renewal are the same as those for the original issue and there is no limit on the number of renewals which can be made.

Somewhere in the legislation, the Government had to declare limits on the number and variety of targets accommodated within the ambit of a single warrant. Section 3(1)(a) of the Act requires the interception of traffic which is

> *sent to or from one or more addresses specified in the warrant, being an address or addresses likely to be used for the transmission of communications to or from –*
>
> *(i) one particular person specified in the warrant; or*
> *(ii) one particular set of premises so specified or described.*

There are further twists to this already complicated clause. In legal terminology, 'person' does not only refer to one individual but also includes 'any organisation and any association or combination of persons'. Similarly, 'address' means 'any postal or telecommunications address' – phone number, telex number or electronic mailbox, for example. Moreover, 'set of premises' can clearly include one or more related buildings.[29]

Labyrinthine or not, this sub-section has a precise objection. The kernel of the warrant, the primary target, is a designated 'person' or set of premises – the latter option might be exploited in the case of a house occupied by suspected but unidentified criminals or spies, or the headquarters of a political party. The main body of Section 3(1)(a) allows taps *on the same warrant* against any line which has been in actual contact with the primary target *and* any line thought *likely* to make contact at some point in the future. The number of warrants was thus kept irrelevant to the number of lines tapped.

146

Furthermore, the conditions of the Act governing amendment of warrants allow instant addition and removal of subsidiary 'addresses'. Such modifications can be made by an official nominated by the warrant – an MI5 case officer, for example – without ratification by the Secretary of State for a maximum of five working days. This should allow enough time to discover whether a suspected associate of the primary target is worth monitoring or not, before ministerial approval is sought.

Section 3(1)(a) is designed for intelligence operations against loosely organised or highly secretive groups. Nevertheless, the latitude available within a single warrant is considerable. Taking the legal wording to extremes, there appears to be nothing to prevent the tapping under a single warrant of the entire membership of, say, Sinn Fein, which qualifies as a 'person' as well as subversive, and anyone who is likely to speak to any party member. The effective limitations on such an exercise are purely practical.

Section 3 of the Act introduces another item to compensate for technical constraints on monitoring a particular line. Any warrant would allow interception of 'such other communications (if any) as it is necessary to intercept' to obtain those explicitly mentioned by the warrant. The Government's declared purpose was to guarantee the tappers 'absolute protection' from prosecution,[30] but the wording of this subsection clearly refers to occasions when spurious traffic is unavoidably intercepted. This would apply in the case of an office switchboard, where an exchange tap might need to record every call passing through that switchboard before extracting those calls conducted on a particular extension.

By the time of the Bill, the criteria of serious crime and national security were no longer sufficient to cover all the Government's intelligence requirements. The Government realised that if no provision had been made for GCHQ and the interception of international communications, the Bill might well have been thrown out amid yet more publicity for the hapless eavesdroppers. A vanguard White Paper, published shortly before the Bill, revealed in circumspect tones an existing practice under which:

the Foreign Secretary authorises interception in accordance with

147

the Government's requirements for intelligence in support of its defence and foreign policies when he considers that this is necessary in the interests of national security or to safeguard the economic wellbeing of the country.[31]

This was the first time that collection of economic intelligence had been officially acknowledged, and this became the main talking point of the White Paper.

The White Paper proposed that authorisation for economic warrants be enshrined in law, noting that 'economic wellbeing' happened also to be the very phrase used by Article 8 of the European Convention on Human Rights. It added that issue should take place 'only if the warrant is with a view to acquiring information about matters outside the country',[32] with one eye perhaps on trades unionists worried that industrial action might automatically attract taps under the clause. Speculation began as to who might be the targets of economic warrants. Opposition spokesman Gerald Kaufman suggested currency speculators dealing in sterling. The Government remained as coy as ever. After its debut appearance, 'economic wellbeing' eventually joined 'serious crime' and 'national security' in the Act to form a new troika of warrant conditions.

GCHQ posed an awkward drafting problem because it collects information on designated *topics* – the oil trade, for example – as well as individuals and organisations. Somehow its operations had to be made legally consistent with the framework for domestic tapping. A format had to be devised which could reasonably describe the target of an international warrant, since the conditions attached to domestic warrants issued under Section 3(1)(a) would not work: the task of listing every *person* located overseas who is likely to discuss oil and every set of premises on which they are likely to do so is obviously impracticable. The second part of Section 3, which deals with 'external' (i.e. international) communications was constructed with great care.

In a warrant issued for international traffic only, there is no need to identify a 'person' or 'address'. A Secretary of State who exercises that option must instead issue a 'certificate' to accompany the warrant, which provides 'descriptions of the intercepted material the examination of which he considers necessary'. In the above example, the appropriate certificate

148

would specify something related to oil. The sole restriction on the content of a certificate prohibits the entry of an address in Britain except in a case of suspected terrorism, where foreign-based groups thought to be operating in Britain can be tapped inside or outside the country under a warrant and certificate.

The reason for the introduction of this new device, the certificate, is not immediately obvious. It might seem more consistent and, indeed, convenient for the prescribed topic to be given on an international warrant just as names and 'addresses' appear on a domestic warrant. There is sound thinking, however, behind this convolution of warrant and certificate. GCHQ's trawling method, described in Chapter 4, has two stages: interception, followed by processing. *Both* stages had to be covered separately.

The solution was the establishment of distinct but inter-dependent authorisation procedures for the two separate technical processes. The certificate specifies the items to be examined from a larger pool of 'intercepted material', which is defined in legal terms as 'communications intercepted in obedience to [a] warrant'. The warrant, therefore, is used to acquire the raw products for the certificate. The Government gave no indication of the details contained on this type of warrant in the absence of names or 'addresses'. The Act merely refers to 'interception of such external communications as are described in the warrant', indicating that the warrant specifies particular routes or circuits. Once the warrant has been executed, the pool of intercepts will be studied to locate and extract items related to the certificate request. The conditions governing the issue, renewal and duration of economic warrants are the same as those for national security.

Under the European Court judgement, the Government was instructed to institute some kind of redress for anyone who had been subject to a tap. Using the courts was considered out of the question. In fact, Section 9 of the Act declares as inadmissable any evidence which 'tends to suggest' that a government official or carrier employee has been directly involved in tapping, whether lawful or not; cross-examination is similarly circumscribed. This is particularly ironic in view of the history of the legislation and almost appears as an oblique act of vengeance against the lawyers who looked too

149

closely at Detective Sergeant Ware's notebook. The Government claimed that if these restrictions were not applied, 'ingenious litigants' would be able to establish whether or not a particular warrant existed.[33] Another justification, once given to the Birkett inquiry, still holds today:

> We are told that in practice the Home Office insists that the power [to tap] should be exercised for detection only, primarily on the ground that the use of the information so obtained, if used in Court, would make the practice widely known and destroy its efficacy in some degree.[34]

In the past, the Government had cited such difficulties with the courts to argue that there should be no legislation at all over tapping. Under European duress, a solution has been found in the form of a custom-built Tribunal to which a plaintiff can apply for an investigation. The Tribunal is composed of five lawyers, each of whom has at least ten years experience and whose seat on the Tribunal is limited to five years. They are equipped with statutory powers to gain access to any relevant documents or other information and each case must be studied in secret session by at least two of them. No statutory provisions were made regarding support staff or finance, but the Government appears to believe that no more than three officials are needed and that the cost of the Tribunal will be roughly £100,000 a year.

The Tribunal began work in April 1986 after, it seems, some difficulty finding premises and a legal luminary will to lead it. The Appeal Court judge Lord Fraser of Tullybelton ultimately agreed to take the chair. He was joined on the Tribunal by Ivor Guild, a senior Scottish lawyer, and three Queen's Counsels from the English courts. The trio were David Calcutt, a recent Chairman of the Bar, Sir Cecil Clothier, an honorary Lieutenant-Colonel in the Royal Signals Corps and head of the Independent Police Complaints Authority, and Peter Scott, a sometime Standing Counsel to the Department of the Environment.

The Tribunal's range is strictly circumscribed. The questions which it is allowed to address are confined to determining the following: first, whether a warrant exists which bears on the complaint; and second, whether the criteria for the issue of that warrant were correctly observed. Under the terms of the Act, a tap with no warrant is *illegal* while a warranted tap that breaks these criteria is *wrongly authorised*. The Tribunal will take action *only* in the latter case, where they have the power to quash the warrant, destroy the associated intercepts and order financial compensation for the aggrieved party. For any other conclusion, however, the Tribunal will simply inform the applicant that there was no improperly authorised tap. There the case will end, with the plaintiff left in a Kafkaesque limbo to ponder one of three possibilities: a tap with a properly authorised warrant, an illegal tap, or a non-existent tap. The Tribunal can offer no further illumination and there is no right of appeal against its decision.

The Act thus restricts the Tribunal's power of investigation on behalf of complainants to ensuring executive compliance with bureaucratic procedure. Efforts to augment the Tribunal's pitiful contribution to civil rights were dismissed. One mild amendment would have conferred an obligation on the Tribunal to inform an applicant if their inquiries suggested an illegal tap, thereby providing an opportunity for the applicant to take court action under Section 1. The Government argued that the proposal was 'anomalous',[35] irrelevant to the Tribunal's function, and unnecessary because the Tribunal 'would no doubt behave like a responsible body' were it to suspect an offence – an eventuality which the Government thought 'not very likely'.[35]

A more fundamental criticism was levelled by John McWilliam MP:

> *If the Tribunal first tries to discover whether or not there is a warrant and then whether there is a tap without a warrant two things will happen. First, the tap will be taken off and secondly, the Minister will be told* [by his civil servants] *that there is not a warrant. That is the wrong way round. The first duty of the Tribunal should be to determine whether the line is intercepted. Its second duty is to determine whether there is a warrant.*[37]

Having fulfilled its Strasbourg obligations, the Government was also concerned to keep the new system under review. The Judicial Monitor introduced at the beginning of the 1980s was transformed by the Act into a 'Commissioner'. The incumbent of this post, Lord Justice Lloyd, retains all of the old Monitor's work on behalf of the Prime Minister as well as acquiring a brief to liaise with and assist the Tribunal.

The Act further endeavours to cope with what Leon Brittan referred to as 'the real mischief', the use made of information obtained by tapping.[38] Some vague controls over dissemination of intercept products are written into Section 6. The numbers and distribution of transcripts or copies of any material and extracts taken from them must be kept to some unspecified 'minimum'. This is a legal version of the need-to-know principle, one of the most basic operational procedures in intelligence work. For international cases in which a certificate is issued, the Secretary of State must guarantee that 'the intercepted material [which] is not certified . . . is not read, looked at or listened to by any person'. In the context of trawling, there is an apparent paradox here; only examination of the intercepts can tell whether or not the contents conform to the requirements of the certificate.

Reactions to the Government proposals were typified by derision rather than semantic confusion. *The Times* scorned the Bill as:

> *one of this Government's 'dumb insolence' measures . . . in which the minimum action possible is grudgingly taken to comply with the letter of rulings under international agreements.*[39]

On practical matters, the lack of specific action over electronic surveillance other than tapping drew most flak. The worst of the criticism followed the February publication of the White Paper and dissipated fairly quickly; the pre-holiday progression of the Bill into law in July attracted not a murmur.

It might seem appropriate that the Thatcher Government should be required to introduce tapping legislation, having already breached the sacred dicta of security on a number of occasions: formal identification of GCHQ, followed by the union ban; Official Secrets Act trials for Geoffrey Prime, Michael Bettaney, and the 'Cyprus Eight' where amnesia might have prevailed with earlier administrations; the discreet effort to make the intelligence services financially accountable. All appear as attempts to assert firmer political direction over

152

the intelligence complex. However, in placing tapping beyond court jurisdiction, the Interception of Communications Act shows that the Government had, on this subject, followed its predecessors in eschewing such control.

As chance had it, the incidents which precipitated official action on tapping affected mainly Conservative Governments, but the attitude of successive Labour administrations confirms a traditionally bipartisan policy of inertia. This is most evident among those Labour ex-Cabinet ministers privileged with an introduction to the 'Cult of Intelligence'[40]: like their Tory counterparts, they are prone to extreme reverence towards its principles and practice.

By 1985, those of Callaghan's ministers who had dealt with tapping while in office had bowed out the Shadow Cabinet. Gerald Kaufman, who led the Opposition attack on the Bill, commented that 'security had become a game played by a self-selected team'.[41] His duel with Home Secretary Brittan was a marked contrast to the deferential manner of the Rees-Whitelaw debate over the 1980 White Paper. Five years on, the same Merlyn Rees, former Home and Northern Ireland Secretary, brought a moment of nostalgia to the second reading of the Interception Bill:

> On the last day of the Labour Government in 1979 after . . . [Callaghan] had conceded defeat, I went back to the Home Office and signed some interception warrants . . . They had to be done that evening.[42]

This touching story of devotion to duty indicates Rees' commitment to the continuity of security. In their effort to forestall Opposition criticism of the Bill, Home Office ministers regularly exploited Labour's adherence to a bipartisan security policy: the use of the same tapping procedures; use of 'national security' in legislation without explanation; and the notorious Harris definition of 'subversion'.

Given the historical precedent, a Labour Cabinet today, once initiated to the intelligence system and faced with the same ruling from Strasbourg, would very likely set off on the same path as Thatcher, Brittan and company rather than eviscerate a major intelligence asset. Unlike the Conservatives, however, the disgust of their own supporters would pose a significant obstacle. Perhaps the production of tapping legislation that would be acceptable to the intelligence complex was a task which only Tories could achieve.

Having constructed the Interception of Communications Act so that tapping is generally illegal except under specified circumstances, the Government proclaimed the new law as a safeguard against the abuse of privacy. But is is clear that, with the help of some inventive drafting, the exceptions comfortably allow current executive practices within boundaries which are both secure and elastic, while the chances of obtaining enough evidence to prosecute an illegal tap (particularly in view of the Act's restrictions on admissability) are negligible. Even then it is not clear who will be the subject of the prosecution – the person who sanctioned the tap or the engineer who fitted it. The Interception of Communications Act is nothing but a cynical gesture towards civil rights.

Chapter 7

The Same the Whole World Over?
Tapping Laws Outside Britain

The previous two chapters have sketched the history and current state of tapping law in the United Kingdom, and described some of the inadequacies of the 1985 Interception of Communications Act. Many of the gaps in the Act were raised in Parliament when it was debated, but it is strange how little reference was made by the opponents of the 1985 Bill to comparable legislation overseas. In fact, once we look at how other countries have handled the control of tapping and bugging, the weakness of British law in these crucial areas of privacy protection becomes apparent.

There is no general right to privacy in English constitutional law, in contrast to the basic law of most countries, and to a series of international treaties to which Britain is a party. These treaties, from the United Nations Declaration of Human Rights downwards, avoid laying down firm guidelines, but they represent the framework of international law within which individual countries have built their detailed tapping legislation. It is therefore worth a glance at what this international law has to say, before moving on to consider specific tapping laws.

The right to have the privacy of one's home and conversation respected is a fundamental human right in international law. It is enshrined in the United Nations Universal Declaration Of Human Rights, Article 12, which states that everyone has the right to the protection of the law against arbitrary interference with their privacy, family, home and correspondence. This principle undoubtedly forbids 'arbitrary' tapping, as a violation of the privacy of one's 'correspondence'. But what makes a particular tap 'arbitrary'? The UN does not help us here. Article 8 of the European Convention on Human Rights, quoted in Chapter 6, is little more specific in these matters.

Despite its vague terms, the European Convention remains as close as international law gets to defining when tapping is, and is not, oppressive or arbitrary. The UN has always avoided laying down more than the very vaguest of criteria, even when it approaches the subject of tapping directly, rather than by way of the general notion of privacy. United Nations Resolution 3348, adopted in 1975, concerns 'The Use of Scientific and Technological Progress in the Interests of Peace and for the Benefit of Mankind'. Article 6 states that:

All States shall take measures to . . . protect all strata of the population from the misuse of scientific and technological developments including their misuse to infringe upon the rights of the individual or the group, particularly with regard to respect for privacy . . .

This principle clearly applies to tapping and bugging technology, but it does so in such a way that an oppressive state could read almost anything into its sonorous banalities.

When international law stops to consider the tapping of *international* telephone lines, it is even broader in its exceptions from the general principle of the right to privacy. The main body responsible for international telecomms law is the International Telecommunications Union (ITU), a specialised division of the United Nations. The subject of international tapping received attention at the ITU's 1975 Conference in the Spanish resort of Torremolinos, where the assembled nations ratified two 'Clarifications' of its Conventions on the international network:

Article 22;113

Members [ie telecomms authorities] *to take all compatible measures, within the system of telecommunications used, with a view to ensuring the secrecy of international correspondence.*

Article 22;114

Nevertheless [members] *reserve the right to communicate such correspondence to the competent authorities in order to ensure the application of their internal laws or the execution of international conventions to which they are party.*

International law is framed to suit the lowest common denominator among signatory states. The unspecific nature of its recommendations as to what activities justify tapping is therefore intentional – a list of specific exceptions from the general right to privacy would command the support of fewer members of the UN, or the European Community.

One theme, however, is clear in all these regulations. It is that of the rule of law. Tapping or bugging (and international law, like that of most nations apart from Britain, recognises no distinction between these forms of electronic surveillance) is considered an 'arbitrary' invasion of privacy if not regulated by the law of the land.

The first conclusion to be drawn from this is that national laws should lay down firm criteria about *who* may legally be tapped. This is where the British system failed, and was duly reprimanded by the European Court, before the introduction of the 1985 Interception of Communications Act. But if the principle of the rule of law is to be followed fully it implies rather more than this.

A first principle of the rule of law is that no one is punishable except for a breach of the law. Tapping is not, of course, a *punishment* for subversive opinions or illegal activities, but if interception is *per se* an infringement of the right to privacy, then a logical extension of the same principle indicates that it should not be used except in cases where a breach of the criminal law is – at least – suspected. As we have seen, this is not the case in Britain. It is, however, a requirement insisted upon by the law in many countries, for example in West Germany and (with some exceptions) the United States. Both these countries will be considered in detail later.

Another principle of the rule of law is the so-called 'Doctrine of the Separation of Powers'. This is based on the idea that, if the law is to be seen as fair, no one body should be able to act as judge and jury in its own case. At the constitutional level this is done by separating the governing ('executive'), law-making ('legislative'), and judging ('judicial') powers of the State so that they are held by different bodies. In this way, the government, parliament, and legal system can balance each other, each able to check any abuse of power by the others.

In the case of tapping law, the logic of this is that where one body wants to tap (usually, in the last resort, it is the Executive branch of government in some form), the authorisation and overseeing of the tap should be placed in the hands of another, separate, body. In practice, this usually means that a judge (or in some cases a parliamentary committee) has to authorise any tapping by the police or security agencies. This is the rule in America, and throughout Europe, except in the United Kingdom.

Finally, the rule of law implies the existence of an effective remedy for breaches of the law. In other words, if someone's conversations are unjustly monitored, recorded, and passed on to others inside the state apparatus, there should be a mechanism to enable this to be discovered, and the victim to receive redress for the invasion of privacy. We have already discussed the inadequacy in this respect of the Tribunal set up by the 1985 Interception of Communications Act. Again, American and West German legislation, as we shall see, offer rather more protection to the citizen in this respect than does British law.

Moving on from international to national law, and from theory to practice, it is apparent that these principles are only *partly* met by an actual set of legislation. Nevertheless, most Western countries manage somewhat better than Britain to protect the citizen from arbitrary tapping.[1]

In nations with written constitutions, tapping is often limited by a constitutional right to privacy, similar to that in the UN Declaration of Human Rights. Such a right does not exist in English Common Law. However, Constitutional guarantees and Bills of Rights are no certain protection. The Fourth Amendment to the United States Constitution promises the right to privacy, but tapping, as we shall show, is rife in America. On the other hand, Belgium, with no great flourishing of constitutional liberties, bans tapping absolutely, in a humble Act governing the operation of Belgium's telephone and telegraph networks.

Called simply the Act of 13 October 1930, the Belgian legislation creates the specific offences of using technical devices for eavesdropping on the public network, and divulging the content, or even the occurrence, of phone conversations. Far from making an exception in the case of State interception, the law in Belgium stipulates particularly strong penalties for State employees caught tapping. They will suffer between fifteen days and six months in prison, as well as a stiff fine, for divulging the content of a call; whereas the corresponding penalty for an ordinary person is a sentence of eight days to one month, together with a lesser fine.

The only material the Belgian State may obtain from telephone calls is 'metering' information, such as the frequency, time and duration of calls, or the numbers dialled from a particular line. Even in this case, the release of such information by the telecomms authority has to be authorised by a judge. In Britain, as we shall see in Chapter 9, metering information is released freely to the police by British Telecom, on request.

Belgian tapping law is unique. No other nation in Europe takes such a libertarian position in the struggle between the individual's right to privacy and the State's urge to tap. Without going as far as Belgium, however, the other European countries all do more than Britain to control Executive tapping. Those that have no constitutional prohibition against unauthorised tapping usually ban the practice in long-standing criminal law. Taps have to be authorised by a judge in almost every case, and permission is usually granted only as a last resort in cases where a serious criminal offence is suspected, though this does not usually seem to apply to the tapping of international calls. Nor are these safeguards peculiar to Europe. Similar procedures exist, for example, in the USA. Compared with other Western countries, Britain is seriously deficient in applying the principles of the rule of law to the interception of communications.

There is no space here for a detailed analysis of tapping laws worldwide. Such an account is, in any case, unnecessary. A couple of case histories between them illustrate a variety of ways in which tapping has been brought under the rule of law more effectively elsewhere than in Britain. Both the United States of America and the Federal Republic of Germany are widely believed, especially by the British Left, to have a history of handling internal dissent in a repressive manner. Yet both these countries protect their inhabitants from tapping to a far greater extent than has even been seriously suggested in the British parliament, by government or opposition.

Modern German tapping law is a model of its kind, but it has not always been so. At the conclusion of the Second World War in Europe, the allied forces in Germany took control of the telecommunications network from the Nazi authorities, and with it the associated tapping facilities. Long after the German Federal Republic achieved statehood in 1949, telephone tapping inside its borders was performed solely by the 'three powers' – the American, British and French armies. This was because the post-war settlement forced an extremely libertarian constitution on the new West German nation. Germany was given a federal structure, with State authorities (*'Länder'*) and parliaments, having comparable local powers to the American States, together with the Federal government and national parliament (*'Bundestag'*) in Bonn. Tapping was, in fact, forbidden to both *Land* and Federal governments under Article 10 of the Constitution (or 'Basic Law'), adopted in 1949, which guarantees the inviolability of postal and telecomms correspondence.

As far as the allied armies were concerned, however, a Convention of 26 May 1952 specified that the Three Powers retained 'the rights . . . heretofore held or exercised by them, which relate to the protection of the armed forces stationed in the Federal Republic'. These 'rights', including the right to tap, were to be kept until 'the appropriate German authorities [had] obtained similar powers under German legislation enabling them to protect the security of those forces'.[2] The allied forces were, moreover, enjoined to co-operate, in these spheres, with the West German authorities. What all this meant in practice was that the military forces of the 'Three Powers' tapped any German phones that they were asked to, with no set procedures to be followed, and no questions asked. Quite junior officials of the Federal and local (*Land*) authorities, themselves forbidden to tap, simply got the British, American or French armies to do it for them. This arrangement was, no doubt, extremely convenient for all concerned, but clearly it could not last forever. In 1963, allegations began to emerge in the press that Article 10 of the Constitution was being evaded in this way, and in the following year an Investigative Committee of the West German parliament, the *Bundestag*, confirmed the story. It became clear that tapping would have to be brought under national control.

It was, however, three years later, 1968, before an amendment to Article 10 finally led to a declaration by the allied powers that the West German State had fulfilled its obligations under the 1952 Convention, and could now look after itself in these matters. Amendment (*Gesatz*) 10, known in Germany simply as 'G10', created exceptions to the basic inviolability of correspondence, which allowed the German State to take over tapping from the Three Power armies.

G10 allows phone tapping and similar forms of surveillance under two separate headings. Section 1 covers interception for the purpose of countering an imminent threat to the security of the State. Section 2 applies to more mundane serious criminal offences. The two types of tap involve different authorisation procedures, and different remedies for those wrongly tapped.

The usual tapping procedure in West Germany is that outlined in Section 2 of G10. This clause had the effect of adding Articles 100a and 100b to the West German Code of Criminal Procedure. These allow the interception of phone calls during, or in the course of, criminal procedures relating to certain serious offences such as genocide, murder, 'white slavery' (*sic*), kidnapping, etc, as well as certain less imminently threatening cases of espionage, terrorism, etc, than those covered by Section 1. Unlike British tapping legislation, but in keeping with the principle of the rule of law, a specific serious offence must have occurred, and other methods of investigation must have failed, or be likely to fail if tried.

The principle of separation of powers is maintained in Section 2 by the requirement that the police or security agencies must obtain a warrant signed by a judge before tapping – except in emergencies, where the Attorney General's office may issue a warrant, subject to confirmation by a judge within three days. The warrant must specify the suspected offence, the purpose and length of the tapping operation, and the way in which the tapping is to be done.

German law also ensures that the involvement of the authorisers does not stop with the scrawling of their signature on the bottom of a piece of paper. Section 2 warrants are overseen by a judge, the Attorney General's office, or a specially authorised senior police officer, whichever is specified by the issuing judge. Whoever is chosen, he or she must

161

ensure that all material irrelevant to the purpose of the tap, as stated on the warrant, is destroyed, including material which is kept at first, but becomes irrelevant later in the investigation. This introduces a degree of control, not only over who is tapped, but over what material is then available to the 'customer' agency which requested the tap. Nothing like this exists in British law where, as we have seen, the most trivial conversations between members of a target's family are eagerly scanned by the intelligence services.

The most dramatic difference between German and British tapping law, however, lies in what happens *after* the monitoring. Under Article 100b of the German Criminal Code, a warrant may only last for three months, with renewal for another three. Once this period is up, and the interception is over, the target must be informed about the tap and supplied with all the material obtained, unless this would prejudice the outcome of an enquiry. This creates an effective judicial remedy against arbitrary tapping, as the victims may then take legal action if they consider the tap to be unjustified.

Section 1 taps involve a slightly different procedure. As with Section 2, the target must be suspected of a particular, and serious, criminal offence, and tapping may only be carried out where other methods of investigation are impracticable, or have failed. Unlike Section 2, however, the offence must represent an 'imminent danger' to the 'free democratic constitutional order', the 'existence or security of the Federation or one of the *Länder*', or the security of the [allied] armed forces'.

Unlike the *judicial* procedure in Section 2 of G10, Section 1 interceptions are authorised by the Executive arm of the State, either a Federal Minister or one of the *Land* authorities for offences within its jurisdiction. With Section 1 taps, a senior civil servant with judicial qualifications oversees the execution of the warrant, examining all the information obtained to find out whether it is legally usable and relevant to the stated purpose of the tap. Only material which passes these tests is passed to the organisation which requested the tap. Only three agencies may apply to tap under Section 1: the Federal or *Länder* offices for the Protection of the Constitution (the *Verfassungsschutz*, West Germany's combined MI5 and Special Branch), the Federal Intelligence Service, and the Military Intelligence authorities.

162

Section 1 taps, because they are not authorised by a judge, lack the judicial remedy through disclosure to the target that characterises Section 2 taps. However, the principle of the separation of powers is maintained, balancing the Executive by the Legislature, rather than the judiciary. Instead of the target being informed about the tapping, the operation is monitored by a special committee of the *Bundestag*, or the relevant *Land* parliament.

The 'G10 *Committee*' consists of five MPs, appointed on a proportional basis from the parties in the *Bundestag*, with a guaranteed Opposition presence. The G10 Committee receives six-monthly reports from each authorising minister (only the Ministers of Defence and the Interior have the right to authorise Section 1 warrants at the Federal level). The Committee also appoints a second body, the three-member 'G10 *Commission*'.

The G10 Commission decides, either of its own volition or at the request of individuals who believe they are being tapped, on the lawfulness of, and necessity for, Section 1 taps. Any interception that the G10 Commission deems superfluous must be withdrawn immediately, and the individual may then have the right of redress in the courts. In practice, the authorising ministers consult with the Commission *before* making any tapping orders, except in the most urgent circumstances. The monitoring procedures are, throughout, similar at *Länder* level.

This parliamentary scrutiny of even the most sensitive taps (from the State security point of view), is much tougher than anything seriously proposed in the UK. Even so, the absence, in the case of Section 1 taps, of a right to notification for the individuals targetted, aroused concern among German civil libertarians. A group of left wing lawyers, led by Gerhard Klass, an *Oberstaatsanwalt* (senior barrister), appealed against the G10 law, first to the Federal Constitutional Court in West Germany, then to the European Court of Human Rights, seeking to have G10 declared unconstitutional, or else a violation of human rights.[3]

Klass and company had an initial success with the Constitutional Court, which declared on 15 December 1970, two years after G10 became law, that Section 1 targets must be notified of the tapping, and supplied with transcripts, *as soon as practicable*, without prejudicing the purpose of the interception. The decision as to when the information could be released, however, still rested with the authorising minister. The appellants pointed out that, in practice, notification could easily be infinitely delayed, leaving the subject of the operation none the wiser, and without legal redress. They took their case to Europe.

There, the Klass appeal stagnated in the muddy bywaters of European justice for eight years. The Judgement of the European Court of Human Rights in the Case of Klass and Others was finally issued on 6 September 1978, just in time to become the case law on which the appellants in the Malone case based their appeal to Europe. The Court came down against Klass, and in favour of the German Government. It concluded that G10, as modified by the Federal Constitutional Court in 1970, was perfectly in line with the European Convention on Human Rights. Tapping in Germany, the European Court ruled, was only performed (in the words of the relevant part of the Convention, quoted in the judgement) when

> *necessary in a democratic society in the interests of national security and for the prevention of disorder or crime.*

The Court decided that, despite the lack of a judicial remedy in Section 1 cases, the G10 law did provide sufficient safeguards against unnecessary tapping.

The European Court decision may have satisfied the West German authorities, but it contained worrying implications for the British Government. As one barrister put it at the time, the Klass judgement made it

> *clear that the English law and practice violate Article 8, 13, and possibly Article 6(1) of the Convention on Human Rights.*[4]

This view was substantiated in the Malone case, and, as we have seen, the law was subsequently changed. The UK 1985 Interception of Communications Act, however, provides far fewer safeguards than does the German G10 legislation.

It would be wrong, on the other hand, to give the impression that G10 is wholly effective in protecting German citizens from unfair tapping. During the 1970s, as the German state experienced outbreaks of both espionage and urban terrorism, the security authorities began to show a willingness to stretch or break the law. Local *Land* authorities were used to carry out operations barely within their legal competence to evade the scrutiny of the *Bundestag*. This happened in 1977, when the government of the *Land* of Baden Würtemburg authorised the bugging of conversations between suspected terrorist prisoners and their defence lawyers.[5]

In the same year, G10 was not bent but broken, in a notorious case which caused the premature retirement of the Head of Military Security (*Militärischer Abschirmdienst* – known, unfortunately, as MAD). MAD became convinced that one of the Defence Minister's secretaries was a Communist spy, and its chief, Paul-Albert Scherer, ordered the bugging and tapping of her home and telephone. Interviewed in the British press three years later, Scherer showed the characteristic arrogance of the secret policeman:

> *We believed we had real grounds for suspecting her. It may have been ungentlemanly, but you do not pussyfoot around in this business.*[6]

It is difficult to tell from the Scherer case whether there was anything unusual about the use of illegal taps. Scherer's attitude might imply that such abuses were common. On the other hand, a spy in the office of a Defence Minister would be an exceptional case for most State security bureaux, so this incident in itself may not indicate any more general avoidance of G10.

Like most national tapping legislation, the German G10 applies solely to cases where a named suspect is having their phone tapped. It does not seem to cover the blanket tapping of international lines to and from the country. It has, for example, been reported that this sort of interception was used over lines from Germany to Switzerland during the hunt for the kidnappers of the German industrialist, Hans-Martin Schleyer.[7]

Despite these deficiences, West German tapping legislation represents a far more serious attempt to preserve the right to privacy than the British legislation. The judicial remedy and parliamentary supervision of tapping are important safeguards of the rule of law in the field of state surveillance. All this in a country which, on any realistic estimate, has been far more threatened by both espionage and terrorism than is the United Kingdom (with the possible, and local, exception of Northern Ireland).

If West German tapping law stands as an example of the advantages of well drafted surveillance legislation, the American experience shows the limitations of the law. It exemplifies how the State can take advantage of confusingly worded laws, or even ignore the law completely, when this suits it. In fact the whole history of American tapping is one of confusion. Despite considerable amounts of legislation in the fields of tapping and bugging, Congress and the judiciary have persistently failed to catch up with the practice of the Executive branch of government and its police, security and intelligence organs.

Ask any American lawyer in the early years of this century about the legal status of 'wiretapping' (as the Americans call telephone interception), and he would probably have answered that it was prohibited under the Fourth Amendment to the US Constitution, which guarantees the right to privacy, and freedom from unreasonable search and seizure of one's person or property. This was not the view taken by Federal agents enforcing the Prohibition laws against the consumption of alcohol, who used the technique on a number of occasions in the 1920s.

At this time, the Prohibition Bureau was probably the only domestic agency to make regular use of phone taps. The official Manual of Rules and Regulations of the Federal Bureau of Investigation referred to tapping as an unethical practice, and in 1924 such surveillance methods were expressly forbidden to the FBI by the Attorney General, Harlan Fiske Stone. The Prohibition Bureau, however, was under the control of the Treasury Department, rather than Mr Stone's Justice Department, and they continued to tap.

Then, in 1928, in the case of *Olmstead v. US*, the Supreme Court decided by a slim majority that tapping was not, as had previously been supposed, against the Fourth Amendment. The Court ruled that, because telephone interception involved no physical entry to premises, it violated no tangible right to

166

privacy under the Amendment. The practical result of the Olmstead judgement became clear in 1930, when the Prohibition Bureau came under the control of the Justice Department. This sharpened the anomaly between the practice of the FBI and that of the Prohibition Bureau, as the two agencies were now under the same department. In the light of the Olmstead ruling, the new Attorney General, William P. Mitchell, felt able to resolve the problem by extending permission to tap to both Bureaux.

The Olmstead ruling, however, created its own problems. There was a wide feeling that tapping ought to be prohibited. Accordingly, in 1934, Congress enacted the Federal Communications Act. This made it a crime to 'intercept . . . and divulge' wire or radio communications. However, the 1934 Act merely added to the confusion. The tappers argued that they could intercept any calls they liked, as long as they did not disclose in court any of the conversations they picked up. The FBI, therefore, adopted the British position of using taps for investigative, but not evidential, purposes.

Unlike the later West German system, the federal nature of the American constitution produced a number of anomalies in tapping law betwen national and local courts. The Supreme Court confirmed, in 1937, that the Federal Communications Act required the exclusion of all material obtained by tapping from evidence in the Federal courts. Two years later, the Court decided that even information *indirectly* derived from covert interception must be excluded, as 'the fruit of a poisoned tree'.[8] However, not only did Federal tapping continue for the purpose of gathering intelligence, but there was no prohibition whatsoever against the use of wiretap evidence in State, as opposed to Federal, courts. The local police continued to tap, and to use the evidence in court.

The Federal eavesdroppers may have maintained that interception without disclosure was perfectly legal, but they received no help in their tapping from the Federal Communications Commission. This body was charged with regulating the American telecomms networks under the 1934 Act, and it held to a much stricter interpretation of the law than did the FBI. This led to the practice, still common in America, of the FBI tapping telephones from the line between the customer's telephone and the exchange, rather than at the exchange itself (as in Britain). With or without the Commission's assistance, tapping had become an important weapon in the FBI's activities, and the practice continued until 1940. In that year, on 15 March, with a European war in full swing, the Attorney General, Robert Jackson, issued Order No. 3343, reinstating the complete ban on covert interception by the FBI issued by Stone in 1924.

Unsurprisingly, the new tough line against snooping did not last long. Less than three months later, President Franklin D. Roosevelt ordered that tapping should be allowed in 'matters concerning the defence of the nation',[9] for intelligence gathering purposes. Not only did the Justice Department now allow taps in espionage and subversion cases, but the Federal Communications Commission was forced, for the first time, to co-operate in the tapping. The implications of this interpretation of the law were spelt out by Jackson in a letter to Congressman Hatton Summers:

The only offence under the present law is to intercept any communications and divulge or publish the same . . . Any person, with no risk of penalty, may tap telephone wires . . . and act upon what he hears or make any use of it that does not involve divulging or publication.[10]

The end of the Second World War brought no diminution in the amount of official tapping in America. The new Cold War and its associated anti-Communist hysteria brought an increase in the amount of covert surveillance of 'subversives', and tapping was also used when kidnapping or sabotage were suspected. Under the Truman administration, Presidential permission to intercept was extended still further to cover murder cases, and the Attorney General, Herbert Brownwell, urged Congress to legislate to permit Federal tapping. Congress, however, refused.

By the mid-1960s, press criticism of the growth in tapping forced President Johnson once again to prohibit interception except in cases involving national security. This category was, however, broad enough to include the black civil rights leader, Martin Luther King, whose phone was tapped on the authority of Robert Kennedy, then Attorney General. According to papers recently revealed under America's Freedom of Information Act, the FBI chief, J. Edgar Hoover, used information about King's sex life gained from taps and bugs in an attempt to discredit the black leader – in blatant breach of the 1934 Federal Communications Act.[11]

The Johnson ruling did have some effect, however, and the overall number of taps performed by the FBI dropped. On the other hand, America's giant equivalent of the British GCHQ, the National Security Agency, began increasingly to turn its 'vacuum cleaner' methods of intercepting international traffic, hitherto applied only to foreign targets, towards domestic criminals and political activists. The NSA was set up in 1952, to bring all American Communications Intelligence (COMINT) under a single Agency, responsible to the President.[12] COMINT, a sub-category of signals intelligence (SIGINT), was defined as 'intelligence produced by the study of foreign communications', but the NSA's interpretation of 'foreign' was a broad one. The NSA began its internal operations in the year of the Cuban missile crisis, 1962, when they set up a joint project with the FBI to monitor the activities of US citizens with Cuban links. By the end of 1967 a wide range of American targets were being intercepted, if not by having their individual phones tapped, then in the course of NSA's sweeps of international telecomms links.

Then, in December 1967, a decision of the Supreme Court in the case of *Katz v. US* reversed the 1928 Olmstead decision, and completely altered the legal context of American tapping. This time, the Court ruled that *all* electronic eavesdropping, where the target had the right to enjoy reasonable privacy, was against the Fourth Amendment – regardless of whether physical trespass was involved in the surveillance or not. The tappers were further embarrassed later in the same year, when the Supreme Court noted, in the case of *Lee v. Florida*, that not a single law enforcement officer had ever been prosecuted under the wiretapping provisions of the Federal Communications Act, passed thirty-four years previously.

Clearly, if official tapping were to continue, the US legislature now had to do something about the state of the law. That 'something' was contained within the manifold clauses of the Omnibus Crime Control and Safe Streets Act 1968. This still forms the basis of the legal framework of communications interception in the United States. Congress declared that wiretapping had become indispensable to the work of law enforcement and security agencies, so it should not be banned, but ought to be regulated by law. Accordingly, the Act sought to ensure the separation of powers by bringing tapping under the control of the courts, at both Federal and State levels.

The Omnibus Act makes it an offence to intercept, or attempt to intercept, without judicial authorisation, any oral or wire communication through the use of any electronic, mechanical or other device. It also forbids the manufacturing, distributing, possessing or advertising of such devices, when done in the course of interstate or foreign commerce, though this does not apply to Federal officials. The wording of the Act means that it applies to both tapping and bugging, unlike the British legislation, which as we have seen, excludes the latter.

FBI tapping was, at last, fully legitimised and brought under judicial control – at least in theory. Under the 1968 Act, the Bureau may, with the approval of the Attorney General's office, apply to a federal judge for authorisation to tap where serious federal offences are suspected. Similarly, State prosecutors may apply to State courts for warrants in cases of murder, kidnapping, gambling, robbery, bribery, extortion, drug dealing, and any crime dangerous to life, limb, and property, and punishable by more than one year's imprisonment. These clauses were aimed at ensuring that no one was tappable except for a suspected breach of the law.

Once application is made, the judge must conduct an enquiry to determine whether or not there is good reason to think:

– *that the person to be tapped has committed, or is about to commit, one of the specified offences;*
– *that particular communications concerning the offence will be obtained through the interception;*
– *that other investigative procedures have been tried out and failed, or why they would be unlikely to succeed if tried.*

If the judicial enquiry goes in favour of the tap, the court may require regular progress reports to be made. Once the conversation has occurred, the judge must without delay be given the recordings of all material intercepted, though the law-enforcement agency concerned may retain a copy for investigative purposes. This is to prevent any tampering with the tapes, which may later be used in evidence as long as the procedures have been followed correctly.

In an emergency, law officers may tap without a warrant, but application to a judge must follow within twenty-four hours. If this retrospective warrant is denied, the judge must notify the target that the tap has taken place, and anyone else considered to have had their conversation unduly intercepted. They may then apply to inspect the material, and can sue if the interception was unjustified. This creates a judicial remedy similar to that in Section 2 of the West German G10 law.

These judicial procedures only apply at Federal level, but, under the 1968 Act, the States had to pass similar legislation if they wished to allow evidence gleaned from interception in their courts. However, the warrant procedures do differ considerably from state to state. The notification of the target where a tap is later disallowed, for example, applies only in Federal cases. As a result of these variations in procedure, the use of tapping in America varies dramatically between different police forces, with two or three states usually accounting for over half the taps. Over the past decade or so, New Jersey has been constantly at the top of the league table, with New York State close behind. Since 1978 these two states have consistently accounted for about half the warrants granted under the Act.

These regional variations are not the only flaws in the Omnibus Crime Control and Safe Streets Act. The wording of the main clause (§2511) was carefully drafted with the assistance of NSA lawyers to exclude most of their eavesdropping activities. The clause forbade 'aural aquisition of wire or oral communictions' (the last two words referring to bugging, rather than tapping). This put the interception of microwave and radio transmissions outside the law – and in America a high proportion of phone calls are sent by microwave for at least part of their route. This clause also permits snooping on mobile telephones, such as carphones, which work on FM radio frequencies. The wording of the Act also excludes from regulation the tapping of signals sent in digital form, which applies to most calls going through the more technically advanced parts of the American telecomms network, as well as

171

to computer communications and transmissions through the new optical fibre technology.

Questioned about the gaps in the legislation, Federal officials have admitted their existence, but say that 'most' interceptions involve a warrant, even where it is strictly unnecessary. With a beguiling honesty, the Justice Department admits that it does not want the law amended to cover the gaps, in case this might hinder law enforcement activities.

Despite the 1968 Act, Federal and local law enforcement agencies continued to tap people suspected of no criminal offence. These illegal wiretaps were used when the authorities wanted to gather information about 'subversives'. Perhaps the most notorious case happened in the town of New Haven, Connecticut, where enormous numbers of people were illegally tapped by the police between 1964 and 1971. The police activity, at first a response to radical political activity in the town, grew into a massive surveillance operation, and ended with 1,238 New Haven residents suing the City authorities, the FBI, and the Southern New England Telephone Company. The citizens received between $1,000 and $6,000 each in out-of-court settlements, depending on how many of their calls had been recorded.[13]

Although they retained this ability to resort, *in extremis*, to illegal tapping, the FBI regarded the 1968 Act as a distinct brake on their activities. It meant that they increasingly had to rely on the NSA's 'vacuum cleaners', which was undesirable because the priority given by the Agency to domestic work tended to vary dramatically, according to other demands on NSA resources and State Department policy.

Under the administration of President Richard M. Nixon, these problems diminished. The illegal tapping of those deemed subversive was authorised directly by the President or the Attorney General, and was used freely, regardless of the law. College professors, government officials, journalists (including a British foreign correspondent), left wing political groups; all of these were spied on, illegally but with impunity, indeed with the active involvement of senior members of the administration; men such as Attorney General John Mitchell, and General Alexander Haig (then Henry Kissinger's deputy).[14]

With the snowballing scandals of the Pentagon Papers and

172

the Watergate affair, however, Congress and the media became increasingly suspicious of the motives of the tappers. Several attempts to secure a legal exemption from the procedures of the 1968 Act in national security cases were staved off by Congress. Meanwhile, the judiciary became anxious to secure strict adherence to the law. In particular, *all* US courts were required to suppress evidence derived from tapping, unless the warrant procedure had been followed to the letter, and several legal cases confirmed the intention of the higher courts to interpret the warrant procedure to the letter.

By the mid-1970s, even the NSA had begun to worry about the vulnerability of some of its activities to the charge of illegality. Previously, the Agency had held that its tapping was based on the vaguely-defined Constitutional powers of the President to take action necessary to preserve the security of the nation – an argument strikingly similar to the 'royal prerogative to tap' theory, as promulgated by successive British governments. In 1976, the combination of post-Watergate feeling in the country and an increasing requirement for the NSA to tap people *inside* the United States led the Ford administration to sanction, for the first time, a bill bringing some of the NSA's activities under judicial control.

The Foreign Intelligence Surveillance Act (FISA), as the bill eventually became, had first been proposed by Senator Edward Kennedy in 1972, and was regularly rejected for the next four years. Even with administration support, the bill once more failed to enter the statute book in 1976, and again in 1977. Finally, six years after it was originally proposed, the Act was passed in 1978.

FISA's purpose was to control NSA interception of American citizens, but its procedures represented a compromise between those who wanted to bring all tapping within judicial control, and those who wanted the NSA to be able to operate in total secrecy, and solely under executive control. The Act therefore brings only *some* of the NSA's operations under the control of a special, secret court, the Foreign Intelligence Surveillance Court, on which sit seven Federal judges, picked by the Chief Justice of the Supreme Court. Unlike all other US courts, the FISC sits in secret session, hears only one argument (the NSA's), and issues almost no public opinions or reports. Even the place where it meets, behind a code-locked

173

door in the Justice Department building in Washington, is supposed to be a secret.

The Court's remit is to examine NSA applications to tap US domestic communications links. These applications usually originate from another agency such as the CIA or the FBI, and must be signed by the Attorney General before reaching FISC. The Court has to decide whether there is 'probable cause' to suspect that the named target is either a foreign power (eg an embassy or trade delegation phone) or an agent of a foreign power. There is no distinction between 'hostile' and 'friendly' foreign powers.

For each tap, the Court has also has to approve a certificate, signed by the Attorney General, which lays out the procedures to be followed to ensure that any information about Americans gathered in the course of the interception is not kept or disseminated by the agency, unless this information relates to the ability of the United States to defend itself against a foreign attack, or sabotage, terrorism, or clandestine activity by a foreign agent. Calls in which one party is an American may not be passed on by the NSA, unless the conversation relates to criminal activities, or to the 'national security, defense, or foreign policy of the United States', and even then the identity of the American cannot be divulged. If these 'minimisation procedures' are followed, the FISC must approve the tap. In the first six years of its existence, the FISC approved every single application to tap presented to it.

In some respects, FISA represents a step forward over the Omnibus Crime Control and Safe Streets Act. Rather than use the carefully worded definitions of the 1968 legislation, it prohibits Federal monitoring of *all* conversations between Americans where they have a 'legitimate expectation of privacy'. The American Civil Liberties Union, however, remain doubtful about how much protection this vague term gives in practice. The flaw, as far as the ACLU is concerned, is that the decision as to whether the parties have such legitimate expectations rests with the Federal prosecutors of the Attorney General's office – which, as we have seen, has itself been involved in illegal tapping on a number of occasions.[15]

Nor is this the only loophole in the 1976 law. The FISC has no power over NSA monitoring of telex and other data communications to or from embassies and other foreign

174

controlled premises, nor does the Court's remit cover the tapping of leased circuits between foreign establishments in the States. These forms of interception were deemed too sensitive for judicial eyes, and are authorised by the Attorney General.

In addition, James Bamford, an American expert on the NSA, has drawn attention to a number of other gaps in the Foreign Intelligence Surveillance Act. Any information about US citizens acquired by the NSA *outside* the States may be kept and disseminated to the CIA, FBI, or whomsoever. The NSA may still tap all international traffic entering or leaving American borders, providing it is done by microwave interception, and they can still scan all data and telex traffic by keyword. What they cannot do is to target Americans by name without a warrant from the FISC, even over international lines (unless the person named is outside US territory at the time).

As far as Bamford is concerned, however, the biggest loophole is that the restrictions in FISA do not apply to information received by the NSA from other signals intelligence agencies, such as Britain's GCHQ. Certainly, the latter have been known to help the NSA by monitoring American citizens. The nature of the UKUSA pact makes it possible, at least in theory, for each member to assist the others to evade their internal eavesdropping laws, by doing their tapping for them. In principle the 1985 Interception of Communications Act covers the activities of the NSA in Britain; however, under the 1952 Visiting Forces Act, American servicemen in Britain are exempt from UK laws while carrying out their duties, and this also applies to NSA civilian staff.

One result of the FISA was an immediate drop in the number of warrants granted under the Omnibus Crime Control and Safe Street Act. In 1973, 864 of these judicial warrants were granted; by 1980, this number had shrunk to 566.[16]

The eighties have seen a slow but steady rise in this figure, to 648 in 1983, but most of these were State level investigations into organised crime. In 1983, one small County in New Jersey, Suffolk County, was taking out more tapping warrants than the whole of the FBI![17]

Warrants under FISA, however, have risen considerably since its inception, from 319 in 1980, to 549 by 1983, and 635 in just the first ten months of 1985.[18] Even so, we cannot assume that these figures include all the tapped 'subversives' in the United States. In 1983, it was reported that tough FBI internal regulations governing the use of wiretaps, which had been introduced by President Ford in the aftermath of the Watergate affair, had been slackened by President Reagan.[19] With American tapping history of exploiting subtle loopholes where possible, and downright illegality where not, it will interesting to see what tapping stories emerge when the papers of the Reagan administration come to light.

Despite its loopholes, and the occasional downright piece of illegality on the part of the law enforcement and security agencies, American law has a number of advantages over the British position as regards electronic surveillance. The 1968 Omnibus Crime Control and Safe Streets Act covers both tapping and bugging, unlike its British equivalent; it ensures a check on Executive power by judicial authorisation of taps; it creates the principle that people should not be tapped except for an actual or suspected breach of the law; and it allows a judicial remedy (in some cases) for illegal tapping by the forces of the state. In all these respects, the Omnibus Act gives far more protection from state surveillance to the American public than is available to their British counterparts under the 1985 Interception of Communications Act. The 1978 FISA, moreover, introduces a level of control over 'vacuum cleaner' interception of foreign lines which would be unthinkable to Britain's GCHQ.

Better than Britain then, but compared with West German law, the American legislation is full of holes. If the German G10 shows the advantages of good tapping law, the American experience reveals not only the disadvantages of poorly drafted laws, but the limitations of passing legislation at all as a means of containing tapping by the state. A determined State Security agency seems able to ignore almost any legislation (even in West Germany – witness the Scherer case).

On the other hand, the very fact that so many cases of illegal wiretapping have come to light in America is a tribute to the openness of US government, compared with Britain. Many of these cases have been exposed under the Freedom of Information Act, and if the American experience has any lesson for the UK, it is that secretive security agencies will feel free to bend or defy any laws, unless restrained by the knowledge that their activities will, eventually, come to light, and to public judgement. In this respect, an alert, investigative press, together with tough Freedom of Information laws (both of which are lacking in Britain), are probably as important as tapping legislation is truly bringing the tappers under the rule of law.

Chapter 8

The Wilder Shores: Covert Surveillance Devices

Perhaps the major difference between British and American tapping law is the distinction, in the former, between tapping proper and the other forms of surreptious surveillance, such as bugging. The fact that, in the UK, such activities are on the fringes of legality, rather than being downright illegal, has allowed the growth of a flourishing private surveillance industry in Britain – a privatised counterpart to the nationalised tapping industry we looked at in Chapters 2–4. The lack of a coherent law against electronic snooping has also encouraged the widespread use of surveillance devices, legal, illegal and semi-legal, by the police and intelligence organisations, either directly or through private sector front organisations.

First, it is necessary to make some semantic distinctions. The terms 'bugging' and 'tapping' are often used interchangeably, but properly refer to different kinds of eavesdropping:

a *tap* is fitted to a telephone or to some part of the telephone network. Its purpose is to pick up both sides of a telephone conversation, and relay the sound to a hidden tape recorder or listener.

a *bug*, on the other hand, is designed to relay conversations within a room; it can therefore pick up only one end of a telephone conversation, if one takes place within the room. A bug can be placed anywhere inside the room, including within a telephone. One kind of bug, the infinity transmitter, works by turning the telephone instrument itself into a bug: sounds in the vicinity of the phone are transmitted through the telephone network while the receiver is on the hook.

a third kind of device functions as a *combined bug and tap*.

178

This involves an infinity transmitter combined with a radio tap, and it is thus often confused with the simple infinity bug, although the latter cannot tap a phone line, as it needs the line itself to transmit its message to the person bugging.

All three forms of aural surveillance device are on open sale in Britain, as is a wide range of visual surveillance and tracking systems. At the end of this chapter, we look in detail at how this equipment works; but it is worth stressing at this point that it is publicly available, and widely used, not just by the authorities, but by private surveillance and industrial espionage organisations.

The distinction between taps and bugs is not a purely technical one: it is intended to have legal force. The Government insists upon a distinction between 'interception' (of telephone conversations), and 'surveillance' (of other conversations). Asked in 1982 to set out this distinction, Home Secretary William Whitelaw told Labour MP Bob Cryer that:

> *The interception of telephone communications covers what is said by both parties to the conversation. Surveillance equipment records or monitors what is said in a specific location, and might thereby pick up what is said by one party to a telephone conversation.*[1]

This distinction may yet cause some problems for the lawyers, as there is no legal definition of 'interception'. The 1985 Interception of Communications Act does not supply one, and *Halsbury's Statutes*, a standard reference work on legal interpretation, were forced to rummage through assorted dictionaries to find an everyday definition. What they came up with was that 'interception' implies an enforced delay in the transmission of the communication – which does not happen in tapping *or* bugging.[2] This raises the interesting possibility that the 1985 Act does not actually cover phone tapping. However, the intention of Parliament was clearly that the Act should cover only the interception of phone calls, and leave bugging wholly unregulated by law; and in the absence of any case law, it is this interpretation we shall use.

Home Secretary Leon Brittan explained the reasoning behind the distinction between taps and bugs during the parliamentary debate on the 1985 Interception of Communications Bill. He declared that telephone conversations:

merit special protection because they are committed by somebody into the custody of a carrier over whom he has no control. Legislation to deal with other aspects of privacy, such as surveillance, gives rise to quite different, and so far unresolved, issues. [3]

Those with less subtle legal minds than the then Home Secretary found it less obvious that these issues were 'quite different'. The *Financial Times*, for example, editorialised that the government had:

deliberately left itself decades behind the times by omitting to consider the wider problem of the extent to which technology enables anyone, authorised or otherwise, to undertake the most widespread, pervasive and intrusive surveillance for whatever reason – criminal, personal, commercial, state. . . .As it is now, we remain with virtually no criminal or civil remedies against most forms of covert surveillance. [4]

Partial and inadequate legal remedies do exist in theory, but even these are impossible to enforce in practice. If anyone breaks into a house to install a bugging device, they can, of course, be charged with breaking and entering (though this is unlikely to happen if they belong to the Security Service), but all this means is that entry is likely to be gained by deception, for example by posing as British Telecom or Gas Board technicians or deploying some other apparently innocent excuse for visiting the building. In this case, only a civil suit for trespass is possible – *if* the bug can be found and its installers identified.

The only laws aimed directly at bugs are the Wireless Telegraphy Acts of 1948 and 1967, which require a licence for bugs that transmit on radio frequencies, and ban the manufacture of those that transmit on certain frequencies reserved for the police. These Acts do not, of course, apply to bugs which use telephone or other wires to transmit the sounds they pick up, rather than radio waves. As the Younger Committee on Privacy, set up in 1972 to look at the law in this area, observed:

180

the purpose of most of these provisions is to safeguard the radio wavelength from unauthorised interference, rather than to protect privacy.[5]

The Younger Committee concluded that 'there is little in either the civil or criminal law to control technical surveillance devices'.[6] This point was emphasised in 1975, when, to draw attention to the legal vacuum, the *New Scientist* planted a bug in the House of Commons, which relayed MPs conversations to a receiver set up on Westminster Bridge. No charges were brought.[7]

The Younger Committee argued against the creation of a general privacy law in the UK, such as exists in most other Western countries, on the grounds that this:

would introduce uncertainties into the law, the repercussions of which upon free circulation of information are difficult to foresee in detail, but could be substantial.[8]

However, they did recommend that 'unlawful surveillance by device' should be made a criminal offence, where it is done surreptitiously.[9] Such laws exist in virtually all Western countries, but not in the UK, despite Younger's recommendation and the golden opportunity presented by the Interception of Communications Act. The only recent legislation that affects freelance operators of taps and bugs is the prohibition against attaching unapproved applicances to the telecomms network, contained in the Telecommunications Acts.

Another way of controlling covert surveillance devices, adopted in many countries, is to ban their manufacture and sale. Younger recommended that 'anyone advertising technical devices with reference to their aptness for surreptitious surveillance' should be guilty of incitement to commit the proposed offence of surreptitious surveillance.[10] This stops well short of prohibiting the manufacture and sale of bugs, and it is certainly not beyond the ingenuity of advertisers to get around such a prohibition. In the United States, where the 1968 Omnibus Crime Control and Safe Streets Act bans the manufacture and distribution of bugs as well as taps, infinity transmitters are on open sale, described as 'burglar alarms', even though they are virtually useless for this purpose.

However, the anti-bug law in America does seem to have been effective in restricting the availability and variety of tapping and bugging devices. Fewer such systems are on open sale in the States than in the UK. Here, a total lack of controls, even on the sale of telephone taps which it is illegal to use, has led to the proliferation of a baroque snooper's arsenal.

The lack of a law against covert surveillance devices has enabled the British police to use the whole range of this arsenal. In place of a legal framework to govern the use of such devices, the police have a set of secret 'Home Office Guidelines'. These were first promulgated in 1977, but did not come to light until 1982, after a parliamentary row about electronic snooping on public telephone kiosks in North Wales.

The story started around Christmas, 1981, when Mr Moses Edwards of Talysarn, Gwynnedd looked out of his window and noticed a couple of men acting strangely in the phone box at the bottom of his garden. When they left, he and his wife went to investigate, and found a miniature radio transmitter hidden behind a panel in the kiosk. Although it was later claimed to be a bug, it seems unlikely that the police would want to intercept only the Talysarn end of telephone conversations. However, we shall never know for sure. The two strange men quickly returned in a white estate car, and seized the device from Mr Edwards. When he threatened to go to the police, he was told, 'You go ahead, it won't do you any good'. Nor did it. When the local police tried to check the number of the white estate on national police records, the computer rejected their query, as the vehicle was protected by a 'Home Office block'.[11]

When the Plaid Cymru MP Daffydd Wigley raised questions in the House about the Talysarn incident, the Home Office admitted that 'a surveillance device which picked up what was said in the kiosk' had been planted.[12] Then, Home Secretary William Whitelaw conceded the existence of 'Guidelines' covering the use of clandestine surveillance devices by the police, but he stalled over publishing them. Only after the *Guardian* newspaper[13] published a leaked version of the police instructions, based on documents from the Isle of Man force, were the guidelines published; the Home Secretary then defused detailed criticism by saying that they were 'under review'.

The 1977 guidelines say that 'as a general principle' the use of covert surveillance devices should be confined to confirming or dispelling a suspicion of serious crime, and that evidence obtained by the use of such techniques should not be used in court, unless the phone conversation was itself the offence. When the Guidelines were issued, this was presented as a limitation on police surveillance, but in fact it simply serves to keep the police use of such tactics out of the public eye.

The main restrictive clause in the Guidelines said that the use of aural and visual surveillance devices (other than binoculars) must be approved by a Chief Constable, or an Assistant Commissioner in the Metropolitan force. However, the Isle of Man document, leaked to the *Guardian* and supposedly based on the Home Office Guidelines, reveals that hidden cameras and other visual devices were authorised by a Chief Inspector. This suggests that such guidelines may be liberally interpreted by local forces, before being transferred into operational instructions. Confirmation of this view comes from the Assistant Chief Constable of Kent, who told a television reporter in 1984:

I do not think that one should be hidebound in developing new [surveillance] *techniques solely because of an obscure piece of paper brought out five or six years ago.*[14]

In the same year, the 'reviewed' Guidelines were announced. They sounded much stricter, using similar wording to the Interception of Communications Act, though substituting a Chief Constable's agreement for a Home Secretary's warrant. Before covert surveillance devices could be used, the new Guidelines said, the Chief Constable must be satisfied that the investigation concerns serious crime, that other methods have failed or would be unlikely to succeed, and that there is good reason to anticipate an arrest and conviction or the prevention of terrorism. However, this casts still more doubt over the question of how the Guidelines are applied in practice: if they are strictly adhered to, why did the Government not include bugging along with tapping in the 1985 Act?

The extent of police use of surveillance devices is impossible to ascertain; nor do we know for sure which targets they are used on, or what devices are used. Not even the Home Office collects such information, which is left to Chief Constables. It is possible, however, to piece together a certain amount of information from public sources, though this is inevitably incomplete due to the fact we have already stressed, that covert surveillance, by its very nature, is extremely difficult to detect.

Most police surveillance is straightforward, and makes no use of fancy devices. As one officer of C11, Scotland Yard's surveillance specialists, told the *Observer* newspaper:

> *Wherever the target goes, you go. If he walks, you walk. If he gets in a train, you get in a train . . . You keep at them day and night. That's the name of the game.*[15]

One step beyond such 'simple surveillance', and entering into the realm of the same guidelines that apply to bugging, is the use of tracking devices. There are two ways of doing this, one involving cameras, the other radio transmitters hidden in the vehicle to be followed. The use of personal trackers, fastened to a suspect person rather than a vehicle, occurs rarely if at all in the course of police work in the UK.

The police are considerably more secretive about their use of aural surveillance devices such as bugs than they are about tracking devices. Police bugs are manufactured by the 'Special Investigations Division' (R12) of British Telecom's research laboratories, based at Martlesham near Ipswich. R12 are said to purchase large quantities of miniature electronic components, including tiny microphones, and in 1979 they demonstrated covert surveillance equipment, including infinity bugs, to German security officials. Bugging research is also carried out at a joint police–MI5 research station at Sandridge near St Albans.[16]

The monitoring of bugs once installed is carried out for the Metropolitan police, and also for the security and intelligence services, at a so-called 'wireless receiving station' in the secluded setting of number 113 Grove Park, Camberwell, London SE5. Festooned with an unusually wide range of radio aerials, the building is officially run by the Technical Services division (C7) of the Metropolitan police, and described in planning documents as used by the 'Police Burglar Alarm Inspectorate'.[17] A building with similar aerials to the Grove Park centre can also be found in Bushey, Hertfordshire. Bugs which transmit their signal via the telephone, such as infinity bugs, as well as combined bugs/taps, are sent to a tapping centre instead.

As well as a wide range of bugs and taps similar to those that are freely available (and which we describe below), the police have access to some special bugging equipment not normally available to the freelance operator. One such system is the surveillance laser, which bounces a thin, invisible beam of light off a window in the room where the targets are talking. Their speech waves in the air set up minute vibrations in the glass, which modulate the laser beam in such a way that the conversation can be decoded back into audible speech at the laser receiver station.

One of the advantages of such a distant surveillance system is that it avoids the illegality involved in trespassing, or even breaking and entering, to install a conventional bug. A C11 officer told the *Observer*:

> *I don't consider civil trespass a serious offence. It's a well-known problem in surveillance.*[18]

One branch of the police force has even less of a problem with illegality. This is the Special Branch, the eyes, ears, and arms of MI5. As such, the Branch is considered with our next group of bugging operators, the British intelligence and security services, who are *not* bound by the Home Office Guidelines covering the police.

The nature of MI5's work involves constant illegality. A journalist who has studied their activities closely told the TV programme on which Cathy Massiter appeared (see Chapter 1) that lawbreaking was:

> *Absolutely routine; there is a section of MI5 which is called A1A . . . whose sole purpose in life is to break and enter property. I've spoken to MI5 officers who've done these burglaries, and it's not just private homes: they'll do offices; they'll do banks; they'll do diplomatic property; no holds barred, doesn't matter.*[19]

A1A have a variety of reasons for breaking and entering, and, as usual in the secret world, each type of operation has an exotic codename. *AZURE* is the term for bugging, whether by installing a simple radio bug, or by more exotic means, such as the 'spike' or 'probe' microphone, like a long, sharp pin, and pushed through the target's wall from an adjacent building. Alternatively, the chosen method could be *CINNA-MON*, the installation of a combined infinity bug and tap in the target's telephone. In theory, this requires a warrant, as it involves phone tapping as well as bugging, but in practice ex-intelligence officers have claimed, *CINNAMON* is often used as an alternative to conventional tapping precisely to get round this requirement.

On the TV programme quoted above, a former clerk with MI5 told viewers how A1A broke into the home of Ken Gill, the General Secretary of TASS (then the draughtsmen's union) and a Communist Party member. His phone was already tapped as a matter of course, but when TASS planned to merge with the AEU, the engineering union, MI5 wanted a closer look:

> *His home had been broken into and a bug placed inside a room to monitor talks between Mr Gill and other trades unionists prior to or during the merger.*[20]

The Special Branch, closer to MI5 than to the rest of the police force, are often involved in such breaking and entering operations, especially where theft may be involved. A police officer is most useful in such circumstances for sorting out any problems that may arise with the local police if A1A are caught in the act.

Breaking and entering is, however, more risky than entry by subterfuge. One ploy is for the operator to pose as an electrician come to repair something; this will provide an explanation for any strange looking equipment he may be seen with. One potential target, a South African exile living in the UK, and suspected of 'subversive' activities while here, told us how a man in overalls claiming to be from the London Electricity Board turned up at his house while he was out. The 'LEB man' asked for him by name and said he had ordered some repair work to be carried out. This was, of course, wholly untrue. In this case, fortunately, his co-residents did not let the visitor in.[21] Another popular pose is as a BT engineer, come to mend the phone: this is a perfect cover for installing an infinity or other telephone bug.

Safer still is the common practice of using BT engineers themselves to install the bugs. The writer Chapman Pincher has described how this works:

> First, they put your telephone out of order, then, when you report it, they say they will come and fix it, and 'fix it' they do.[22]

When such a telephone-based device is installed for the Security Service, whether by real or imitation BT technicians, BT's engineering records are doctored to make sure no ordinary engineer will turn up and discover the bug. BT Area offices keep a 'Fault Card' for each line on their patch, on which visits have to be marked; when a bug has been installed, the card is marked in such a way that the usual engineers are instructed to refer any reported faults to a special section in the Area office which deals with security liaison.[23]

When the Government announced its intention to privatise BT, and withdraw its monopoly of some telephone services, this presented MI5 with a problem: if BT engineers were no longer to have automatic access to every phone, how were they going to install bugs? The solution that was found was to retain the monopoly over the local network all the way up to the first phone socket, rather than up to the junction box as might seem more logical. Other telecomms companies have lobbied hard against this aspect of the monopoly, as fitting sockets could be a lucrative business, but have met a brick wall in trying to persuade the Government's telecomms regulator, OFTEL. The sole reason is to ensure that BT engineers can still be used for fitting MI5 bugs.

The use of such BT staff can, of course, cause problems for MI5. On at least one occasion a trades union official has been told by a BT engineer that he had been bugged. The technician was quoted as saying, 'We often do it to villains, but I thought by the look of your bookshelves you were just an ordinary trades unionist'.[24] Sometimes, therefore, MI5 will use a different sort of outsider to do the dirty work – a professional bug operator. The strange world of these free-lance eavesdroppers is considered below.

Apart from journalists and trades union activists, other obvious targets of MI5 bugging include left-wing political parties and pressure groups – the same sorts of people as appear in the 'Fear of Tapping' catalogue, in fact. In 1975, a battery-powered radio transmitter was found in the headquarters of the Communist Party, fixed behind a small dais in the Party's main lecture room, where its Executive Committee met regularly.[25] A decade later, the National Council of Civil Liberties had its telephones 'swept' for signs of bugging. Several of them showed indications of bugging.[26]

The CPGB bug was a fairly simple device, about the size of a small transistor radio, but much tinier devices are available to the security service. In 1975, *The Times* published a photograph of a bug smaller than a 2p piece,[27] and by the early 1980s much smaller bugs still were openly available, some designed to look like miniature electronic components, undistinguishable from the legitimate contents of a telephone or, say, a modern washing machine, except to a real expert.

One device said to be very popular with MI5 is a bug that can be made to look like an electrical plug or socket. Instead of transmitting its signal by conventional radio waves, it imposes a Very Low Frequency 'carrier current' signal onto the mains electrical wiring of the house, enabling conversations to be picked up from anywhere within range of the same electricity sub-station that serves the target premises.

Another bugging technique is apparently reserved for the intelligence services and (in Northern Ireland) the Army. According to one report, even the Special Branch of the Royal Ulster Constabulary is not allowed to use the system, which is operated in Northern Ireland from an 'Army Landline Interception Centre' in Belfast. The technique is called 'Radio Frequency Flooding', and little is known about how it works, but it is said to be 'extremely difficult to implement, very range-limited, and requires an abundance of costly equipment'.[28]

In contrast to MI5, much of the Secret Intelligence Service (MI6)'s bugging and tapping occurs overseas. A classic operation of this kind, codenamed *PRINCE*, involved the construction of a 1,400 foot tunnel from West Berlin, under the border with East Germany, in order to tap underground telephone cables from a nearby Russian air force base. That was in 1955.[29] Two decades later, the Russians repaid the compliment from the West, and dug a similar tunnel under the US embassy in Moscow, in order to install and maintain bugging equipment to which microphones elsewhere in the building were attached.[30]

Diplomatic bugging within the UK is often carried out by MI5. According to the Labour MP Dale Campbell Savours, speaking under Parliamentary privilege in July 1986, the recently-banned memoirs of former MI5 agent Peter Wright contain the allegation that targets have included the West German and French embassies in London.[31] On another occasion a British intelligence official was forced to 'retire early', after being caught in the act of bugging the United States embassy.[32] However, it was MI6 themselves who were involved in one of the most famous diplomatic buggings of recent years – the Lancaster House affair.

The 1979 Lancaster House Conference was organised by the British Government to arrange a settlement between the competing factions in the liberation struggle to create Zimbabwe out of Rhodesia. Determined to ensure a diplomatic triumph for the hosts, MI6 bugged the hotel and conference rooms of the main participants, including Robert Mugabe (later to become Prime Minister of Zimbabwe), and his main rival, Joshua Nkomo. Valuable information about the negotiating positions of both men was fed to the British Foreign Secretary, Lord Carrington, each morning.[33] Unsurprisingly, the other participants began to suspect that something was up, and Nkomo persuaded a British backer, Tiny Rowland of the Lonhro corporation, to pay for his hotel room to be 'swept' to detect bugs. None were found, and the company which did the search, Diversified Corporate Services Limited (DCS), was itself later discovered to have extremely close links with British Intelligence.[34] The conference was an immense success for the British.

DCS's business was partly straightforward commercial security work; partly the training of agents (mostly from overseas) in surveillance, bugging, tapping, . 'surreptitious entry', and debugging; and partly freelance work for MI6 in the same areas of speciality. Three intelligence officials con-

189

firmed to the *New Statesman* that the company worked for MI6 on a number of occasions. DCS's debugging services were hotly sought after: Joshua Nkomo was following Harold Wilson, who hired DCS staff for this purpose in 1975 when he suspected that he was being bugged by MI5. Whether Nkomo and Wilson would have been deterred by the company's links with those suspected of doing the bugging in the first place, had the two leaders been aware of it, it not recorded.

The hiring of others to do dubious tasks that the intelligence services do not wish to be seen to be involved in has a number of advantages for the official agencies. In particular, it enables them to distance themselves from any unpleasant repercussions if the surrogate agents get caught in the act. Apart from DCS, a number of other companies and individuals have been involved in this sort of work; one of them is a former MI6 technician turned security consultant named Lee Tracey, who in 1981 told the TV programme *Panorama* about his work as a freelance tapper for British Intelligence:

> *The job of doing the routine tapping is, of course, the job of the Home Office and MI5 and Special Branch, but they're the routine tapping of people on a boring long-term consistent basis . . . The kind of jobs I would do would be the ones that we would call 'black bag jobs' . . . It means that I would have to gain entry by my wits, preferably invited in. The common movie idea of burglary is very seldom used, but is used, obviously has to be used, because there are occasions when that's the only way.[35]*

Tracey claimed that he had done 'About five or six hundred . . . black bag' jobs for the intelligence services, some seventy of them in the UK. He said that none of these had involved a warrant, but that the Home Secretary was not aware that such unauthorised taps occurred.

Another former intelligence officer who ran a company which has done work for the official security world is Peter Hamilton. His firm, Zeus Security Consultants, claim their job is 'to provide Security Services of all kinds to Government and other authorities'.[36] Its directors include Lord Chalfont and former Metropolitan Police Commissioner Sir James Starrett. In 1983 Zeus was commissioned to gather information about objectors to the proposed Sizewell nuclear reprocessing plant. Hamilton hired a detective agency named Contingency Services, based near Sizewell and run by one Vic Norris, who told the *Observer* in 1985:

> *We have a couple of very good imitation lefties. They know the score, they know the patois that these people use. They can drop names. They have got connections . . . I do the work that the Home Office don't want their own people to do because its too precarious or dirty.*[37]

Even the police seem to have taken up this privatisation of covert surveillance in recent years. In 1984 the Report of the Commissioner of the Metropolitan Police noted that the Met had hired a company named Anacapa Sciences Limited to train four 'intelligence and surveillance' teams to monitor targetted criminals.

Peter Hamilton of Zeus Security is a member of the Institute of Professional Investigators. In 1985, so were 850 other security experts, mostly former policemen and intelligence officers, but including thirty *serving* members of civilian or military intelligence, together with an unknown number of serving policemen and POID officers. Seminars have been held for the IPI at the RAF Security School based at RAF Newton in Nottingham, and at the Royal Military Police School in Chichester.[38] But the IPI are just one part of the British private surveillance and counter-surveillance industry, which has mushroomed over the past fifteen years, fostered by the absence of British laws against covert surveillance.

In the 1980s, bugging is big business. When the first professional bug merchant arrived in the UK from America in the mid-sixties, his business soon collapsed; apart from the Special Branch, no one in Britain seemed very interested in buying bugs and taps. After the 1968 Act banning bugging in the United States, however, Britain became an increasingly important base for manufacturers and distributors of bugs and taps, which were then imported into America, and the home market expanded as demand grew to meet supply. By 1973, one manufacturer was claiming to have supplied more than 250 British companies with surveillance devices in the previous year, and the UK bugging industry had a turnover in excess of £1 million.[39] In 1975, the original American 'bug merchant' returned to the UK 'rubbing his eyes in disbelief' at the size of the British market, and claimed that 'Britain is as actively engaged in the manufacture of electronic surveillance items as America ever was'.[40]

The UK bugging industry today includes manufacturers and retailers of bugging equipment, as well as a wide range of companies offering bugging or anti-bugging services. A cursory glance through the Central London Yellow Pages reveals some eighteen companies offering 'electronic surveillance' or 'counter-surveillance' as a service to their clients. The retail trade, in particular, is concerned to maintain appearances, and stresses its counter-surveillance and bug detecting role, rather than bugging itself. However, virtually all the companies seem to sell bugs and taps, as well as expensive counter-measures purporting to detect these devices.

Not all these companies can boast the illustrious contacts and clientele of, say, Diversified Corporate Services. Nevertheless, there is no lack of market among the paranoid and the inquisitive for surveillance and counter-surveillance equipment and services, and virtually no regulation over the trade. Over-hyping and exaggeration thrive in such an environment. One of the most notorious companies in the industry is the American-based Communication Control Systems Inc., which does business in the UK from 'The Counterspy Shop' with premises near the American Embassy in London's exclusive Mayfair district.[41]

CCS was founded by an American named Ben Jamil, whom we have already met as 'the first American bug merchant'. His first bug company was called International Telephone Supply Inc. (ITS), formed in 1962 and selling antique-style telephones as well as taps and bugs. In 1966 Jamil was indicted by a Federal Grand Jury for bugging offences, but the charges had to be dismissed due to the confused state of American privacy law at the time (see Chapter 7). It was following this experience that Jamil first tried, unsuccessfully, to move his retail operation to the UK. Britain was still useful, though, as a base from which to import bugs into the USA in the wake of the 1968 Act. Then, in 1970, the US parent, ITS, collapsed, and investigations began into its shady finances. It was discovered that Jamil had borrowed money from a creditor whose principals included a mafioso.

Two years after the ITS collapse, Jamil re-emerged at the head of a company named Communication Control Corporation, Inc. (CCC), which concentrated on the sale of virtually useless, but expensive, counter-surveillance equipment. In 1975, CCC, too, went bankrupt, and Jamil founded CCS, selling virtually the same range of products. Among his customers in the mid-seventies were the millionaire Adnan Kashoggi, the Shah of Iran, and the Greek government, to whom he apparently sold a large quantity of non-functioning bugging equipment.

In 1977, Jamil moved into the British market and set up an office in London's Belgravia district. The office was, according to police sources cited by the *New Statesman*, raided later in the year by a team from Scotland Yard's Special Branch and Anti-Terrorist Squad. A number of offensive weapons were confiscated, including CS and MACE gas canisters and a dartgun known as the 'Taser' which fired a barb attached to a device capable of delivering a massive electric shock. Undeterred by the police interest, CCS went on to open the 'Counterspy Shop' two years later and, according to a US customs official, continued to import teargas and dart-guns from its American parents, as well as telephone 'scrambling' equipment, bugs and taps, for sale in the shop.

By 1984, as well as the New York HQ and the London shop, CCS had branches in Miami, Chicago, Houston, and Beverly Hills, a catalogue printed in four languages, including Arabic, and sales in excess of $20 million a year. Nor does the hypocrisy of the bug sellers lag behind their profitability; in 1985, CCS's Vice President, in his capacity as a 'countermeasures expert', told the *Daily Express* that 'Our business is for right, it is not for evil . . . If you . . . had been a victim [of bugging] you would come apart at the seams. People feel as they do after being raped'.[42] Meanwhile, CCS were selling the 'State Of The Art Smallest Surveillance Tape Recorder' and a tapping device called 'the Telephone Spy . . . Now you can monitor all telephone calls made by an employee or spouse without his/her knowledge'.[43]

CCS are, admittedly, an extreme example. More typical perhaps are two recent arrivals on the British bug retailing scene: Cumberworth Surveillance, based in Kingston-upon-

Hull, and Lorraine Electronics Surveillance (also known as Ruby Electronics) of Leyton in north-east London. These outfits have virtually identical catalogues, containing a range of bugs, taps, and combined systems. Both companies point out that the devices they sell are illegal to use in Britain, and claim that 'it should be understood that our products are supplied for export'. This is despite the fact that the London firm sells a tap which is 'housed in an "exchange" standard BT wall socket'; such sockets are not used outside the UK.[44]

Aside from the bug retailers, a major sector of the UK bugging industry consists of those offering surveillance services to firms. In 1973 the *Sunday Telegraph*[45] reported that some forty individuals and six firms were engaged in industrial espionage, and this is now perhaps the main area of use for bugging devices (outside the police and intelligence services). Covert surveillance is used, not just by industrial spies, but by those that hunt them. A manual of company security, co-edited by Peter Hamilton of Zeus Security and published in 1985, says that:

> *Management is only justified in initiating secret surveillance if a need has been demonstrated. This need can range from a reasonable suspicion based on information, which by itself is not conclusive, to the discovery that a member of staff is removing confidential material without authority.*[45]

The manual goes on to reassure the company executive that 'the police are essentially human and quite capable of the Nelson touch in appropriate circumstances'.

In reality, as opposed to pulp fiction, industrial spying is used for much more than simply obtaining secret formulae. Finding out how much of it goes on is, however, a difficult task, as most companies that find their premises infiltrated by a human or electronic spy prefer to keep quiet about it, for fear of damaging their reputation. Nevertheless, a handful of industrial bugging cases have come to light and these illustrate the range of commercial uses to which electronic surveillance devices may be put.

The obvious aspect of industrial espionage is the gathering of information about competitors' activities. Known cases of bugging that seem to fit into this category include one in 1967, when a bug was found attached to the telephone of the senior partner in an engineering firm. An industrial spy was found, camping in a nearby field with a receiver and tape recorder in his tent; police were quoted as saying, 'We are making enquiries into this case. Industrial espionage as such is not an offence'.[47] Another story involved the bugging of hotels used for business conferences; a 'counter-espionage expert' told the *Guardian* that hotels near Heathrow airport had been bugged on at least six occasions in the mid-seventies. The spies were said to include both those employed by specific companies to bug their rivals, and freelance operatives, hoping to sell any intercepted information to the highest bidder.[48]

Another type of industrial espionage involves keeping an eye (or an ear) on employees rather than competitors. In 1980, North Westminster licensing magistrates were told that a casino in central London had a whole 'electronic bugging network' installed, with phones tapped and hidden cameras everywhere to watch the activities of staff and customers.[49] A recent case of staff surveillance was suspected in 1983, when staff on the local newspaper *The Brighton Evening Argus* discovered a bug in the room in which they held their union meetings, which was relaying their proceedings live to a receiver in the Editor's office. The Managing Director of the company (a subsidiary of the giant Westminster Press chain) expressed bewilderment about who might have been responsible for the bugging. After a strike by journalists and printers on the paper, an 'independent enquiry' was set up as part of the return to work agreement; but it failed to find out who was responsible for the bugging.[50]

In recent years the takeover boom in British industry has proved to have been a boom area for the bugging and counter-bugging experts (who, as we have seen, are often the same people). Merchant bankers Hill Samuel, takeover specialists, have their offices 'swept' for bugs several times a year, and during the recent takeover battle between high-street electrical retailers Currys and Dixons, the former held their board meetings, appropriately, to the sound of dozens of transistor radios at full volume, to foil bugs.[51] One case in which bugs were actually found concerned the Birmingham brewers Davenports, who were fighting off a bid from the rival Wolverhampton and Dudley brewery when they discovered a tiny bug taped to the underside of a small table near the chairman's seat in the boardroom. Davenports' rivals immediately denied responsibility, and condemned the bugging. The perpetrator has not been found.[52]

It is not only industrial spies, though, that use bugs and taps. Freelance private detectives, criminals, and private individuals may join the covert surveillance game for fun and profit. As early as 1959, a Post Office employee was convicted under the Prevention of Corruption Act for taking money from a bookmaker to tap a line relaying dog-racing results.[53] Another bookie in 1967 admitted paying a private detective agency to place a bug in the phone of a man he suspected of robbing him of £1,000.[54] Before the change in the divorce laws, private detectives were also used to tapping phones in divorce cases – a practice which led to the only known successful prosecution for tapping, that of Graham Blackburn in 1974 (see Chapter 5). Ten years later, no prosecution occurred after someone tapped the phone of champion jockey, John Francome, and offered the tapes (which reputedly contained evidence that Francome had broken racing regulations) to the *Daily Mirror*. Although an injunction preventing the *Mirror* from publishing transcripts of the tapes was upheld by the Court of Appeal, the paper was allowed to keep the identity of the tapper secret.[55]

The technology sold by the bug and tap retailers in the UK is remarkably consistent from shop to shop, although prices tend to vary considerably. As well as bugs, taps and combined devices of all shapes and sizes, they sell receivers of various kinds to pick up the radio signals emitted by the bugs, etc. Usually these are transistor radios, able to receive higher, 'air band' frequencies in the 108–120MHz range, as well as the standard VHF radio band of 88–108MHz. They also sell tape recorders (sometimes miniature ones) with a slow-speed function to avoid regular tape changes. In addition, the would-be operator can obtain so-called 'Vox' (voice activation) devices, which will switch the tape recorder on when a sound above the background level is detected, and thus avoid redundant taping.

Finally, the bug retailers sell 'counter-surveillance' equipment, bug and tap detectors of varying reliability.

The most commonly available type of bug is battery operated. It works by picking up any conversation within the room in which it is installed with a microphone, and relaying it in the form of a radio signal to a receiver somewhere between a hundred yards and a quarter of a mile away. The distance over which a radio bug can operate depends on the power of the bug and receiver, and the environmental conditions through which the signal has to travel. As a general rule, however, the longer the range, the larger and more powerful the bug has to be, and this increases the risk that the device may be detected. Battery bugs may be divided into three main types:

i. Miniatures

Although expensive versions may be as small as a sweetcorn kernel, the most widely available miniatures go down to approximately 2cm^3. With miniatures, the small size itself is the main aid to concealment. A physical search may well fail to reveal a miniature fixed somewhere inconspicuous, while the low power of these devices means that even an electronic 'sweep' (see below) may fail to find one.

ii. Agent Transmitters

These are designed to be secreted about the person. The eavesdropper then transports the bug into the target premises and stays there while the bug transmits its signal to a receiver elsewhere. Agent devices are usually larger, more powerful, and hence more easily detectable than miniatures – although even the most paranoid may baulk at passing a detector over all their visitors. Common disguises include bugs posing as signet rings and pens. Another sort of agent transmitter does not use radio signals, but transmits sound to a miniature tape recorder also hidden on the agent; these are usually sold built into briefcases, which appear perfectly normal, inside and out, to a cursory inspection.

iii. Concealment Packages

These are bugs disguised as something else, which may be placed on the target premises and left to transmit any sounds. A frequent gambit is to build such bugs into common kinds of ashtray, table lamps, and similar items of office or room furniture. The ideal concealment device is specifically designed to blend in with the fittings in the room to be monitored, otherwise the appearance of a strange ashtray (or whatever) may arouse the target's suspicion. Another solution is to use the concealment package in such a way that the target aids his own bugging; Lee Tracey claims to have done this when he

> *put a bug into a pocket calculator which was . . . given to the person to be bugged. It was intended that the victim would generously take the bug into meetings with him and supply the power by replacing the calculator batteries whenever needed.*[56]

Most of these battery-operated bugs are not really suited to long-term surveillance, as the batteries need changing regularly.

Most *mains powered* bugs work, like battery bugs, by transmitting radio signals to a VHF/Air band receiver. Unlike battery systems, however, the source which powers the transmitter is mains electricity, and therefore these bugs are usually hidden in electrical appliances. Commonly available versions are disguised in a standard 13 Amp plug socket, which can be fixed to the wall in place of the normal one, or in a two-way adapter plug. Both these work normally, as well as housing bugs. As with battery bugs, mains systems are easily available over the counter or by mail order from British suppliers. Unlike battery bugs, they will carry on broadcasting for years, using the target's own electricity supply.

More sophisticated are the *Carrier-current* devices, used by the police and intelligence services but also commercially available, using Very Low Frequencies between 50 and 300 KHz to transmit their signal along the mains electrical wiring of the house itself, rather than by sending radio waves through the atmosphere like other bugs. To pick up the conversations in a room bugged in this way, all one need do is plug a receiver into the mains supply of another building operating off the same electricity sub-station.

Among the most commonly available covert surveillance devices are 'telephone powered' bugs. They are often tiny, designed to look like the electronic components in the telephone instrument where they are housed. Alternatively, they can be installed along the line to the exchange, typically in the junction box. The most famous telephone powered bug is the inifinity transmitter. This is not a radio bug but, like the carrier current systems, sends its messages along the wires to which it is connected – in this case the telephone line, rather than the mains electricity network. The name 'infinity bug' is derived from the original American manufacturer's claim that room conversations could be picked up from an 'infinite' distance away, using the international telephone network.

Infinity bugs are not, strictly speaking, transmitters at all; the transmission of the sounds they pick up is done by the phone system. An infinity in fact consists of a tone-controlled switching device, coupled with a microphone and amplifier. The switch is designed to cut off the telephone 'hook switch', which keeps the phone dead when the handset is down, and to activate the microphone and amplifier. It does this when it hears a particular electrical signal or audio tone. On the original model, the sound that activated the bug was a tone at around 440Hz, which is produced by the 'C' note on a harmonica, giving the infinity its American nickname of 'the harmonica bug'. Once an infinity has been installed in the victim's phone, all the operator need do is dial the target's number, and send the activating tone down the line (usually by blowing a whistle or harmonica into the mouthpiece).

The tone should prevent the target's phone ringing, but if it does not, all the dialler need do is pretend to be a wrong number, and then generate the tone again when the target hangs up. Once activated, the infinity bug will transmit sounds from within the room where the target phone is installed to the eavesdroppers's phone. Anyone ringing the target will get the engaged tone, but if the target lifts the receiver, the bug cuts out, and the phone may be used to make a call. Once the eavesdropper gets bored and hangs up, the phone returns to normal.

All the devices mentioned so far can be detected by a thorough electronic search or 'sweep'. For the real professional with time or money to spend, preferable alternatives fall into two categories, the ultra-simple, and the extremely complicated.

The most primitive kind of bugging consists simply of

wiring a microphone hidden in the room to an amplifier and tape recorder elsewhere. This is undetectable by normal means, providing the microphone and wires are securely hidden, as it dos not emit radio waves or change the current on a telephone line. The problem lies in getting enough time on the target premises to install the wiring. Otherwise, this simple method is the best. A 'security expert' told the *Guardian* in 1977 that, using such methods, and given about four hours, he could bug a room so that:

> *You could bring in a dozen experts and the only way they could be absolutely sure the room was bug free would be to tear the room apart and rebuild it.*[57]

Where there is insufficient time for such an operation, two complex systems also provide considerable security against detection; one is radio frequency flooding (see above), the other involves the use of a 'field effect transmitter' (FET) or 'passive reflector'. This is a tiny, flat piece of metal, about a quarter of the size of a postage stamp, which can be hidden in the wall, behind the plaster, or simply secreted about the room somewhere. The FET is very difficult to detect, as it does not transmit anything itself. Instead, the operator beams a powerful radio wave at it from outside the room. The reflector is designed to change (or 'modulate') this signal according to the sounds in the room, and then send it back to a receiver, where the eavesdroppers may listen to or record any converation occurring in the bugged room. These devices first came to public attention in 1952, when one was found inside a carving of the Great Seal of the United States, which was a present from the Soviet government to the US embassy in Moscow.[58] This device, however, was some three quarters of an inch in diameter, whereas modern reflectors are much smaller. Radio frequency flooding may work in a similar way, though it appears not to require the installation of a reflector.

Two other devices worth mentioning, which can easily be acquired by the freelance, are the special microphones which can be used for eavesdropping. 'Parabolic microphones' can be pointed into a room from outside and record a conversation from a considerable distance. 'Spike microphones' are thin, pin-shaped devices which are inserted through a wall of the target room.

Moving from bugs to taps, from the (just) legal to the illegal, we find that the necessary equipment is equally widely available. Not that tapping necessarily requires specialised components; performing a direct tap on a telephone line is simplicity itself. All you need is a set of high-impedance headphones, with a capacitor attached to keep out the telephone line current. The headphones may then be fastened onto the telephone wire with crocodile clips, once the wire has been bared of its plastic coating. The trouble with this method, as we have already noted, is the risk of detection. No one wants to be caught by the police or a BT engineer while dangling off a pole with a pair of headphones. Direct taps are rare in covert surveillance, then, but they have been known to be fitted to distribution cabinets in the street, notably by the IRA to tap British Army phone calls and to investigate their own members.[59]

A more sophisticated method is the 'inductive' tap. One widely available version looks like a rubber sucker with a couple of wires attached. The sucker hides an induction microphone, which contains a coil; when a current passes through the line (i.e. when a call is taking place) it creates a magnetic field which induces a corresponding current in the induction coil. Obviously, these sucker devices are useless for covert surveillance, though they are often used by people to tape their own phone calls. However, other inductive devices can be disguised as common desk items, or fitted along the telephone line. These contain a radio transmitter similar to that used in a radio bug, which may be picked up by the usual VHF receiver. Inductive taps do not need to be physically connected to the line, but may be used up to four feet away. The problem with these taps is that they usually produce a poor quality signal, and easily pick up interference from other electrical appliances.

A third kind of tap works in a very similar way to radio bugs, drawing its power from the telephone, and transmitting phone conversations on VHF frequencies. These fall essentially into two categories: those connected in *series* to the telephone circuit, and those connected in *parallel*. The former draw their power from the telephone line, the latter can be battery operated for greater power. The main advantage of a parallel tap, though, is that it may be used on an extension phone or a switchboard line, rather than only on a single direct line.

One of the most common series taps looks exactly like the microphone in the mouthpiece of the telephone, and works in the same way, except that it also houses a tap. In the United States, where they are often used by law enforcement agencies, such devices are known as 'drop-ins', as they need only be dropped into the telephone handset once the mouthpiece is unscrewed. In the UK, telephone microphones are attached by two screws to a couple of wires in the handset, but this only adds a minute or so to the work needed to install one of these taps, which are easily obtainable in Britain.

Another easily obtainable series tap is housed in a replacement for the normal BT plug-in phone socket. Like the 'drop in', a couple of minutes with a screwdriver, and the amateur tapper has a workable and hard-to-discover tap installed on the target's line. Both types of tap will work for years on the power provided by the telephone current, without needing to be touched.

There is nothing new about combining a bug with a tap in one unit. Primitive versions involved a 'third wire' being installed alongside the normal pair in the telephone cable to transmit recorded phone calls, while the 'bug' element was provided by a hook-switch defeat system. These were first mentioned in 1952, in the *Sunday Pictorial* article quoted in Chapter 1,[60] and 'exposed' a second time five years later by Chapman Pincher in the *Daily Express*.[61] Third wire systems were, of course, difficult to install, and their use was restricted to the police and MI5. They are now wholly obsolete.

Most combined systems now use a radio bug, powered by the telephone current, together with a series tap connected to the same radio transmitter. The eavesdropper can listen to all room conversations until the telephone handset is lifted, whereupon the bug cuts out and the tap allows eavesdropping on the phone call. Combined systems like this sound exotic, but can be purchased over the counter for around £140.

If someone suspects that he or she is being tapped or bugged, what can they do about it? In reality, precious little. Potential targets can, if they wish, spend a lot of money on debugging devices and tap detectors; or hire the services of a counter-surveillance 'expert' to perform an electronic search or 'sweep' of their premises. However, such methods are fraught with inadequacies: no equipment is available, or even conceivable, that could detect all known bugs and taps, despite the 'universal' claims of some manufacturers of debugging devices.

Bug detectors work by scanning radio frequencies (usually only the VHF and 'air band' frequencies used by the most common bugs) to detect a signal emanating from a bug. One problem here is bugs which operate outside the usual frequencies. Another is bugs which use telephone or mains transmission rather than broadcasting radio signals (though some carrier current devices may be detected, using a device marketed by a company called Argen Security).[62] A third problem is low power bugs, which can be difficult to detect unless the scanner is within a couple of feet of the transmitter. Finally, directly wired microphones, FETs and similar sophisticated devices are not susceptible to discovery by the usual bug detector sweeps. Metal detectors can be used to find hidden wiring, microphones, and even FETs, but they have to be extremely sensitive to find something as small as a modern bug, and can be fooled by hiding the eavesdropping device behind something innocent and metallic, such as central heating pipes.

Tap detectors are even more useless. They work by measuring telephone power voltages, to see if anything is siphoning current off the line. Ironically, this can detect some *bugs* that are undetectable by normal radio scanners (ie the infinities and other telephone bugs), but it will not detect most taps. Neither direct taps nor proper exchange taps can be detected in this way, nor can any taps which are not powered by the telephone current. On the other hand, some crossed lines which lead to the famous 'squeaks and farts' may well cause a drop in line voltage. This was inadvertently illustrated by the Plaid Cymru MP Daffydd Wigley, who bought one of these devices, which lit up when a variation in line voltage occurred:

I remember one particular instance when a fairly important person was speaking to me over the telephone and there was a click on the phone about four seconds after the conversation had started . . . He said 'Ah, they are bugging us again' and the second the click had come on his end, the light had come on mine.[63]

A professional de-bugger will carry out all the above tests, and also perform a thorough physical search of the premises. This may be of considerable use in detecting many of the devices used in industrial espionage, but is unlikely to find evidence of the biggest operators of all, the police and intelligence services; especially given the close relationship between the latter two and the 'de-bugging experts'. These are almost invariably experts in bugging as well as de-bugging, and, as we have seen, some are involved in still more dubious activities. There was something rather strange about the NCCL arranging to have their premises swept in 1985 by a man with a history of spying on trades unionists engaged in industrial disputes. Perhaps the story of the Lancaster House sweeps contains a lesson for many potential clients of the de-buggers.

Another danger with de-bugging is that it can give a false sense of security. In this it is akin to the use of 'scramblers' to encode telephone conversations; de-scramblers are fairly easily obtainable for those prepared to look for them, as are bugs which are difficult to detect.

An alternative approach for those who fear they may be bugged is to set up false leads for the eavesdroppers, following the old trades unionists' trick described in Chapter 1. In the last analysis, there is no defence against bugging and tapping. It is worth repeating (and extending the application of) the words of those who should certainly know what they are talking about, British Telecom:

The telephone is vulnerable to eavesdropping and interception and is not a secure means of communication. Caution must therefore be exercised when it is necessary to discuss sensitive matters on the telephone. Conversations should be in guarded terms.[64]

These days, this can apply to conversations in a room, as well as over a telephone.

Chapter 9

Not Quite Tapping . . .

Apart from its uses for tapping and bugging, there are less well-known ways in which the police and security services can use the telephone system to their advantage. One of these is traffic analysis, the study of the 'external' characteristics of phone calls, such as the numbers dialled from a particular phone ('metering'), or the origins of calls to a particular phone ('tracing'). The analysis of such 'externals' has been brought to a high science by GCHQ, which has two divisions devoted to traffic analysis called S and T. The techniques they use were developed during the First World War, with military applications in mind, in particular as an attempt to extract *some* information from signals too heavily coded to be decypherable. Today, GCHQ's traffic analysts use Tandem computers to analyse externals. Little is known about the present activities of GCHQ's traffic analysis division, but it seems reasonable to assume that military and diplomatic matters still dominate its work; nevertheless, much of the expertise acquired in such areas would be transferable to the analysis of external telephone signals.

The term 'active measures', on the other hand, refers to more overt activities than bugging, tapping or traffic analysis, such as selectively cutting off particular lines at strategic moments. Both traffic analysis and active measures have legitimate uses in telecommunications; metering, for example, is used as a check by British Telecom when customers dispute their bills, while selective cut-offs may be necessary when a telephone exchange becomes severely overloaded. It is other applications, however, which interest the police and intelligence services.

When a telephone subscriber picks up the receiver and dials, the number dialled tells the local exchange where the call is going. Together with the length of the call, and the time and day it is made, this determines the cost of any particular telephone conversation. But the exchange equipment does not have to remember all the numbers dialled in order to bill customers. For billing purposes, directly dialled telephone calls are measured in units; the length of conversation available for one unit varies according to the time of day and the distance between the caller and the called.

In the local telephone exchange a meter attached to each subscriber's line simply clocks up the accumulating units, rather like a car milometer. There is no record of which numbers are dialled. Four times a year, each meter is photographed, using a vast camera that snaps a hundred meters at a time. The number of units recorded on the film are typed into British Telecom's huge accounts computers, which send out the subscribers' quarterly bills. The system is clumsy, but usually accurate, and it provides no information that could interest anyone other than BT and its customers. Only when a telephone subscriber makes an operator-connected call does BT record the number called, and this is duly listed on the caller's next quarterly bill.

From time to time, telephone customers question the accuracy of their bills. When this happens, BT can connect a device called a 'meter check printer' (MCP). As its name implies, this enables a check to be made on the subscriber's meter reading. It prints out the numbers dialled from the line to which it is connected, the time and duration of outgoing calls, and the time (but not the source) of incoming calls.

Internal BT regulations stipulate that an MCP may be used in cases of queried bills, repeated complaints about the telephone service where engineers can find nothing wrong with the line, and obscene or threatening phone calls where the identity of the caller is suspected. A stock of MCPs is held in every telephone area, but their use is restricted, according to BT because of the expense involved. One former exchange employee told us that 'For some reason, they were never available on demand, and could only be got at a week's notice'.[1]

In fact, BT staff have to compete with the police and security services for the use of MCPs. It is these, and similar devices, that are used for the accumulation of 'metering' information on the phones of suspected subversives or criminals. This process was described by High Court judge Sir Robert Megarry as 'a cousin of what is generally regarded as telephone tapping'.[2] When calls are monitored in this way the contents of the conversation remain private, but metering reveals the extent of a person's social, political, or criminal contacts with others, and can enable intelligence analysts to build up a broad picture of a target's life.

The POEU, whose members install the MCPs, told the European Court during the Malone case that:

> While metering provides less information than tapping, it does not require a warrant, it involves less manpower effort and cost, and the information which it does provide . . . can be of considerable benefit to the police, in suggesting lines of enquiry or suspects to interview.[3]

But metering has wider uses than this. Apart from simple lists of someone's telephone contacts (which can be particularly useful, for example, for positive vetting), it can indicate patterns of behaviour. If the target always rings John Smith and Mary Jones after speaking to Fred Bloggs, this can reveal quite a lot about lines of communication within the organisation being watched, whether that is an environmental pressure group, a trades union involved in industrial action, or, indeed, a criminal conspiracy.

Metering can also be used in conjunction with conventional telephone tapping. Here it helps to screen out some of the inevitable useless information produced by a tap, to reduce the volume of mundane calls that are recorded. Equipment designed to read the dialled telephone signals is connected to the target line, along with the usual tapper's tape recorders. The whole thing is computer controlled, and can be programmed to record nothing except when the target dials particular selected numbers, or simply to screen out certain numbers, and record the rest. Equipment for doing this is actually available on the open market; one supplier, Communications Devices Ltd. of Byfleet, Surrey, offers both telephone and telex versions of such 'second generation monitoring systems', with the claim that they are 'designed for police, national security and intelligence applications and priced accordingly'.[4]

It is difficult to discover the extent to which the MCP and other devices are used by the police and MI5. Of its nature metering information is not usually produced in court; unless a phone call is itself the illegal act (for example, an obscene call or a computer hacker tapping into someone else's database), its 'external' details are usually more useful as intelligence material than evidence. No overall figures are available, because no warrant or court order is required; metering information is simply arranged and supplied by BT on request. Nevertheless, it is clear, as the POEU claimed to the European Court of Human Rights, that metering 'is used for much more than enabling the Post Office (now BT) to ensure that a subscriber is correctly charged'.[5]

The difficulty in finding out just *how* much more it is used is illustrated by the fact that, to illustrate their evidence on metering to the European Court, the POEU could find no British court case in which the MCP was mentioned, and instead referred to an example in which the POID used a similar BT device called a tone detector printer (TDP), to collect metering information for the police.

BT regulations describe the process by which the police obtain metering information:

> the normal procedure recommended by the Home Office is that such requests should be made through police channels to the Post Office Investigation Division – telephone numbers listed in the Police Almanac.[6]

On receiving such a request, the Investigation Division would have to go through an MCP control officer in the target's local telephone area office. This functionary (according to one source usually a middle grade manager in the local traffic division with other 'security' functions as well) allocates all local MCPs, whether the information is sought by the Security Service looking for a list of some Communist's friends, or by an irate telephone subscriber with a three figure bill. The machine will be connected, usually, by a local technician in the exchange, who is very unlikely to know why the MCP is being attached. The machine is connected in parallel to the normal traffic meter, but transcribes the dialled numbers, rather than simply clocking up call units.

These administrative procedures are much less onerous than those governing tapping. As judge Robert Megarry pointed out in the High Court in 1979: 'This process is carried out without a warrant and without the administrative safe-guards laid down for telephone tapping proper'.[7] The distinc-tion is illustrated by the police use of metering in the 'Operation Julie' drugs case. In June 1976, Detective Inspec-tor Dick Lee arranged for metering equipment to be attached to the line of Henry Todd, the suspected organiser of a drugs ring:

> *Help was sought from the Post Office Investigation Branch, and they fitted a meter to his telephone . . . for security reasons* [Inspector Lee] *decided not to put a full scale tap on Todd's phone at this stage.*[8]

Todd's meter was left on for over six months, until he moved to another address when a meter was promptly attached to his new line. There are no set time limits for the use of meters, which may be on a line for years.

It is not just the police, security services and BT that use metering information. Today, anyone who works for a large organisation, whether public or private, is likely to have the calls from their office phone metered. Owners of office switchboards (Private Branch Exchanges, or 'PBXs', in tele-comms jargon) may now buy their own meters (or have them built into the more advanced PBXs). These are used to show how the internal phone network could be rearranged more efficiently, by indicating the areas of high phone usage, and to detect illicit private use of company telephones. An official study[9] of the use of such 'extension logging' equipment in government departments found savings of 20–30% in call charges could result. Like the MCP and TDP, call loggers, going under names like 'Tel-Tag' (used by the Metropolitan police for their own telephone system), 'Call Analyser' and 'Telemanager', can be programmed to print out the numbers dialled from each extention phone. Even single line loggers are available; the wonders of high technology allowing us all to meter our own phones.

Conventional metering equipment cannot reveal where calls *to* a targeted subscriber come from. The reason for this is that, while telephone calls carry a signal indicating where they are going – ie, the dialled number, there is nothing to show where a call comes from. Finding the source of a call *to* a target phone requires another sort of traffic analysis called 'call tracing'. Traditionally, this could only be done by a telecomms engineer physically following the path of the electrical current back to its origin, while the call was actually in progress. This was a tedious and lengthy process which would often end prematurely, when the caller hung up before the call was traced. By the early 1980s, however, the police were able automatically to identify the source of a call from a public call box, if not from a private telephone.

The method used for this is probably based on techniques developed in the mid-1970s, during the hunt for an obscene phone caller whose anti-social tastes ran to pestering nurses on duty at West Country hospitals. The calls always emanated from public call boxes, and the police tried a variety of ways of tracing them, before calling in a Home Office wireless officer named Jim Westcott. He hit upon the notion of analysing the paytone 'pips' which indicate to the caller the need to feed the coinbox. Although the pips were supposed to consist of a 400Hz tone, it was discovered that the tones on different call boxes in fact varied slightly around this figure. On close analysis, each phone box has its own tone 'signature'. Once all the local phones had had their signatures recorded, these could be compared with the police recordings of the obscene calls. Using this discovery, the police were able to track down and arrest 'Paytone Jim', as they nicknamed the obscene caller.[10]

Five years after the capture of Paytone Jim in July 1981, the Home Secretary, William Whitelaw, announced in Parliament in answer to a question from Labour MP Renee Short, that:

A study is being undertaken, at the request of my department, by British Telecom into the feasibility of identifying automatically the telephone numbers of those calling for assistance from the police and fire services.[11]

BT told the press that the system involved 'sophisticated

and expensive electronics'. 'We have shown that it is feasible and we have left it up to the Home Office to say whether we should go further,'[12] said a spokesman. The Home Office do, indeed, seem to have given the go-ahead, because the POEU told the European Court during the Malone Case (see Chapter 6) that:

> *Since the bombing of the Harrods store in London just before Christmas, the Metropolitan police have showed a remarkable facility for tracing hoax calls: there have been four prosecutions in as many weeks . . . Clearly BT has some kind of technical facility (which is not the meter check printer) for tracing a call back to its destination, and it is obvious from the prosecutions that the police are receiving such information from BT.*[13]

The system announced by William Whitelaw, presumably the same one referred to by the POEU, is only attached to 999 numbers, but more flexible call tracing equipment has also been reported to be available. In 1985, a woman suffering from obscene calls was told by the Metropolitan police that:

> *there were only a few tracer machines for the whole of London, and these only recorded the numbers from which callers were calling; the operator* [who was already monitoring her line in an effort to deter the caller] *could not listen in.*[14]

Even these machines, however, seem to be restricted to detecting calls from public call boxes. With private phones, there is no signal that can indicate where a call comes from. In the case of the more advanced PBXs, however, calls from within the system can be traced. This is because these machines are computer controlled, and, for call logging purposes, store in their memories the information, for example, that Extension 9876 called Extension 4321 at such and such a time. To trace the source of the call received by 4321 only requires the running of a simple program to search the PBX computer database for which extension called that number at that time.

Apart from coinbox calls and internal calls through advanced PBXs, simple, automatic call tracing remains a tappers' dream, so long as the present generation of British telephone exchanges remain in service. Practical constraints ensure that both call tracing and metering in general present a definite, but limited, threat to civil liberties. MCPs and similar forms of metering involve the police in persuading British Telecom to carry out the expensive process of attaching a special piece of equipment to the target subscriber's line, checking it regularly and processing the tape output. The big black box is highly visible to BT staff working at the exchange, which, as we have seen in the case of tapping proper, is very bad for security, Metering is, for these reasons, probably an unusual, if by no means unknown, method for the police and security services to use.

All this, however, is due to change in the very near future. The dream of automatic call tracing is becoming a reality with the new, computerised System X telephone exchanges. These store in their vast memories all the numbers dialled from each line. This means that information about who is calling whom is constantly available, exactly as it is for some PBX calls. Once BT adopts digital exchanges, the whole public telecomms network will be like a series of interlinked and communicating advanced PBXs.

The 'call logging' information produced by digital exchanges like System X can be printed out on a customers' bill, or accessed by means of commands typed out on a computer terminal linked to the exchange (but possibly located miles away). Furthermore, dialled digits will be stored for months in BT's billing computers, so that retrospective metering and call tracing may be carried out on anyone who arouses suspicion: for example, someone who comes into contact with a person who has already been targetted. This facility is referred to by the manufacturers of System X, Plessey, in a publicity leaflet which lists 'malicious call identification' among the services available on the digital exchanges.[15]

BT will, therefore, possess all the metering information the police and Security Service could desire – without going to the time, expense and risk of installing any special equipment on the line. The information will be available to *everyone*. With computers to sort this data and look for patterns, a vast amount of so-called low level intelligence may be gathered, for a fraction of the cost and effort of present-day tapping and metering. Moreover, such metering will be impossible for exchange workers to detect.

In these circumstances, the use of such information by the authorities is bound to increase dramatically, unless new legislation restricts their acquisition of traffic data from BT. The new metering systems are, however, being introduced with no mention of their intelligence applications, in the innocuous name of 'itemised billing'.

Bascially, itemised billing involves replacing the current dialled unit meters with equipment that automatically records all called numbers. Telephone bills can then be sent out with each call made listed individually on the bill, with the called number and cost, just as operator connected calls are shown under the present BT system.

Itemised billing has been the rule in many Western countries (for example, the United States) for many years. Unless it is done through digital exchanges, however, it does not facilitate call tracing – there are just too many practical problems in sorting manually through every subscriber's metering printout. In the United States, moreover, the multiplicity of different telephone networks means that even when they are fully digitalised automatic call tracing is unlikely to be practicable across the whole country. In Britain, System X heralds very different, and more threatening, possibilities.

Since the privatisation of BT, the Government's telecomms watchdog OFTEL has been keen to introduce itemised billing into the UK as soon as possible, as required by Section 37 of BT's operating licence, issued under the 1984 Telecommunications Act. A pre-digital version first went on trial in March 1983, in the Bristol area, and later extended to London, Edinburgh, Leicester, and Shrewsbury. However, the system ran into a number of technical problems, mostly due to its incompatibility with the normal BT billing computers, which process the charge unit information from the photographs of subscribers' meters. The two systems consistently produced contradictory information, which meant that the bills had to be sorted out by hand.

In 1985 the itemised billing trials were abandoned, and BT now intends to bring the system in, as it first intended, with its System X exchanges. Orders have been placed for ICL 'System 25' minicomputers, which will be used in tandem with the new exchanges to produce itemised bills. System X is already being introduced throughout the country, along with so-called 'System Y' exchanges (which have similar facilities), but the programme will not be completed until the next century. As the number of digital exchanges grows, so will the authorities' capacity to gather private traffic information on all of us.

The current legal framework within which metering operates is wholly inadequate to control these developments. Until the mid-1980s, metering in any form was wholly unregulated by British law. In principle, British Telecom could hand over a list of the calls made by one of their customers to anybody who cared to ask. In practice, of course, BT internal regulations have always restricted the circulation of metering information, whether in the form of MCP printouts, itemised bills, or the results of call-tracing exercises.

The official position on metering rests on the view that there is:

a fundamental difference between the disclosure of the contents of a communication and the disclosure of so-called metering information.[16]

The reason for this distinction is that whereas tapping proper involves the interception of private conversations, the information provided by 'metering' consists only of

signals sent to [BT] . . . and makes no use of communications to any other person.[17]

It is technically true that the numbers dialled by a caller are – in one sense – a message sent to the telecommunications network, to indicate where to send the call. BT, when introducing itemised billing, makes great play of the fact that no more information is collected than when an operator connects the call. However, with the collection of 'low level' intelligence, it is the cumulative amount of data, and the ability to sort it electronically that count. We can choose which calls to put through the operator, and a list of those calls would reveal very little about any given person's life. On the other hand, with the metering of *all* someone's calls, as we

214

have seen, the authorities can gather a considerable amount of information that most of us would consider 'private'.

The question of whether the provision of metering information to the police is in breach of our right to privacy was considered by the European Court during the Malone case. Malone believed that calls from his Vauxhall home had been metered, though this was based entirely on the circumstantial evidence that twenty locations he had recently phoned, including the auction houses Sotheby's and Christies, were visited and searched by police after his arrest in 1977. The information leading up to these raids could have been gathered by orthodox tapping.[18]

During the course of the Malone case over the next seven years, the Crown consistently denied that any metering had taken place. The Megarry judgement in February 1979 ruled that the alleged metering was, in any case, not illegal, and the judge recommended no specific legislation to cover the acquisition of traffic information. When the case came before the European Court, however, the POEU, as an expert interested body, submitted written evidence describing the administrative practices under which the police were able to procure meter records. The union asserted that the fact that a particular conversation had taken place should be safeguarded in the same way as the conversation itself.

The union's evidence altered the European Court's perception of the metering issue and, in August 1984, it ruled that, whether or not Malone himself had been subject to traffic analysis:

> *The records of metering contain information, in particular the numbers dialled, which is an integral element in the communications sent by telephone. Consequently, release of that information to the police without the consent of the subscriber . . . amounts to an interference with a right guaranteed by Article 8* [of the European Convention on Human Rights].[19]

By this time, however, the British Government had moved to bring metering under the law. Section 45 of the 1984 Telecommunications Act put skeletal controls on the release by BT of traffic information by forbidding telecomms companies from intercepting or disclosing any 'message' transmitted through the network or any 'statement of account', outside their normal work, except in obedience to a warrant or 'in connection with the investigation of any criminal offence or for the purposes of any criminal proceedings'.

This wording contained no 'national security' clause, a lapse which the Government sought to correct the following year in the Interception of Communications Act, Schedule 2, of which prohibits the disclosure of 'any information concerning the use made of telecommunications services provided for any other person', except in cases of criminal investigation or proceedings 'in the interest of national security or in pursuance of the order of a court'. A document asserting reasons of national security and signed by any Government minister, or by the Attorney General or Lord Advocate, is to be taken by the courts as conclusive evidence that metering was carried out for such purposes. 'National security' covers, in this instance, the same range of targets as the tapping sections of the Act.

In practice BT will simply comply with police requests, given the practical constraints associated with current metering techniques. The wording of the clause is modelled on the Data Protection Act, another piece of legislation which seeks to exempt the state from the requirements of openness and respect for privacy that every other person and organisation in society must obey.

The 1985 Act, therefore, simply enshrines the official distinction between tapping and metering. There *is* a real difference, but as the POEU have noted, 'it is one of degree, rather than kind'.[20] The technological advances now occurring make it more important than ever to regulate the amount of metering that goes on, and to limit its targets. Without such legislation, it is difficult to believe that metering in Britain is only carried out when 'necessary in a democratic society', as the European Convention on Human Rights requires.

Traffic analysis, like tapping and bugging, is essentially a covert activity: ideally, the target never realises that anything is going on. Active measures, on the other hand, involve the police and intelligence services using the telephone system overtly, in order to further some tactical aim such as disrupting the activities of those perceived to be the State's enemies. For example, cutting òff the telephones of key trades union

216

organisers at the key moment of a strike can be a most effective measure, disrupting lines of communication and causing chaos.

The general heading of 'active measures' can cover a wide range of activities. At its crudest, it includes the well-attested use of threatening and obscene phone calls by the South African security forces to intimidate opponents of apartheid: at its most sophisticated, the term can be applied to the British Government's plans to cut off the telephones of most of the population in the event of war or severe civil emergency. Between these extremes lie a number of possible active measures, but evidence of such activities is hard to come by, and allegations of selective cut-offs are invariably hotly denied by BT and the Home Office. Nevertheless, there have recently been a number of such allegations.

One strange story is that of Hilda Murrell, an elderly rose grower and anti-nuclear campaigner found murdered close to her home near Shrewsbury in 1984. At first the police claimed simply that her home telephone had been torn out of its socket at the time of the attack. After a number of people, including Tam Dalyell MP and the writer Judith Cook, pressed for further enquiries and made a few of their own, it transpired that Hilda Murrell's telephone had been dealt with in a different, and considerably more sophisticated way. According to Cook:

> An informed source from within British Telecom was to tell me later that the junction box had been unscrewed and only the green wire cut. Then the box was screwed back on again. The result was that while the line was obviously dead to anybody trying to ring out on it, any caller ringing in would hear the phone ringing as if all were in order but the occupant of the house was either out or not answering. Later, it was proved that a number of people had rung that particular number but had received no reply over the days before Hilda's body was found.[21]

A number of other suspicious circumstances led Tam Dalyell MP to accuse the intelligence services of murdering Hilda Murrell, but a police enquiry found no hard evidence to sustain this charge.[22] However, the knowledge of telecommunications necessary to disconnect the telephone in the way described is not usually possessed by the average house-breaker; on the other hand, Section A1A of MI5, responsible for break-ins, would certainly know how to do this.

The year before Murrell's death, there had been allegations that trades unionists had had their phones cut off at a strategic moment in an industrial dispute. Leaders of the POEU claimed that their home phones were put out of order at the same time that BT senior management was 'locking out' engineers working to rule in the international telephone exchanges.[23] In this case, though, there was no breaking and entering involved; the phones could have been disconnected at the local exchanges, or along the wires between the exchanges and the unionists' homes.

One-off disconnections like this, and indeed the Murrell case, are impossible to prove even to the satisfaction of a sympathetic observer, never mind the public at large. However, when cut-off incidents happen in a regular pattern, to a large number of people, over an extended period of time, it becomes the credibility of official denials that is at stake. Such a series of events has occurred with CND members involved in campaigning against American Cruise missiles in Britain.

The authorities claim that a great advantage of Cruise missiles is that they are mobile enough to move around the country on the back of huge lorries, so they can present no fixed target to enemy (Russian) strikes. The CND Cruise-watch campaign aims to ridicule this concept by showing that the vehicles engaged in Cruise exercises can be tracked around the country by ordinary people, armed only with telephones, patience, and the capacity to stay awake into the small hours of the morning: we can assume that if this is so, the facilities available to the Russian armed forces could also trace Cruise, rendering its *raison d'être* meaningless.

Cruisewatch members communicate the whereabouts of the missile convoys to each other by passing phone messages from person to person, down a so-called 'telephone tree'. From the time of the third nocturnal Cruise excursion in June 1984, just three months after Hilda Murrell's death, the telephone tree began to suffer from its own form of Dutch Elm disease. Many of the tree contacts reported their phones out of order, either sending the engaged tone to callers though no one was on the line, or simply going dead.

At the end of the year, CND publicised a dossier of such events.[24] The June Cruise exercise had seen five tree contacts with phones out of action, in July it was three tree contacts, plus CND headquarters and the London office of the womens' peace camp at Greenham Common airbase. Exercises in October and November repeated the pattern. The stories of played-back conversations recounted in Chapter 1 may be another part of the same campaign of telephonic harassment of CND. Since December 1984, when CND started publicising the cut-offs, the incidence of faults on the nights the Cruise convoys ride has declined. CND told us that mysterious things do still happen, particularly to Cruisewatch telephones in isolated parts of the country, but they are considerably rarer than in 1984.

It is true that our antiquated telephone network is prone to malfunction at any time, but it stretches coincidence beyond its limits to attribute all the CND stories to technical problems. We have already seen, in Chapter 2, that in the early 1980s the Government was prepared to stretch the rules to combat CND, and the balance of evidence, admittedly circumstantial, lends a lot of credence to CND's accusations.

The ultimate in active measures is British Telecom's Telephone Preference Scheme (TPS), defined in official instructions as:

> *a means of withdrawing outgoing service for most subscribers on an exchange so that service to preference subscribers may be safeguarded during civil or military emergencies, from the effects of congestion* [ie all lines engaged] *or loss of public power supplies.*[25]

Every telephone subscriber is allocated a secret 'preference category'. The vast majority are in Category 3, 'not entitled to preference in any emergency, civil or military'. In such circumstances, we would be unable to use our telephones at all, though the authorities would be able to ring us, for example to issue instructions.

Category 2 subscribers are normally limited to less than ten percent of the connections on any exchange; they are entitled to outgoing service in an emergency, because they are:

lines . . . required in a civil or military emergency for the maintenance of law and order, for the continuance of the various public services, for the distribution of essential supplies and generally to maintain the life of the community.

Category 2 includes 'Employers Associations', such as the CBI (though not the TUC), the homes of magistrates, sheriffs, lords lieutenant and judges (though not justices of the peace, solicitors, or law centres), and the homes of MPs and 'Key' council officials (names to be notified to BT by 'the Authority concerned'), but not elected Councillors.

During a 'war emergency', even Category 2 lines would be withdrawn from outgoing service, and only the highest category allowed the means of telecommunications. These Category 1 lines consist of:

only those lines required by the authorities responsible for the Fighting Services and essential public services to retain control of their organisations.

They are limited to less than two percent of the lines on any exchange, and consist largely of Government departments, suppliers of essential commodities such as oil and foodstuffs (distributors, but not retailers), and official bodies such as the BBC and IBA, and British Rail. Private homes are not usually included in Category 1.

In the local telephone exchange, all lines are wired according to their preference category, so that, for example, all Category 3 lines can be disconnected simultaneously. In modern exchanges, the system is started by the exchange manager inserting and turning a key into a lock in the side of the switching equipment. The system is then 'primed', and can be triggered to operate the preference system by simply keying two secret code numbers on an exchange telephone, which can be done from a remote position. In the older mechanical exchanges, a row of switches has to be thrown by an engineer to achieve the same effect.

So far, the system has only been used once in earnest, in 1975, when a telephone exchange in Newcastle was damaged in an explosion.[26] The preference scheme has never been operated on a national basis, except (on a purely theoretical

220

basis) during military exercises, when British Telecom takes a full part in the war games. In such circumstances, BT's main liaison point for the Ministry of Defence is a headquarters unit called LCS/ETA6 'Defence Enquiries', which took a major role in a nuclear war exercise codenamed 'Fanfare' in 1984, which was designed to test BT's emergency procedures.[27]

However, the TPS awaits, not just the prospect of nuclear war, but any serious unrest, such as a national strike. A Home Office circular states that the decision to operate the scheme rests on balancing:

> *service and economic considerations against security risks (of letting the exchange operate for a few days or weeks without preference) having regard to conditions at the particular exchange and current international or industrial tensions.*[28]

The secrecy surrounding the scheme is such that even those individuals who are assured of a place in Category 2 are not told of the fact. This is because some places (the BT instructions quoted above instance educational institutions) are on the TPS because they are to be requisitioned as Government stores, etc., in times of crisis.

The existence of the TPS proves nothing about the other 'active measures' of which BT and the Government have been accused, but it shows the degree to which British Telecom is bound up in the Government's defence and counter-subversion policies. The purpose of this chapter has been to show that the links between telecommunications and civil liberties are not confined to what is usually understood as tapping. Traffic analysis techniques and active measures are made easier and easier by advances in technology, and should be widely understood and discussed if the activities of the State in these areas are to be brought under public accountability, and informed by a sensitivity towards human rights, rather than an obsession with secrecy.

Chapter 10

The Future of Tapping

The advances in traffic analysis techniques outlined in the previous chapter are not the only changes in telecomms technology that should be of interest to anyone concerned about electronic eavesdropping. A number of developments are in the offing – System X, optical fibre cables, the so-called 'Integrated Services Digital Network' (ISDN) which will carry TV pictures and computer data on the same channels as phone calls; even, eventually, videophones – all of which carry implications for tapping.

The key thing that links these changes is that they all make use of *digital* signals, rather than the analogue signal that carries speech through the telephone network as a continuously varying electrical current. The new breed of high-tech telecomms engineers now refer to the latter – fondly or contemptuously – as 'POTS', Plain Old Telephone Service, and indeed phone calls will ultimately form only a small part of the digital telecomms system of the future. The notion of moving information around by encoding it in a digital form is today familiar to many people as the way computers work, so before examining the potential of digital phone tapping it is worth looking at computer communications, and at the distant relative of tapping known as 'hacking'.

Computers work by storing and moving around information, in the form of 'Bits', short for BInary DigiTS (computing is full of duff acronyms). In a digital system, data is encoded as strings of '0's and '1's, which, in a computer, are represented by the presence or absence of electrical pulses going through the millions of switches embedded in the microprocessor that make up the guts of the computer. The flow of bits, and thus the flow of information, is controlled by 'programs', instructions either held inside the computer hardware or fed in (as *software*) from devices plugged into the computer memory, such as keyboards or disk drives.

*Micro*computers, such as the machines in many homes, usually have only one screen and keyboard attached. Larger *Mini*computers and *Mainframes* often have many such terminals attched to them, and sometimes these can be quite a distance away from the main computer. Even microcomputers based miles apart from each other may be linked together, so that they can exchange information. On many occasions, then, computers need to communicate over a distance. Computer data may be transmitted, just like telephone signals, down cables or over high frequency and microwave radio systems. Over long distances, it is usually sent along normal telephone lines, after being changed, by a device known as a 'Modem' (MOdulator/DEModulator), out of its digital, on-off, form into a wave-like signal which can be carried by the analogue telephone network we currently enjoy.

Intercepting computer data can be done in one of two ways. If it passes through the phone system, or even a direct wire, it can be picked up by any of the normal amateur phone-tapping methods, though naturally the snooper needs a suitable terminal, rather than a telephone handset, to make the signal intelligible. Journalist Barry Fox described one occasion on which he tapped an 'electronic mail' system, which sends data messages between computer terminals:

We tape-recorded the warbling sound that goes down the telephone line when an electronic mail communication is in progress. We taped only our own data but this is the kind of recording which can be made during a crossed line, by deliberate tapping, or even using an inductive loop near someone's telephone line. We then played back the tape recording through a low-fi loudspeaker, near the handset of a telephone hooked up to an electronic mail system. As if by magic the warble came up on screen as a replica of the original text, including our secret passwords![1]

BT also runs several specialist data transmission services for major data users, using an advanced technique called 'Packet Switching', which cannot be intercepted using these simple methods, though it should present no problems for profession-

223

al tappers, who can pick the traffic up at the appropriate exchange.

More common than computer tapping is *hacking*. A computer which can be dialled up on the telephone to allow its legitimate users to communicate with it from a distance may also be accessed by anyone with a computer and modem who wants to find out what is in the memory. The hacker needs to understand how to control the computer they have accessed, and most large organisations try to keep their data secret by restricting access to those who have an authorised user identity code and one or more passwords. Only when these are fed into the central processing unit (CPU) will the computer allow access to its memory.

Hackers obtain this information, and the telephone numbers which will enable them to dial up the computer, in several ways: sometimes, they have inside information leaked by someone who knows the computer system. On other occasions, trial and error may lead a hacker to penetrate a system. Once obtained, codes and phone numbers are quickly passed around the hacking community. Books on hacking techniques, such as *The Hacker's Handbook*, are readily available; terminals as simple as a standard home computer system can be used, and modems that will communicate with most major computer systems can be bought for around £100 (at 1986 prices).

Most hackers do it purely for fun, though the techniques can be used to commit computer crimes. When hacking is discovered, it is often because the interlopers have left some cryptic message in the system. Even when this happens, hacking is rarely prosecuted. However, recent precedent, in the case of the Prestel hackers, shows that it can be illegal in Britain, strangely enough under the forgery laws. The case also illustrates the use of some new interception techniques.[2]

Prestel is a computerised information system run by BT. It allows subscribers to set up or access information databases and to swap messages by depositing them in electronic 'mailboxes'. In 1984, a computer enthusiast named Robert Schifreen stumbled upon an astonishingly simple code sequence (ten 2s as an identity code, followed by the password '1234') which belonged to a former senior manager with Prestel, and had not been deleted from the system when he left. This enabled Schifreen to get into, not the main Prestel computers, but a special development computer used by Prestel staff testing new ideas.

A few months later, he accessed the same computer again. This time he discovered in one of its files the ID codes and passwords of Prestel's Systems Manager and Systems Editor. Computing systems managers and editors have a lot of power to move around and change the files on their computers, far more than ordinary users, and it was clear to Schifreen that this had a lot of hacking potential. He called a friend, Steve Gold, who knew the Prestel System well because he operated a message system called 'MicroMouse', for computing hobbyists.

Schifreen and Gold became very familiar with the Prestel system. They left messages in the files of a company named Timeframe, who provides a business information service for the retail industry, and read through the 'letters' in several mailboxes, including the Duke of Edinburgh's, where they left a note saying 'I do so enjoy puzzles and games. Ta ta! Pip!' In their innocence, the pair actually confessed about their activites to Prestel, to enable them to plug the security gap. Prestel responded by changing all users' codes. However, they also told the newly-created BT Investigation Department (BTID), formed out of the POID with similar targets and powers to its predecessor, but also containing a number of specialist computer detectives among the thirty-two investigators on its staff. The Prestel hackers were to be their first targets.

Even when the identity of the hackers was known, bringing them to trial certainly took time and ingenuity. The BTID (without, apparently, the need for any kind of warrant or permission) attached two pieces of equipment to Schifreen's and Gold's telephone lines. One was an ordinary metering device, called the 'Miracle Call Logger'; the other was a 'Data Monitor', which selects and records only *data* transmissions down the line to which it is attached, and not ordinary voice conversations.

By early 1985, Schifreen was beginning to embarrass BT by publicising his exploits in the computer press and on television, and in March BT had enough evidence from their interceptions to call in the police. The pair were charged with 'uttering a false instrument with the intention of inducing someone to accept it as genuine', under the 1981 Forgery and Counterfeiting Act. The 'instrument' in question was a floppy disk on which the codes for access to Prestel were stored. In April 1986, after a lengthy trial, they were fined a total of £1,300, with £1,000 costs: they could have gone to gaol.

Computer data is not the only kind of information which can be turned into bits and transmitted in digital form; the human voice, too, can be encoded like this. This is the principle used by the digital PBXs and System X exchanges mentioned in the last chapter, and also that of modern transmission systems, such as 'pulse code modulation' (PCM), which turns telephone signals into digital form to transmit them at high speed through the more advanced parts of the UK trunk network. The main advantage of digital methods for the network operator, such as the PBX owner or BT, is simply that they can handle many more calls much faster than conventional telecommunications.

In a conventional telephone network, the sound of the human voice is converted into an electrical current, which takes a form analogous to the speech pattern; as the sound of the voice on the telephone changes, so does the shape of the electrical signal on the line. In such a system, the *switching* of this current is done in one or more exchanges by making a physical connection within the exchange machinery, allowing the signal to flow from one part of the exchange to another, and eventually out to another exchange or to the called telephone. The path of this flow through the switches is determined solely by the number dialled and the physical configuration of the exchange.

In a *digital* transmission system, on the other hand, sound is converted in a series of bits, each string of digits corresponding to a particular voice sound level (the method of sampling and coding is similar to the techniques used to create high quality digital LP records). Digital *switching*, whether in an advanced PBX or a System X exchange, is accomplished by powerful ('Large Scale Integrated' in the jargon) microchips. Digital exchanges are, in effect, giant computers; they move information around in the same way as more conventional computers, but that information happens to be digitally encoded human voice signals. Like the movement of data

226

through a computer, the path of a call through these exchanges is controlled by software programs stored within the system, and by instructions typed into a terminal attached to the exchange. As we shall see, this has important implications for the tappers.

If the main benefit of digitalisation for the network operator is in the areas of speed and capacity, for the ordinary user it provides a wide range of new facilities to add to the POTS. Some of these, such as short-code dialling and redialling of engaged calls, are available built into modern telephones themselves, courtesy of the ubiquitous microchip. Other services come with digital PBXs; these include three (or more) way 'conference calls', 'call diversion' (which allows extension users to 'forward' their calls to another extension), and the call-logging facilities discussed in the previous chapter. System X and other digital local exchanges offer all these, and more, to all those connected to the exchange, rather than just customers with special phones or advanced private exchanges. These facilities, which BT calls 'star services', are possible because of the *programmable* nature of digital systems. They sound quite attractive as options for the telephone user but the same programs, only slightly modified, made the tappers' lives much easier.

When customers key out the codes for a star service on their telephones, this activates a particular program in the exchange. Other programs are run from computer terminals attached to the exchange. When System X begins to predominate in the network, much of this work will be done from Operations and Maintenance Centres (OMCs), each of which will control up to thirty local System X exchanges. According to BT,[3] the functions of an OMC are maintenance, service management, network management and customer billing, but in fact they will also carry out official tapping on behalf of the police and intelligence services.

In its essence, all conventional tapping consists simply of attaching an extension telephone to the target's line. Whether this is done at the exchange by professionals or by the methods described in Chapter 8, there is always a physical tap somewhere on the target's line which can be seen, if not by the tapped person then by BT engineers. Even with GCHQ's trawling techniques, tapping equipment in the form of microwave aerials, strange sets of connections in the international exchanges, and so on can be discerned by the trained eye. Digital tapping is different. The tap leaves no physical presence anywhere; it is literally invisible, and makes no discernable changes to the telephone circuit being tapped.

Instead, it works by utilising the conference call programs built into digital switching systems. However, instead of openly bringing together a number of callers so they can have a many-sided conversation, a secret third phone is brought into the line by keying a few codes into the exchange terminals in the Operation and Maintenance Centre. No technician in the target's exchange will ever be able to discover the tap, and only engineers with high security passes (probably from management rather than technical grades) will ever know what has happened. Ultimately, the tappers' customers could even do it themselves, if provided with suitable terminals and instructions.

Contrary to assertions by BT,[4] digital exchanges make tapping easier in a number of ways. Taps can be installed more easily and quickly, so they are cheaper to set up, and the security risks inherent in traditional tapping are eliminated. No longer will the strangely-marked yellow vans sneak towards exchanges at night, but the lines into the tapping centres are likely to be busier than ever, and still more reels will be added to the continuously turning banks of tapes inside Tinkerbell's descendants.

Digitalisation, however, offers more to the tappers than just improvements in operational efficiency and security. As the National Council for Civil Liberties have pointed out,[5] the invisibility of System X taps could encourage the growth of unauthorised tapping as a result of informal contacts between the police and BT staff. At the moment, the risk of such taps being detected probably acts as a deterrent to such activities; in the future this risk will be negligible. Trawling, too, will potentially become easier. The 'network management' facilities which are built into digital exchanges to enable them to route calls wherever they want will allow particular circuits to be routed through a point in the network where a suitable 'trawling net' is installed; this could be a metering device, a voice or speech recognition system, or a data monitor.

We have already seen in the last chapter how digital PBXs

228

and System X exchanges both offer similar call logging or metering facilities, and for tapping, too, digital PBXs give the snoopers System X-like facilities. In the past, large private switchboards presented a problem for the tappers: they either had to monitor *all* conversations going through the system (and then screen the innocent calls out, manually or by the use of expensive voice recognition equipment), or, alternatively, to fit a tap between the target extension and the PBX. This latter necessitated either getting the permission of the person running the PBX or setting up a 'black bag job', involving breaking in or using deception to gain access to the premises where the private network is installed. In principle, digital PBXs offer a solution to this problem; they have 'conference call' programs which can be modified to create invisible taps, just like System X. The problem is that the modifications are not built in. However, engineers assure us that with sufficient knowledge of how a particular PBX works, a tapper can dial in and key a series of codes which will activate the conference call program and allow silent interception of a particular extension.

The Government's telecommunications regulatory body, OFTEL, now requires manufacturers of large digital PBXs to lodge with them:

> *a copy, in machine readable format, of the full listing of all stored commands or other stored information contained in the approved system. With this must be an explanatory commentary, in English.*[6]

This requirement is more onerous than it appears to the inexpert eye. 'Machine readable' means in binary digits, '0's and '1's, and these 'machine-code' instructions for a large digital PBX would cover hundreds of thousands of pages. OFTEL will need a number of large warehouses to house this information for all the machines on the market. Specialist engineers have told us that there is no legitimate reason why OFTEL should need this information: all the technical details of how a new PBX works that might conceivably be required are available from the British Approvals Board for Telecom-munications (BABT), which tests all new PBXs exhaustively before they are able to be connected to the BT system. What these listings will do, though, if passed on to experts in the tapping establishment, is enable them to understand the conference call programs enough to tap an individual extension, and more than one source has told us that this is, in fact, the purpose of the OFTEL regulation.

As far as PBXs are concerned, digitalisation is already with us, although it is not clear whether any manufacturers of large private exchanges have yet actually deposited all this information with OFTEL. Where System X is concerned, however, the digitalisation timetable has been slipping further and further into the distance, owing to technical problems with the system's operating software. First unveiled as early as 1979, there is still, at the time of writing, only one System X local exchange operating, at Baynard House in the City of London (though there are a number of digital trunk exchanges in the network). BT and Plessey are, however, now believed to have overcome most of the software difficulties, and System X will be progressively installed over the next ten years.

By the mid-1990s, we should have a largely digital network. To speed up the process, BT have decided to buy a number of AXE 10 digital exchanges for the Swedish based manufacturer, Ericsson. Dubbed 'System Y' by the press, these exchanges are fully compatible with System X, and as far as tapping is concerned, they have very similar facilities. The role of digital telecommunications in the new technology era which we are entering has been described as analogous to that of the railways, canals, and roads during the industrial revolution; for tapping its impact will be just as revolutionary.

Despite the interception and traffic analysis facilities of System X, digital speech transmission need not necessarily work in favour of the tapper. Encryption has cropped up at intervals throughout this book with reference to telegram and telex transmissions, but not in the context of telephone conversations. Cyphers, by their very nature, act on discrete quantities, such as the individual letters of a written message, but cannot be applied directly to a continuous signal like analogue speech. By contrast, digital transmission reduces all communications, spoken or not, to an exchange of bits, so that any suitable encryption method can be applied uniformly to voice, text, data, facsimile or video.

Since the First World War, Britain's cryptographic industry

230

has operated under the tight control of GCHQ and its predecessors. Although it has proved impossible to dissuade enthusiastic amateurs from devising new, and sometimes effective, cyphers and cypher equipment, the SIGINT establishment has acted quickly to thwart any commercial manifestations which might hamper their own activities. The Patent Office, to which hopeful cypher wizards invariably turn to guard against plagiarism, offers an ideal monitoring mechanism. In 1951, one Christopher Henn-Collins filed a patent application for a coding machine, only to have a secrecy order lodged against the design by the Patent Office.[7] In February 1984, a similar fate befell a system, developed by the Barnsley company JLC Data, for preventing unauthorised copying of computer disks. The company's method appears to have borne an unwelcome similarity to GCHQ's own disk security system.[8]

GCHQ has been obliged to relax its stranglehold over cryptography slightly in the last few years, following a rapid increase in business demand for encryption products. This is partly accounted for by the growth of commercial data communications, especially in the financial sector, where security is at a premium; but it also derives from provisions in the 1984 Data Protection Act which requires the custodians of personal data to guarantee the security of that information during transmission. GCHQ nonetheless retains a dominant influence in the field. A plethora of small companies have now joined the established contractors – GEC–Marconi, Plessey and Racal – to exploit the new market.

For many years, the leading commercial encryption system was IBM's LUCIFER cypher by virtue of its adoption, in a revised version, by the American Government in 1977 to serve as the nation's Data Encryption Standard (DES).[9] The DES cypher is generally carried on a specially designed microprocessor, which is fitted into a customer's computers. (It is possible to implement any cypher as a software program, but the encryption process is generally much slower.) The DES cypher works by putting uncoded data through a mathematical procedure called an 'encryption algorithm'. The precise effect on the input data, however, is governed by the choice of a single binary number, known as the 'key'. Changing the key used with the cypher alters the encrypted data stream; the

231

algorithm is characteristic of an individual cypher, and cannot be changed. The LUCIFER cypher is constructed symmetrically, so that the same key is used for both encryption and decryption. The idea is that only the sender and the recipient know the key, so that an eavesdropper, who may be aware of the algorithm, must nonetheless test many different keys in order to decode the intercept. The number of possibilities rises as the number of digits in the key increases; the longer the key, the more secure the cypher.

LUCIFER's original key contained 128 bits, but by the time the cypher was formally chosen for the US Data Encryption Standard, it had 'mysteriously' shrunk to 56 bits. The National Security Agency, which was intimately involved in the development of LUCIFER, was widely held to be responsible. The agency was further accused of rigging the cypher in various ways to ensure that it could still read LUCIFER–encrypted traffic.[10]

Until very recently, the Data Encryption Standard was the only commercial cypher available as a microprocessor device. Following the Reagan administration's imposition of rigorous controls on advanced technology trade from 1980 onwards, potential DES users outside the United States, including those in Britain, encountered increasing difficulty in obtaining the necessary export licences. Among them was British Telecom, who needed an encryption process for their new 'SatStream' satellite business service.[11]

SatStream, which came into service in 1984, offers private circuits via the European Communications Satellite to Western Europe through a small dish aerial, typically twelve feet in diameter, installed on the customer's premises. With a similar arrangement at the far end, BT and the other carriers involved in the service need only allocate satellite channels as appropriate: there is no switching, and no call on any other part of BT's network. (BT also maintains its own SatStream earth stations with orthodox links to private circuit customers.) According to the corporation:

the broadcast capability of SatStream allows customers' transmissions to anywhere in Europe with relatively small and cheap earth stations. This is a significant advantage over the terrestrial network, but at the same time it makes the links more vulnerable to eavesdropping . . . The unauthorised reception of SatStream traffic would require considerable expertise and financial investment; nevertheless it was decided to develop an optional encryption facility to provide for the total security of sensitive customer data when this is required. This facility renders the data on the SatStream link entirely unintelligible to all except the intended recipient stations.[12]

Although DES was initially favoured by British Telecom, the cypher was found to have technical limitations when used on high-speed data channels carrying digital video and satellite transmissions. Fortuitously:

an alternative, unencumbered algorithm was made available by British Telecom Cryptographic Products, which was internationally adopted for exclusive use on the SatStream service. This algorithm has been called TACA (Telecommunications Administrations Cryptographic Algorithm) and uses a 96-bit keyvariable.[13]

This home-grown algorithm, known within the corporation as B152, can also operate with a 64-bit key. In the second half of 1984, BT's research laboratories at Martlesham in Suffolk designed a microprocessor, entitled B-Crypt, running on this shorter key. Since further development under the supervision of BT's Data Security Laboratory in Ipswich, B-Crypt is shortly expected to go into commercial production, at the Hughes Microelectronics plant in Scotland. British Telecom is looking to establish B-Crypt and the B152 algorithm as European standards, but has denied that it has any similar aspirations further afield.[14]

B-Crypt's resistance to cryptanalysis has undoubtedly been thoroughly investigated by GCHQ, to whom British Telecom submitted it, apparently in the hope of having it approved for sale to government departments. Although it is far better adapted for satellite transmission, B-Crypt does not seem to be significantly stronger than DES, which, at the time of its adoption in 1977, was expected to last no more than ten or fifteen years before a general solution was found. Once again, though, the relationship between GCHQ and British Telecom may prove more important than the inherent properties of the cypher: the question of whether or not GCHQ can decode fully encrypted SatStream transmissions is academic while the possibility exists that the agency has access to the cypher keys. Since these are under BT control, the possibility is a real one.

SatStream proved to be a popular service with BT's large business customers. In the summer of 1985, SatStream links were opened to North America, attracting a number of prestige clients, including the US Embassy in London, the *Financial Times*, the electronics group Texas Instruments, and the Canadian-based multinational Massey-Ferguson. Private satellite circuits are one of the fastest-growing parts of British Telecom's international business: GCHQ Cheltenham, as ever, will be listening in.

Another increasingly popular telecommunications facility is 'Cellular Radio', which links portable telephones (often in cars) to each other, and to the normal telephone network, by using radio signals in the 900MHz region, just below microwave frequencies. Both BT's 'Cellnet' and the rival 'Vodafone' network run by Racal work by dividing the country into a number of 'cells', each with a receiver station which also acts as an exchange to switch calls coming in from the portable telephones within its ambit. As callers move about from one cell to another, the telephone automatically locks onto the appropriate receiver.

The concept of portable telephones has been a popular feature of science fiction for decades, and unsurprisingly the new systems (if not their cost) have been met with considerable acclaim. Sometimes, however, this has gone too far: one *Guardian* journalist cited as an advantage of portable systems 'freedom (presumably) from the attentions of the tappers'.[15] The writer presumes too much; there is no such freedom. The tappers can intercept such transmissions in one of two ways, either by trawling through the radio waves using techniques akin to those used on microwaves, or by using the clause in the telecomms legislation which forces the network operators to co-operate with official tapping 'in the interests of national security'. The operators will then have to allow tapping at the receiver stations, which can be carried out in a similar way to local exchange tapping.

The introduction of Cellular Radio, expansion of small dish services, and System X, are only three parts of BT's program-

234

me of technical development over the next couple of decades. Perhaps even more important is the installation of optical fibre cables in the UK trunk network, in place of the copper wire or coaxial cables used until recently. The latter can handle digital transmission, with digital pulses replacing the analogue signals of earlier systems, but optical fibres can carry many more digital calls much faster and less expensively. Instead of an electrical signal, they have a laser or a Light Emitting Diode (LED – a similar device to that used to light up the numerals on some pocket calculators) which flash pulses of light down a glass tube. The glass is carefully manufactured so that it does not refract any of the light out of the cable, but reflects the signal down through its core at the speed of light, the on-off pulses of the light source representing digital bits. By 1990, fifty per cent of the trunk network will be optical fibres. For international routes, the comparatively low cost of optical fibres threatens, in the long run, the financial viability of the satellite system. The first submarine optical fibre cable, between Broadstairs and the Belgian port of Ostend, is due to come into operation in 1987, followed in 1988 by the first transatlantic system. Ultimately, the major telecomms countries aim to encircle the globe with vast capacity optical fibre cables.

Optical fibres are said to be untappable. Certainly, it is impossible to use a conventional direct or induction tap along such a cable, but, as we have seen, practically nobody taps into main cables in any case. The professionals do it at the exchange, the amateurs at the target phone or along the line between telephone and junction box. Optical fibre transmission does not affect exchange tapping, while the local network from telephone to main distribution point (and probably further) will remain electrical rather than optical for the foreseeable future because the advantage of optical fibres – their large capacity and low cost – is wasted when only one phone call at a time is required. Until the telephone cable from one's home carries cable TV pictures, or videophones are installed in place of telephones, the freelance tapper's skills will still be in demand.

For the near future, then, the untappability of optical fibres is largely irrelevant, except for government and other high security phone systems, which may well become all-optical and defeat tapping. It is possible that freelance tapping will eventually be rendered technically impossible, but it would be making a big assumption to claim that no means of tapping optical fibre cable will ever be invented.

In the long term, a network based on digital exchanges linked by powerful optical fibre cables can carry much more information than simply phone calls. Computers, cable television systems, facsimile machines (which send copies of pictures through phone lines), videophones and other devices will all be sending digital signals through such a telecomms network, called the 'Integrated Services Digital Network' (ISDN). As an ISDN develops, it will first be of use to business and other organisations that use many computers and sophisticated office equipment, but ultimately such services are expected to be extended to the home. The more important telecommunications becomes in our lives, the more information about us can be obtained by tapping.

The science fiction prospect of videophones replacing telephones, so that callers can see, as well as hear, the people they are talking to, may, in fact, not be far ahead. Videophones have been technically feasible for decades, the problem has been the cost of transmitting moving pictures, which take up a thousand times more cable capacity than speech signals. However, a solution has now been found; instead of transmitting the whole picture throughout the 'call', a computer picks up *changes* in the picture (for example, a slight movement by the person being filmed), and sends only the change down the line. This takes up significantly less capacity than sending the whole picture, and makes videophones look economically feasible in the era of fibre-optics and System X.

Videophones are a tapper's dream. Equipped with cameras as well as microphones, and programmable, they could easily be modified to offer the snooper a combined bug, tap and visual surveillance system; the satirical nightmare of George Orwell's *Nineteen Eighty-Four* would become a reality. By then, unless society has evolved ways of controlling covert surveillance by the state, we will run the risk of becoming a society with no private space, anywhere.

Alongside these advances in telecommunications technology will come new tapping techniques. Perhaps the most important developments are likely to be in the areas of speech and

236

voice recognition, where the cost and reliability of equipment are likely to improve considerably over the next few years, especially now that the commercial potential of such systems is recognised. As this technology improves, and with the advanced call logging and tracing facilities offered by System X, trawling techniques are increasingly likely to be used for all sorts of taps.

According to one expert, the British intelligence complex has been looking at ways of avoiding the brute force, Cray approach to speech processing. Small computers could be equipped with specially built 32-bit microprocessors, each of which can search for between five and ten key words, with a success rate of seventy-five percent, while tolerating background noise of up to half the strength of the signal itself. The Royal Signals and Radar Establishment has shown great interest in the Inmos 'Transputer', a 32-bit processor with built-in memory storage and communications facilities, which will allow a more flexible internal design for computers and simplify the kind of pattern-matching used in voice and speech recognition. This approach may well finally overcome the eavesdropper's worst problem, which is not the installation of the tap or bug, but processing the results to exclude irrelevant material.

Trawling, however, is unlikely ever wholly to supersede the conventional tapping of all calls from a particular line: for important targets no other method will do. As far as such interception is concerned, it seems likely that the police and intelligence services would prefer to be able to do their own tapping, rather than relying on the System X Operations and Maintenance Centres. Any such increase in the independence of the tappers from the telecom carriers is likely to make unauthorised tapping easier.

Only in the area of freelance tapping does the current technology trend promise to *reduce* the level of eavesdropping, and we have already expressed our doubts about the extent to which this is likely to happen in practice. Even if it does, the freelance snoopers are likely simply to turn to bugging as an alternative source of information. The demand for industrial espionage seems to be rising and, especially with the current state of the law, the number of companies offering electronic covert surveillance services is almost certain to increase with it. The future looks bright for the practitioners of the black bag job.

The orthodox tapping establishment also seems set to grow. Recent years have seen an increasing concentration on the part of the police on public order and counter-subversion, in which they are following the realignment of the intelligence services towards 'the enemy within', rather than foreign espionage. In foreign affairs, too, 'economic' targets (based in the UK, even though the warrants are signed by the Foreign Secretary) seem to be replacing diplomats and the like as a tapping priority.

As information gathering becomes more and more important to the State and other bodies, and the technologies of both telecommunications and tapping become increasingly efficient, so the risk to our civil liberties will rise as well. Bureaucracies have their own internal momentum, and will always seek to widen the scope of the empires they control: when comparatively free from public scrutiny and legal constraints, as the tappers are in the UK, they are likely to succeed. Any overall assessment must conclude that the tapping industry, in all its manifestations, both public and private, looks set for a boom period in the last decade and a half of the twentieth century.

In this chapter, and throughout the book, we have concentrated on the technology of tapping. Given the boundlessness of the State's appetite for information, interception is limited only by technological boundaries. Moreover, as in the case of the American Omnibus Crime Control and Safe Streets Act, a law designed for the technology of a previous era will fail to control tapping. However, we are not technological determinists; the technology-driven expansion of tapping we predict for the near future is not inevitable although the process of halting it, and reasserting the civil right to privacy, will not be an easy one in the UK. More than in any other Western nation, the culture of secrecy is embedded deep in the British unwritten constitution.

This means that an improved anti-tapping law would not be enough. At its best, such legislation might, for example, restrict tapping to cases of serious crime (which would include espionage and terrorism, but certainly not 'subversion'), include bugging and other forms of electronic surveillance, and bring an element of judicial or parliamentary scrutiny into

238

the granting of warrants. However, in the absence of effective democratic controls over MI5, SIS, and GCHQ (with its UKUSA treaty obligations to tap), the experience of our own and other countries indicates that a loophole would be found, or illegal methods used. Moreover, judicial control would be no control, in the present state of the legal system. Trust in the intelligence establishment is a driving force in the world of judges; once the magic words 'national security' are spoken, all concern for individual liberty flies out of the window. As Professor Graham Zellick, editor of the journal *Public Law*, said of MI5 and SIS:

> *The courts know nothing of their existence, and, to exacerbate the problem, run from questions of national security as a fox does from hounds.*[16]

This has meant that successive governments, of all parties, have been able to resort to the magic words whenever they felt threatened by public disclosures of their eavesdropping activities. This has been necessary perhaps primarily because in Britain telephone tapping has been conducted in an environment in which most people maintain a profound cultural antipathy towards snooping of any kind, and an ingrained, often indignant support for the individual right to privacy – even if this concept is not recognised in the law of their land. Consequently, even the discussion of tapping is forbidden.

Telephone tapping is one of around a hundred topics about which the Government will not answer detailed questions from MPs. Press enquiries have been deflected by more subtle means. On the one hand, there is the lobby system, whereby the Government maintains an unhealthy conviviality with the media by leaking whatever suits the political purposes of the day. On the other, there is the 'Defence, Press, and Broadcasting Committee' of the Ministry of Defence, where executives from the press and broadcasting organisations hold regular meetings with senior civil servants to agree on those areas which should not be mentioned in the media without reference to Whitehall. The Committee's conclusions are relayed throughout the mainstream media in the form of 'D-Notices'.

There are currently eight D-Notices, each of which lays out

239

a number of unmentionable topics. Number Six, issued in March 1986, is entitled *British Security and Intelligence Services*. It asks, amongst other items, that:

> *nothing should be published . . . about details of the manner in which operational methods, including the interception of communications, are actually applied and of their targets.*

D-Notices are issued as requests and have no force in law; the law's only sanction is the threat of exclusion from informal access to privileged information from the inner sanctums of Government. The flaw in the system became apparent when publications with no interest in, or likelihood of receiving, such information, and no representation on the Defence, Press and Broadcasting Committee, began simply to ignore D-Notices. By the late 1970s, more mainstream publications were following suit, and the system fell into disrepute.

The Government's ultimate weapon for suppressing media coverage of embarrassing subjects is Section 2 of the 1911 Official Secrets Act, which outlaws the receipt of official information by any 'unauthorised person'. This much derided and unwieldy piece of legislation was last used against journalists in the 1978 Aubrey, Berry, Campbell prosecution, which concerned the disclosure of information about Britain's signals intelligence capability. Although the jury returned guilty verdicts on some of the charges, the Labour government of the day suffered a public relations mauling, especially from its own supporters, for its efforts on behalf of State secrecy. The pressure for a revamped secrecy law grew, but, by the time Whitehall had drafted suitable legislation, it was 1979, and the newly-elected Thatcher administration was in power.

Although it was touted as freedom of information legislation, the object of the draft Protection of Official Information Bill was not to lift the veil of secrecy surrounding the hidden recesses of the State, but to ensure more successful prosecutions than were likely under the discredited 1911 Act. The kernel of the legislation was the creation of six categories of 'official' information, disclosure of which would become an imprisonable offence. Number four concerned:

> *Information obtained by reason of the interception of . . .*

240

telecommunications conversations, messages or signals in pursuance of a requirement imposed or authorisation given on behalf of the Crown, and information relating to the obtaining of information by reason of any such interception.

In other words, the Bill gave D-Notice 6 legal force by forbidding any mention of the targets and methods of state-sponsored phone tapping. Fortunately for the reader's right to peruse this book, the bill was stopped in its tracks by the exposure of art historian and royal functionary Anthony Blunt as a Soviet agent. The press and parliament realised that this disclosure would have been illegal had the 1979 Bill been law, and the Bill was withdrawn.

No further attempts have been made to revamp British secrets law and create a replacement for the D-Notice system. Instead, the Government has begun to use the Civil Law of Confidence against former employees who seek to expose State malpractices. This has the advantage of not requiring a jury trial; a claim is instead heard before a judge 'in Chambers', who may approve an injunction against the publication of the information. At least three books have recently been halted in this way, including the memoirs of former MI5 agent Peter Wright, and *GCHQ: The Negative Asset*, an account by ex-employee Jock Kane of corruption and malpractice inside Britain's SIGINT empire.

The lesson of the 1979 Protection of Official Information Bill is an important one. Many civil libertarians pin their hopes on a Freedom of Information Act, but, unless the wording produced by the Whitehall mandarins is scrutinised extremely closely, any such measure runs the risk of simply replacing the unjust, but unworkable, Official Secrets Act with an unjust, but efficient, 'Freedom of Information' Act.

Neither a better Interception of Communications Act, nor freedom of information legislation will guarantee that we avoid the Orwellian prospects of a high-surveillance future. Far more important is open discussion and debate, together with public pressure to lift the miasma surrounding the secret state. This is a larger task than merely passing one or two pieces of legislation: it requires the ending of the subservient attitudes of the judiciary, parliament and the media towards questions of national security.

241

The forces pressing for this are currently few in number, but ought to be much larger. We have indicated a large range of people who are subject to tapping, not just political parties and pressure groups, but business executives, trades union members, and anyone who makes an international phone call. If all these were to add their voices to the already-convinced civil libertarians, the pressure for change might become irresistible.

References

INTRODUCTION

1   quoted in *The Socialist Register* 1979, p.279
2   *Computing*, 19 January 1984
3   *Business Week*, 24 October 1983

Chapter 1: FEAR OF TAPPING

1   House of Commons Hansard, 12 March 1985, col 241
2   Command 7873, '*The Interception Of Communications In Great
        Britain*', H.M.S.O., April 1980
        Command 9843, '*The Interception Of Communications*',
        H.M.S.O., February 1985
3   House of Commons Hansard, 12 March 1985, col 184
4   ibid., col 210
5   ibid., col 202
6   *Daily Express*, 20 October 1983
7   *Police Review*, 15 February 1985
8   *Observer*, 5 August 1984
9   see for example:
        The Sunday Times, 3 February 1980
        New Statesman, 9 February 1980
        Post Office Engineering Union, '*Tapping The Telephone*', p.10
10 House of Commons Hansard, 12 March 1985, col 158
11 ibid.
12 House of Lords Hansard, 26 February 1975, col 947
13 House of Commons Hansard, 11 July 1984, col 481
14 House of Commons Hansard, 12 March 1985, col 160
15 Interception of Communications Act (1985), section 2(3)
16 House of Commons Hansard, 12 March 1985, col 160
17 20/20 Vision, *MI5's Official Secrets*, Channel 4, 8 March 1985
18 quoted in *Observer*, 24 February 1985
19 20/20 Vision, *MI5's Official Secrets*, Channel 4, 8 March 1985
20 ibid.
21 ibid.

243

22 letter to *The Times*, 12 March 1985
23 Hampstead Group, Committee of 100, '*Mail Interception and Telephone Tapping In Britain*', p.7
24 ibid, p.8
25 ibid.
26 *The Sunday Times*, 17 February 1985
27 see Campaign for Nuclear Disarmament dossier, '*Telephone Problems At Times of Cruise Exercises*', 1985, p.8
28 *The Times*, 2 October 1978
29 House of Commons Hansard, 28 February 1985, cols 460–461
30 *The Sunday Times*, 3 February 1980
31 letter to *Guardian*, 5 March 1985
32 *New Statesman*, 1 February 1980
33 20/20 Vision, *MI5's Official Secrets*, Channel 4, 8 March 1985
34 ibid.
35 *New Statesman*, 1 February 1980
36 *The Sunday Times*, 3 February 1980
37 *The Times*, 4 February 1980
38 *The Leveller*, 18 September 1981
39 *Post Office Engineering Union Journal*, January/February 1984
40 *Guardian*, 19 May 1984
41 *Guardian*, 30 April 1984
42 20/20 Vision, *MI5's Official Secrets*, Channel 4, 8 March 1985
43 ibid.
44 *Guardian*, 4 May 1984
45 J. Coulter et al. *State Of Siege*, p.46
46 quoted in *Guardian*, 7 April 1984
47 see for example complaints by the 'Society For Individual Freedom', reported in *The Times*, 4 February 1970
48 quoted in *The Times*, 10 January 1980
49 quoted in *The Times*, 5 February 1980
50 *Guardian*, 19 December 1985
51 see Chapter 5
52 *The Times*, 4 February 1980
53 ibid.
54 *Observer*, 3 February 1980
55 *The Times*, 4 October 1974
56 Tony Bunyan, *The Political Police in Britain*, p.207
57 *The Times*, 29 July 1976
58 *The Times*, 4 February 1980
59 *Guardian*, 20 May 1981
60 *Daily Telegraph*, 20 November 1978
61 *Wiltshire Echo*, 19 August 1965
62 *The Times*, 2 September 1965

63 *Police Review*, 15 February 1985
64 *Guardian*, 28 November 1984

Chapter 2: THE TAPPERS AND THEIR TARGETS

Historical accounts of British intelligence can be found in:
Christopher Andrew, *Secret Service*; James Bamford, *The Puzzle Palace* (dealing with signals intelligence); and Tony Bunyan, *The Political Police in Britain*.

1 Anthony Verrier, *Through The Looking Glass*, p.26
2 Public Records Office, CAB 93/5 (file withheld)
3 Christopher Andrew, *Secret Service*, p.368
4 see for example: Nigel West, *A Matter of Trust: MI5 1945–72*,
     p.46
5 ex-MI5 officer Peter Wright, quoted in World In Action, *The Spy That Never Was*, Granada TV, 16 July 1984
6 clause 2 of the Maxwell-Fyfe Directive, quoted in part in
     Command 2152, 'Lord Denning's Report', para. 238
7 see for example:
     The Sunday Times, 12 December 1976 (re. Harold Wilson and
        the National Union of Seamen)
     Barbara Castle, *The Castle Diaries, 1946–70*, Weidenfeld and
        Nicolson, 1984, p.542 (re. Communist Party influence on
        AUEW)
8 *Observer*, 10 March 1985
9 Tony Bunyan, *The Political Police in Britain*, pp.276–7
10 *Observer*, 17 March 1985
11 published information on MI5:
     Observer, 3 March 1985
     Guardian, 17–19 March 1984 [series]
     Computing, 1 March 1984
12 *Guardian*, 2 December 1985
     information from London Borough of Haringey Council
13 *Guardian*, 13 December 1985
14 see Command 7873, '*The Interception of Communications in Great
        Britain*' para 22; Command 283, '*The Birkett Report*', para
        104
15 see for example: *Computing*, 19 September 1985
16 quoted in: *New Statesman*, 2 February 1979
17 James Bamford, *The Puzzle Palace*, p.311
18 Anthony Verrier, *Through The Looking Glass*, p.212
19 *New Statesman*, 2 February 1979

20 James Bamford, *The Puzzle Palace*, p.315
21 quoted in: James Bamford, *The Puzzle Palace* p.333
22 quoted in: *New Statesman*, 2 February 1979
23 James Bamford, *The Puzzle Palace*, p.xiv
24 *New Statesman*, 19 November 1982
25 *The Times*, 2 April 1984
26 James Bamford, *The Puzzle Palace*, p.xx
27 ibid, p.xxi
28 *The Times*, 21 November 1985 (advertisement)
29 David Kahn, *The Codebreakers*, p.266
30 Command 8787 (The Franks Report), pp.95–6
31 *New Statesman*, 19 November 1982
32 *Observer*, 3 March 1985
33 James Bamford, *The Puzzle Palace*, p.287

Chapter 3: LOCAL EXCHANGE TAPPING

1 see: *Police and Constabulary Almanac*, R. Hazell & Co, Henley, 1986, p.7
2 House of Commons Hansard, 7 February 1985, col 1125
3 Dick Lee and Colin Pratt, *Operation Julie*, p.206
4 Home Office, *Consolidated Circular to the Police on Crime and Kindred Matters*, 1977, paras. 1.70
5 *New Statesman*, 1 February 1980
6 Post Office Engineering Union, *Tapping the Telephone*, p.20
7 quoted in: *The Leveller*, no.21, December 1978
8 see for example:
   J. Atkinson, *Telephony*, Pitman, 1948, pp.775–6
   New Statesman, 9 February 1979
9 Nigel West, *A Matter of Trust: MI5 1945–72*, pp.18–9
10 Command 283, *The Birkett Report*, para 115
11 *The Sunday Times*, 20 June 1971
12 see: Peter Wright, ex-MI5 officer, quoted in *The Spy Who Never Was*, World In Action, ITV, 16 July 1984
   Public Records Office, DEFE 7/300 and 301 (withheld until 1991)
13 *Evening Standard*, 4 July 1973
14 Control Centres house operator staff who serve a number of local exchanges
15 *The Sunday Times*, 3 February 1980
16 ibid.
17 *New Statesman*, 1 February 1980
18 The process of fitting this sort of tap takes a matter of minutes.
19 *Observer*, 5 August 1984

Post Office Engineering Union, *Tapping The Telephone*, p.19
New Statesman, 1 February 1980

20 *Post Office Engineering Union Journal*, August 1980
21 see: Duncan Campbell, *War Plan UK*, p.169, p.191ff
    Post Office Telecommunications Journal, Spring 1970
22 information from Westminster City Council records
23 James Bamford, *The Puzzle Palace*, p.97
24 *The Sunday Times*, 3 February 1980
25 *New Statesman*, 1 February 1980
26 Dick Lee, *Operation Julie*, p.161
27 quoted in: 20/20 Vision, *MI5's Official Secrets*, Channel 4, 8
    March 1985
28 Command 7873, *The Interception of Communications in Great
    Britain*, para.15
29 *Panorama*, BBC1, 2 March 1981
30 *New Statesman*, 1 February 1980
31 ibid.
32 Home Office press officer, February 1985
33 *New Statesman*, 3 April 1981
34 *The Times*, 12 February 1982
35 information from Greater London Council and Westminster
    City Council records
36 *New Scientist, 28 February 1985*
    Observer, 5 August 1984
37 see: *The Sunday Times*, 27 February 1983
38 *New Statesman*, 3 April 1981

Chapter 4: TRAWLING

1   House of Comons Hansard, 2 April 1985, col. 1158
2   Rupert Allason, *The Branch*, p.22
3   James Bamford, *The Puzzle Palace*, pp.329–330
4   see: Command 283 *The Birkett Report*, para. 47
5   James Bamford, *The Puzzle Palace*, pp.xxiii–xiv
    New Statesman, 2 February 1979
    Time Out, 21 May 1976
6   *The Times*, 11 July 1957
7   House of Commons Hansard (written answers): 27 January
    1983, col 487; 7 February 1983, col 245; 22 February 1983,
    col 377
8   quoted in: James Bamford, *The Puzzle Palace*, p.171
9   quoted in: *New Statesman*, 21 February 1986
10 *Time Out*, 13 May 1983
11 *National Times* (Australia), 6 May 1983

12   Desmond Ball, *A Suitable Piece of Real Estate*, p.73
13   *The Times*, 2 February 1967
14   ibid.
     Private Eye, 21 June 1968
     Duncan Campbell, *The Unsinkable Aircraft Carrier*, pp.167–169
15   James Bamford, *The Puzzle Palace*, p.333
16   *Haagsche Courant* (Holland), 30 March 1983
17   *The Sunday Times*, 11 April 1982
18   *Guardian*, 6 July 1963
19   Patrick Beesly, *Room 40*, p.2
20   *Haagsche Courant* (Holland), 30 March 1983
21   *Covert Action Information Bulletin*, no.11, December 1980
22   This cable would have been laid by the invading Argentinian
     forces with the intention of maintaining secure
     communications with the mainland.
23   *The Sunday Times*, 20 June 1971
24   Charity registered with Charity Commissioners no.260106
25   *New Scientist*, 28 February 1985
26   Christopher Andrew, *Secret Service*, pp.400–401
27   Public Records Office, FO 850/283. Official Circular no.38,
     dated 28 July 1950, title as cited
28   Duncan Campbell, *The Unsinkable Aircraft Carrier*, pp.164–165
29   interview with former NSA official, February 1985
30   Chapman Pincher, *Inside Story*, p.245
31   *Computing*, 24 July 1980
32   James Bamford, *The Puzzle Palace*, p.245
33   ibid., p.250
34   *Observer*, 29 September 1985
35   *National Times* (Australia), 20 May 1983
36   Duncan Campbell and Steve Connor, *On The Record*, Michael
     Joseph, 1986, p.296
37   quoted in: *Guardian*, 27 January 1986
38   quoted in: *New Statesman*, 21 February 1986
39   Peter Lambley, *The Psychology of Apartheid*, pp.180–181
40   George M. White, *Speech Recognition, an idea whose time has
     come*, Byte, January 1984, p.213
41   John Holmes, former head of Joint Speech Research Unit,
     quoted in: *Guardian*, 30 August 1984
42   survey by Electronic Engineering, May 1982
43   M.J. Hunt et al., *Automatic Speaker Recognition for Use over
     Communication Channels*, record of the annual proceedings of
     the US Institute of Electrical and Electronic Engineers
     (IEEE) International Conference on Acoustics, Speech and
     Signal Processing, May 1977

44 M.J. Hunt, *Further Experiments in Text-Independent Speaker Recognition Over Communication Channels*, ibid., April 1983
45 ibid.
46 J.S. Bridle, *An Efficient Elastic-Template Method for Detecting Key Words in Running Speech*, paper to British Acoustical Society, April 1973
47 R.M. Chamberlain, J.S. Bridle, *A Dynamic Programming Algorithm for Time-Aligning Two Indefinitely Long Utterances*, IEEE Int. Conf. Acoustics etc., March 1983
48 *Covert Action Information Bulletin*, no.11, December 1980
49 interview with former NSA official, February 1985
50 J. Coulter et al., *State of Siege*, pp.46–47
51 *Private Eye* no. 607, 22 March 1985

Chapter 5: TAPPING, PARLIAMENT AND THE LAW

1 Command 283, 'Report Of The Committee of Privy Councillors Appointed To Inquire Into The Interception of Communications', chaired by Sir Norman Birkett QC, [henceforth 'Birkett'), para 9
2 ibid., para 31
3 ibid.
4 ibid., para 15
5 letter to *The Times*, 12 June 1957, from Edward F. Iwi
6 House of Commons Hansard, 29 October 1947, col 840
7 ibid., col 880
8 House of Commons Hansard, 3 December 1947, col 63
9 House of Commons Hansard, 11 January 1948, col 2096
10 House of Commons Hansard, 31 July 1952, col 1665
11 Account of the Marrinan case is largely based on: Birkett, paras 91–101. See also: *The Times*, 8 June 1957 and 11 June 1957
12 House of Commons Hansard, 6 June 1957, col 1461
13 House of Commons Hansard, 7 June 1957, col 1571
14 House of Commons Hansard, 27 June 1957, col 413
15 quoted in: H. Montgomery-Hyde, *Norman Birkett*, p.1
16 quoted in *The Times* 29 June 1957
17 *The Times*, 29 June 1957
18 Birkett, para 8.
19 ibid., para 53
20 ibid., para 50–52
21 ibid., para 70
22 ibid., para 64

23 ibid., para 68
24 ibid., para 107
25 ibid., para 56
26 ibid., para 129–131
27 ibid., para 95
28 ibid., para 100
29 ibid., para 153
30 ibid., para 101
31 ibid., para 175–6
32 Kenneth O. Morgan, *Labour In Power 1945–1951*, p.416
33 quoted in: *The Times*, 8 June 1957
34 quoted in *The Times* 7 September 1957
35 House of Commons Hansard, 31 October 1957, col 1260
36 *The Times*, 1 November 1957
37 *Daily Express*, 1 November 1957
38 quoted in: *The Times*, 31 December 1959
39 H. Montgomery-Hyde, op.cit., p.567
40 *The Times*, 32 December 1959
41 House of Commons Hansard, 3 December 1959, col 1388
42 Birkett, para 124
43 *The Times*, 18 November 1966
44 letter to *The Times*, 25 November 1966, from Dr Cyril Bibby
45 quoted in: *The Times*, 17 July 1970
46 House of Commons Hansard, 1 February 1973, col 1784–5
47 *The Times* (Law Report), 16 March 1968

Chapter 6: TAPPING LAW IN THE 1980s

'Megarry judgement'	Judgement of Sir Robert Megarry, Malone *v.* Commissioner of Police, All England Law Reports 1979, Vol.2, pp.621–650
European Court Documents European Commission 8691/79	European Commission of Human Rights, application no. 8691/79, James Malone against United Kingdom, report of the Commission, 17 December 1982
European Court:	European Court of Human Rights, Malone Case (4/1983/60/94); judgement delivered, 2 August 1984
Cour (83) 94	Memorial of the Government of the United Kingdom to Court, 14 October 1983

Cour (83) 42	Request of the European Commission of Human Rights bringing the case before the Court, 16 May 1983
Cour/Misc (84) 39	Note of Court hearing, 20 February 1984 (morning)
Cour/Misc (84) 40	ibid. (afternoon)
C (84) 57	Malone judgement, press release, 2 August 1984
Cour (85) 29	Text of settlement between applicant and UK Government, 18 March 1985

1 Megarry judgement, p.624
2 European Court, Cour/Misc (84) 40, p.1
3 European Court, Cour (83) 94, p.3
4 European Court, Cour/Misc (84) 39, p.27
5 Megarry judgement, p.621
6 ibid., p.631
7 ibid., p.638
8 European Commission 8691/79, p.2
9 European Commission 8691/79, pp.48–52
10 Command 7873, '*The Interception of Communications In Great Britain*', H.M.S.O., April 1980, para 4
11 ibid., para 8
12 Command 8191, '*The Interception of Communications in Great Britain (Report by the Rt. Hon. Lord Diplock)*' H.M.S.O., March 1981, p.2
13 Post Office Engineering Union, *Tapping The Telephone*, p.4
14 Public Records Office, 1955 Cabinet Papers, quoted in: *Guardian*, 2 January 1986
15 quoted in: *The Times*, 11 July 1980
16 Command 8191, p.2
17 *The Times*, 4 March 1981
18 Command 8191, p.2
19 Command 7873, para 10
20 House of Commons Hansard (written answer), 21 February 1982
21 see: *Guardian*, 8 January 1986
22 Command 8092, report of the Royal Commission on Criminal Procedure, (chair: Sir Cyril Phillips), January 1981, paras 3.56–3.60
23 House of Lords Hansard, 21 February 1984, col 637–8
24 House of Lords Hansard, 19 March 1984, col 1033
25 European Court, C (84) 57, p.5

26 Command 9438, 'The Interception of Communications',
        H.M.S.O., February 1985
27 Command 7873, para 9
28 Interception of Communications Act (1985), Section 4(1)(b)
29 ibid., Section 10(1)
30 House of Commons Hansard, 2 April 1985, col 1141
31 Command 9438, para 10
32 ibid., para 22
33 House of Lords Hansard, 6 June 1985, col. 917
34 Command 253 (The Birkett Report), para 152
35 House of Lords Hansard, 6 June 1985, col 952
36 House of Commons Hansard, 2 April 1985, col 1160
37 House of Commons Hansard, 12 March 1985, col 211–2
38 ibid., col 157
39 *The Times*, 6 March 1985
40 from John Marks and Victor Marchetti, *The CIA and the Cult of
        Intelligence*, Knopf, New York, 1974
41 House of Commons Hansard, 3 April 1985, col 1244
42 House of Commons Hansard, 12 March 1985, col 179

Chapter 7: THE SAME THE WHOLE WORLD OVER?

1 for a comparative study of tapping legislation in Europe, see:
        Council of Europe Legal Documentation and Research
        Division *Legislative Dossier No.2 – Telephone tapping and the
        recording of telecommunications in some Council of Europe
        member states*, Council of Europe, Strasbourg, May 1982
2 Article 5 §2 of the Convention of 26 May 1952 *On Relations
        Between The 3 Powers And The Federal Republic*, as amended
        by the Paris Protocol of 23 October 1954
3 account of Klass case from: European Court of Human Rights
        Case of Klass and Others – Judgement, Council of Europe,
        Strasbourg, 6 September 1978
4 P.J. Duffy, *The Case of Klass and Others – Secret Surveillance of
        Communications and The European Convention on Human
        Rights*. Human Rights Review, April 1979, p.34
5 see: S. Cobler, *Law, Order and Politics In West Germany*
        (London, Penguin, 1978); also *Guardian*, 18 March 1977
6 *Sunday Telegraph*, 7 December 1980
7 *Guardian*, 24 September 1980
8 case of *Nardone v. United States*, 308, US 338 (1939); quoted in
        Richard E. Morgan, *Domestic Intelligence* p.89, fn5

9   Clive Morrick, *Tapping Telephones In The United States*, New Law Journal, 14 June 1979
10 quoted in: Richard E. Morgan, *op.cit.*, p.89
11 *Guardian*, 16 September 1985
12 material in this chapter concerning the US National Security Agency and the Foreign Intelligence Surveillance Act is drawn mainly from: James Bamford, *The Puzzle Palace*, particularly chapters 2, 6, and 10
13 *New York Times*,
    4 March 1984,
    13 May 1984,
    13 September 1984
14 James Bamford, *The Puzzle Palace*, pp.249–250
    New York Times, 8 January 1981
    New York Times, 30 October 1984
15 *New York Times*, 13 September 1984
16 *New York Times*, 29 April 1982
17 *New York Times*, 3 June 1984
18 *New York Times*, 19 October 1984
    The Times (London), 27 November 1985
19 *Guardian*, 9 March 1985

Chapter 8: THE WILDER SHORES

1 House of Commons Hansard, 4 May 1982, col 13
2 Halsbury's Statutes: Current Statutes Service vol. 45 issue 4, pp.3–4 (Butterworths 1985)
3 House of Commons Hansard, 7 February 1985, col 1119
4 *Financial Times*, 8 February 1985
5 Command 5012, 'Report of The Committee on Privacy' (chair: Sir Kenneth Younger), H.M.S.O., July 1972 [henceforth 'Younger'], para 421
6 ibid., para 520
7 *New Scientist*, 10 July 1975
8 Younger, para 664
9 ibid., para 53(ii)
10 ibid., para 564
11 *The Times*, 11 February 1982
12 *Guardian*, 11 February 1982
13 *Guardian*, 24 February 1982
14 quoted in: *Policing London* no.6, February/March 1983
15 *Observer*, 15 December 1985
16 *New Statesman*, 1 February 1980, 8 February 1980
17 ibid., information from Southwark Council records

18   *Observer*, 15 November 1985
19   20/20 Vision, *MI5's Official Secrets*, Channel 4, 8 March 1985
20   ibid.
21   interview with South African exile, February 1982
22   Chapman Pincher, *Inside Story*, p.143
23   *New Statesman*, 8 February 1980
24   *Guardian*, 19 April 1984
25   *Guardian*, 5 February 1975
26   *Guardian*, 30 March 1985
27   *The Times*, 8 February 1975
28   John S. VanDewerker, *State of the Art of Electronic Surveillance*,
        submission to the US National Wiretap Commission, 1976,
        para 1.1.2.5., p.166
29   Nigel West, *A Matter Of Trust: MI5 1945–72*, p.73
30   *Guardian*, 3 June 1978
31   House of Commons Hansard, 21 July 1986, col 52
32   *New Statesman*, 22 February 1980
33   *Observer*, 24 September 1984
34   *New Statesman*, 22 February 1980
35   *Panorama*, BBC1, 23 February 1981
36   *Observer*, 27 January 1985
37   ibid.
38   *Observer*, 3 February 1985
39   *The Times*, 8 June 1973
40   Ben Jamil, founder of Communication Control Systems, quoted
        in: *Sunday Telegraph*, 13 June 1975
41   account of Jamil's career mainly drawn from: *New Statesman*, 7
        March 1980
42   *Daily Express*, 21 March 1984
43   information from Communication Control Systems
44   information from Cumberworth Surveillance and Lorraine
        Electronics Surveillance
45   *Sunday Telegraph*, 15 June 1973
46   P. Hamilton et al., *Handbook of Security*, Kluwer Publications
        (1985) Chapter 3.9, pp.07–08
47   *The Times*, 11 March 1967
48   *Guardian*, 1 February 1977
49   *Guardian*, 6 March 1980
50   *Guardian*, 17 November 1983
51   *Observer*, 2 February 1986
52   *Observer*, 26 January 1986
53   *The Times*, 22 October 1959
54   *The Times*, 1 September 1967
55   *Guardian*, 25 August 1977

58   John S. VanDewerker, op.cit., para 1.3.5, p.177
59   Frank Doherty, *SIGINT* Used by Anti-State Forces: A Case
        Study of Provisional IRA Operations, published in: Celina
        Bledowska (ed.), *War and Order*, pp.117–123
60   *Sunday Pictorial*, 30 March 1952
61   *Daily Express*, 1 November 1957
62   *International Security Review*, 1978
63   J. Davies, Lord Gifford, T. Richards, *Political Policing In
        Wales*, Welsh Council for Civil and Political Liberties (1984),
        Ch.6, pp.39–40
64   British Telecom, Staff Security Manual; extract quoted in:
        BSSRS, *Technocop*, p.45

Chapter 9: NOT QUITE TAPPING

1   There are thought to be an average of two to three MCPs per
        exchange
2   judgement of Sir Robert Megarry, Malone *v.* Commissioner of
        Police of the Metropolis (No.2), All England Law Reports
        [1979], Volume 2, (henceforth 'Megarry judgement'), p.639
3   European Court of Human Rights, Malone Case (4/1983/60/94):
        COUR (84) 8, Written Comments Submitted by the Post
        Office Engineering Union – Received 26.1.84 (Henceforth
        'Malone Case: POEU Comments') p.21 para 80
4   information from Communications Devices Ltd.
5   Malone Case: POEU Comments, p.23, para 94
6   GPO Telecommunications Instruction D1 COO21 ptII (June
        1979), p.7, para 34
7   Megarry judgement, p.639
8   Dick Lee and Colin Pratt, *Operation Julie*, p.101
9   HM Treasury (Central Computer and Telecommunications
        Agency) Information Technology Series No.1, *Telephone
        Extension Logging*, H.M.S.O, April 1983, p.8, para 5.4
10   *Top Security*, May 1977
11   House of Commons Hansard, 17 July 1981, col 284
12   *Guardian*, 23 July 1981
13   Malone case: POEU Comments, paras 82–83, p.21
14   *Observer*, 1 September 1985
15   Plessey Group, *System X: The Optimum Solution*, 1981
16   David Waddington (Home Office minister), House of Commons
        Hansard, 3 April 1985, col 1312
17   European Court of Human Rights, Malone Case (4/1983/60/94):
        Cour (83) 94, Memorial of the Government of the UK
        received 14 October 1983, p.44, para 350

18 European Court of Human Rights, Malone Case (4/1983/60/94): Cour/Misc (84) 40, note of Court hearing 20 February 1984 (afternoon), p.32

19 European Court of Human Rights, Malone Case (4/1983/60/94): judgement, 2 August 1984

20 Malone case; POEU Comments, para 89, p.22

21 Judith Cook, *Who Killed Hilda Murrell?*, p.17

22 ibid., p.83, p.117

23 address by Phil Holt (President, Post Office Engineering Union) to public meeting at Conway Hall, London, 13 October 1983

24 Campaign for Nuclear Disarmament, *Reports of Telephone Problems at Times of Cruise Exercises*

25 GPO Telecommunications Instruction D1 BOO12 (1980), p.1 para 1; quoted in: *Time Out*, 23 January 1981

26 Duncan Campbell, *War Plan UK*, p.234

27 letter to BT trades unions, 30 March 1984

28 Duncan Campbell, *War Plan UK*, p.235

Chapter 10: THE FUTURE OF TAPPING

1 *New Scientist*, 25 April 1985

2 full account of Gold/Schifreen trial in: *Telelink*, June 1986

3 A.A. Waliji, *The Architecture of System X, Part 4, The Local Administration Centre*, Post Office Electrical Engineering Journal, vol. 73, April 1980 [Local Administration Centre was the original title for OMC]

4 see for example: *New Scientist*, 24 April 1980

5 *New Scientist*, 23 October 1980

6 *New Approval Scheme Announced for Dealerboards*, Department of Trade and Industry, *Ringing The Changes*, 3 July 1985

7 Patent no. 1605232, see: *New Scientist*, 30 January 1986

8 *Computer News*, 1 March 1984

9 see for example: Data Security in Financial Networks, *Communications*, August 1985

10 James Bamford, *The Puzzle Palace*, pp.344–9

11 *Electronics Times*, 23 January 1986

12 C.B. Brookson & S.C. Serpell, *Security on the British Telecom SatStream Service*, paper to the Institution of Electrical Engineers, International Conference on Secure Communication Systems, 22–23 February 1984 (reprinted with amendments in: *British Telecom Technology Journal*, Vol.2 No.3, July 1984)

13 ibid.

14 *Electronics Times*, 23 January 1986
    Computer Weekly, 20 June 1985
    Telephone Engineer and Management, 1 December 1984
15 *Guardian*, 4 April 1985
16 Quoted in *Guardian*, 13 January 1986

Glossary of Terms and Acronyms

analogue	describes signals which vary continuously, such as speech
AZURE	MI5 codename for surveillance through an installed bug
BABT	British Approvals Board for Telecommunications
bit	binary digit (takes value 1 or 0)
BRUSA	Britain–United States signals intelligence treaty, superceded by UKUSA (see below)
BT	British Telecom
BTI	British Telecom International (division of BT)
BTID	British Telecom Investigation Department
C7	Metropolitan Police technical services division
C11	Metropolitan Police criminal intelligence division
cable vetting	interception of telegrams
cable censorship	another term for 'cable vetting'
carrier	an organisation which operates a public telecommunications system (like British Telecom)
CCS	Communication Control Systems Inc. (US)
CCU	Civil Contingencies Unit (section within the Cabinet Office)
cepstrum	mathematical expression used in speech analysis
CIA	Central Intelligence Agency (US)
CINNAMON	MI5 codename for surveillance through a combined bug and tap installed inside a telephone

CND	Campaign for Nuclear Disarmament
COCOM	Co-ordinating Committee for Multilateral Export Controls
COMINT	Communications Intelligence (a sub-category of SIGINT)
Commissioner	judge appointed to review the operation of the 1985 Interception of Communications Act
Committee of 100	group of 1960s peace activists independent of CND which promoted non-violent direct action (sit-downs etc.)
CPGB	Communist Party of Great Britain
CPU	central processing unit
CSO	Composite Signals Organisation (part of GCHQ)
DCS	Diversified Corporate Services Ltd.
DES	Data Encryption Standard (US)
digital	describes signals composed of a series of binary digits
DTMS	Diplomatic Telecommunications Maintenance Service
DOE	Department of the Environment
externals	facets of a communication other than the contents (e.g. source, destination, duration)
FBI	Federal Bureau of Investigation (US)
FBU	Fire Brigades Union
FET	Field Effect Transmitter
FISA	Foreign Intelligence Surveillance Act
FISC	Foreign Intelligence Surveillance Court
G10	Gesatz 10, amendment to the West German Constitution concerning tapping
GC&CS	Government Code and Cypher School
GCHQ	Government Communications Headquarters
GMC	General Medical Council
GPO	General Post Office
group switching centre	British Telecom trunk exchange
hacking	unauthorised entry into a computer system

259

HARVEST	IBM-built processor used by National Security Agency for automatic scanning of telex messages
HF	High Frequency (radio signal)
IBM	International Business Machines Inc. (US)
ICL	International Computers Ltd.
ILC	International Licensed Carrier
INTELSAT	International Telecommunications Satellite Organisation
IPI	Institute of Professional Investigators
ISDN	Integrated Services Digital Network
IT4/NE1	IT4: Operations Division, British Telecom International NE1: Network Efficiency section, Special Investigation group
ITS	International Telephone Supply Inc.
ITU	International Telecommunications Union (agency of the United Nations)
JIC	Joint Intelligence Committee
JIO	Joint Intelligence Organisation
JSRU	Joint Speech Research Unit (part of GCHQ until 1985, now attached to the Royal Signals and Radar Establishment, Malvern)
JTLS	Joint Technical Language Service (part of GCHQ)
Judicial Monitor	judge appointed by the Government between 1981 and 1985 to review official tapping operations, superceded by the 'Commissioner' (see above)
jumper	connecting wire between the two sides of the MDF (see below)
junction	a circuit between two exchanges
key word	word occurring in a telephone conversation which triggers a recording device in an automated tapping system
LED	Light Emitting Diode
local exchange	a telephone exchange to which customers are connected directly

260

local network	comprises a 'local exchange', its customers' telephones and the lines between them
logging	an umbrella term covering 'metering' and 'tracing', generally used in relation to digital switchboards
LUCIFER	data encryption technique developed by IBM
MCP	Meter Check Printer
MDF	main distribution frame, exchange equipment which sorts incoming customer lines into numerical order
metering	monitoring of the destination of calls made on particular lines
MI1b	War Office code-breaking section (First World War)
microwaves	radio signals used for high-capacity ground and satellite communications
MINARET	National Security Agency domestic surveillance programme
modem	device for converting analogue signals to digital signals and vice versa
multiplexing	technique used to transmit a large number of telephone conversations through one cable or radio path simultaneously
NCCL	National Council for Civil Liberties
NDC	Non-Allied Diplomatic Communications
NCU	National Communications Union
NSA	National Security Agency
OFTEL	Office of Telecommunications, regulatory authority for Britain's telecommunications industry
OMC	Operations and Maintenance Centre
PBX	Private Branch Exchange
PCM	Pulse Code Modulation, a technique for converting analogue signals into digital signals
POEU	Post Office Engineering Union
POID	Post Office Investigation Division
PSA	Property Services Agency (part of

	the Department of the Environment)
R12	Special Investigations Division, British Telecom Research Laboratories
R18	Speech Recognition, Synthesis and Coding Division; British Telecom Research Laboratories
REPRIEVE	tapping equipment, used by Australian intelligence
RFF	Radio Frequency Flooding
RHYOLITE	American signals intelligence satellite
Room 40	common name for Admiralty code-breaking section (First World War)
SAS	Special Air Service
Satstream	British Telecom business satellite service
service observation	monitoring of telephone conversations for quality control purposes
SIGINT	Signals Intelligence, information derived from intercepted communications and other transmissions
SIS	Secret Intelligence Service
STE	Society of Telecom Executives
switching	establishing a connection between customers
TDP	Tone Detector Printer
TKO	Trunk Offering, operator facility for breaking into a line
TOWROPE	MI5 codename for telephone tapping
TPS	Telephone Preference Scheme
Traffic Analysis	analysis of 'externals' (see above)
trawling	process of intercepting and filtering a large volume of communications to extract significant items
Tribunal	body of senior lawyers, established under the 1985 Interception of Communications Act, to which victims of suspected tapping may complain
trunking	technique for transferring the traffic from a given number of lines onto a

262

	smaller number of lines
trunk network	the part of the telephone network which provides customers with long distance links
UKUSA	United Kingdom/United States signals intelligence treaty (1947), also signed by allied states
Y service	responsible for operating radio monitoring stations, evolved into Composite Signals Organisation
ZIRCON	proposed British signals intelligence satellite

Select Bibliography

Carol Ackroyd, Karen Margolis, Jonathan Rosenhead and Tim
    Shallice, *The Technology of Political Control*, Pluto Press, 1980
Philip Agee, *Inside The Company: CIA Diary*, Penguin, 1975
Rupert Allason, *The Branch*, Secker and Warburg, 1982
Christopher Andrew, *Secret Service: The Making of The British
    Intelligence Community*, Heinemann, 1985
J. Atkinson, *Telephony*, Pitman, 1948
Crispin Aubrey, *Who's Watching You?*, Penguin, 1981
Cyril Aynsley and Peter Hedley, *The D Notice Affair*, Michael
    Joseph, 1967
Desmond Ball, *A Suitable Piece of Real Estate*, Hale & Iremonger
    (Australia), 1980
James Bamford, *The Puzzle Palace*, Sidgwick and Jackson, 1983
Patrick Beesly, *Room 40*, Oxford University Press, 1984
G.B. Bleazard, *Introducing Satellite Communications*, National
    Computing Centre, 1985
Celina Bledowska (editor), *War and Order*, Junction Books, 1983
BSSRS Technology of Political Control Group, *TechnoCop: New
    Police Technologies*, Free Association Books, 1985
Tony Bunyan, *The Political Police in Britain*, Quartet, 1977
Duncan Campbell, *The Unsinkable Aircraft Carrier*, Michael Joseph,
    1984
Duncan Campbell, *War Plan UK*, Paladin, 1983
S. Cobler, *Law, Order and Politics in West Germany*, Penguin, 1978
Judith Cook, *Who Killed Hilda Murrell?* New English Library, 1985
Committee of 100 (Hampstead Group), *Mail Interception and
    Telephone Tapping in Britain*, reprinted edition published by
    Attila Publications, June 1973
Hugo Cornwall, *The Hacker's Handbook*, Century Communications,
    1985
Jim Coulter, Susan Miller and Martin Walker, *State of Siege: Politics
    and Policing of The Coalfields*, Canary Press, 1984
CSE [Conference of Socialist Economists] Communications

Group,*Hunt on Cable TV: Chaos or Coherence*, Campaign for Press andBroadcasting Freedom, 1982

Hilary Draper, *Private Police*, Penguin, 1978

M.T. Hills and B.G. Evans, *Telecommunication Systems Design*, George Allen and Unwin, 1973

Andrew Hodges, *Alan Turing: The Enigma of Intelligence*,Counterpoint, 1983

Peter Hain (editor), *Policing The Police, Volume 2*, John Calder, 1980 [Chapter 2: Duncan Campbell, *Society Under Surveillance*]

Jim Hougan, *Spooks*, William Morrow Inc. (USA), 1978

Institution of Electrical Engineers, *International Conference on Secure Communication Systems*, IEE Conference Publication no.231, February 1984

Institute of Electrical and Electronic Engineers (USA), records of the annual International Conference on Acoustics, Speech and Signal Processing

Francis Jacobs, *The European Convention on Human Rights*,Clarendon Press, 1975

David Kahn, *The Codebreakers*, Weidenfeld and Nicholson, 1974

Peter Lambley, *The Psychology of Apartheid*, Secker & Warburg, 1980

Peter Laurie, *Beneath The City Streets*, Granada, 1979

Dick Lee and Colin Pratt, *Operation Julie*, W.H. Allen, 1978

David Leigh, *The Frontiers of Secrecy*, Junction Books, 1980

Ronald Lewin, *The American Magic: Codes, Ciphers and The Defeat of Japan*, Penguin, 1982

Robert Lindsey, *The Falcon and The Snowman*, Penguin, 1981

Brenda Maddox, *Beyond Babel: New Directions in Communications*,André Deutsch, 1972

D. Madgwick and T. Smythe, *The Invasion of Privacy*, 1974

H. Montgomery-Hyde, *Norman Birkett*, 1964

Richard E. Morgan, *Domestic Intelligence*, University of Texas Press,1980

Chapman Pincher, *Inside Story*, Sidgwick and Jackson, 1978

Thomas Powers, *The Man Who Kept The Secrets: Richard Helms and the CIA*, Simon and Schuster, 1979

Post Office Engineering Union, *Tapping The Telephone*, POEU, 31 July 1980

Gill Reeve and Joan Smith, *Offence of the Realm: How Peace Campaigners Get Bugged*, CND Publications, 1986

Sydney F. Smith, *Telephony and Telegraphy*, Oxford University Press, 1978

Edward R. Teja and Gary Gonnella, *Voice Technology*, Reston Publishing (USA), 1983

Anthony Verrier, *Through the Looking Glass*, Jonathan Cape, 1983
Raymond Wacks, *The Protection of Privacy*, Sweet & Maxwell, 1980
Nigel West, *MI5: British Security Service Operations 1909–45*, The Bodley Head, 1981
Nigel West, *MI5: A Matter of Trust*, Coronet, 1983
John Wingfield, *Bugging*, Robert Hale, 1984

Official Papers (published by HMSO)

Command 283, *Report of the Committee of Privy Councillors appointed to inquire into the Interception of Communications*, September 1957,(chaired by Sir Norman Birkett)
Command 2152, *Lord Denning's Report*, September 1963 [investigation of the Profumo affair]
Command 5012, *Report of the Committee on Privacy*, 1972, (chaired by Lord Younger)
Command 7873, *The Interception of Communications in Great Britain*, April 1980
Command 8092, *Report of the Royal Commission on Criminal Procedure*, January 1981, (chaired by Sir Cyril Phillips)
Command 8191, *The Interception of Communications in Great Britain: Report of the Rt. Hon. Lord Diplock*, March 1981
Command 8787, *Falkland Islands Review: Report of a Committee of Privy Councillors*, 1983, (chaired by Lord Franks)
Command 9438, *The Interception of Communications in the United Kingdom*, February 1985
H.M. Treasury (Central Computer and Telecommunications Agency), *Telephone Extension Logging*, Information Technology In the Civil Service Series No.1, April 1983

Television Programmes

Panorama, BBC1, 23 February 1981
Panorama, BBC1, 2 March 1981
MI5's Official Secrets, 20/20 Vision, Channel 4, 8 March 1985
The Spy That Never Was, World In Action, Granada, 16 July 1984

Papers published by the Council of Europe, Strasbourg

European Treaty Series, no.5: European Conventions and Agreements, Vol. 1, 1949–61, 1971
Report of the European Commission of Human Rights, application no. 8691/79, James Malone against United Kingdom, report of

the Commission, adopted 17 December 1982.

European Court of Human Rights, Malone Case (4/1983/60/94):

Request of the European Commission of Human Rights bringing the case before the European Court of Human Rights, Cour(83) 42, 16 May 1983

Memorial of the Government of the United Kingdom, Cour (83)94, 19 October 1983

Letter of 21 September 1983 from the General Secretary of the Post Office Engineering Union to the Registrar of the Court, Cour (83) 95

Written comments submitted by the Post Office Engineering Union, Cour (84) 8, 26 January 1984

Note of the hearing held on 20 February 1984 (morning), Cour/Misc (84) 39

Note of the hearing held on 20 February 1984 (afternoon), Cour/Misc (84) 40

Memorial of the applicant concerning Article 50 of the Convention, Cour (84) 18, 17 February 1984

Judgement of the Court, 2 August 1984: Press release re. judgement, C (84) 57, 2 August 1984

Text of settlement between the applicant and the United Kingdom Government, Cour (85) 29, 18 March 1985

Legal Documentation and Research Division

Legislative Dossier No.2 – Telephone Tapping and the Recording of Telecommunications in some Council of Europe member states

Index

271